contents

introduction			9
chapter 1	starting off		15
chapter 2	how to form a band		19
chapter 3	the audition		25
chapter 4	**personal stuff**		29
	practise		*29*
	vocals		*44*
	busking		*48*
	networking		*52*
chapter 5	**solo performers/covers**		57
	gigging abroad covers		*65*
	agents, covers circuit		*67*
	other routes		*69*
	basic songwriting		*72*
chapter 6	the road test		81
chapter 7	rehearsals		89
chapter 8	**equipment**		99
	guitars		*99*
	bass guitars		*108*
	guitar amplification		*117*
	the public address (pa) system		*121*
	vocal microphones		*126*
	keyboards		*129*
	musical equipment insurance		*131*

THE ART OF GIGGING

chapter 8	**your first gigs**	**133**
	staging your own gig/event	*140*
	artist/band biog/photo/website	*141*
	the venue	*144*
	the musicians union	*151*
chapter 10	**choosing which route to take**	**153**
	covers v original	*153*
	sending out demos	*162*
	splitting the song royalties	*165*
	protecting the copyright of the songs	*167*
	artists to keep an eye on	*171*
	local radio air-play	*181*
chapter 11	**your image**	**185**
	the front person	*186*
	choosing a name	*189*
	choosing a manager	*196*
chapter 12	**studio & home recording**	**201**
	studio recording	*201*
	production music libraries	*208*
chapter 13	**music & the industry**	**211**
	the performing rights society (prs) and	
	the mechanical copyright protection society (mcps)	*216*
	other useful contacts	*221*
	music industry websites	*222*
in my liverpool home		**227**

introduction

I never set out to write this book intentionally, it just happened.

Friends, family and people I would meet in every day life would constantly ask me for advice for their son, daughter, niece, nephew, singing dog.. etc.

I would find myself repeating the same advice over and over again.

I don't mind at all, I love talking about anything to do with music, but it always seems to be when you are just lining up your cue to pot the black in your local.

The amount of times I have heard the words ' My daughter has the most wonderful voice' or 'My son is in a band and they need some equipment. Where is the best place to get it? Oh, and some gigs and a manager and so on'.

It would then take me so much time to advise on their next move within the industry as regards moving on and improving the situation they were currently in. Now remember, I am in the middle of a game of pool!

A particular close friend, Alan Binks, explained to me that his daughter was moving down to London as a university student and would like to try to earn some money doing some gigs as a singer.

I decided the best thing would be to write down some tips and advice on the basic equipment she would need and some info on agents and basic gigging tips that she could then use as a 'check-list'.

As explained throughout the book, having the talent is one thing, but amassing the knowledge, resources, equipment, etc, and then getting yourself into a position where you can entertain people with a view to earning some money is another.

Like any trade, the entertainment industry is not something you can just jump into. You have to learn the basics and learn about the industry you are getting involved in. There has to be some kind of an 'apprenticeship' of sorts.

A performing artist, whether they are a guitarist, singer, drummer, keyboardist, etc, should have some knowledge or they simply will not succeed, or at the very least they may have to learn the long, hard way as I did.

There are so many short cuts and simple tips that an experienced gigging musician can pass on to a 'starter'. This in turn can make things much simpler and should also save the 'student' a lot of money, time and heartache in the process.

Another reason for writing this book is that I noticed a 'niche' in the market for the side of the industry which, for some reason (including snobbery), most music industry books seem to by-pass.

That by-pass jumps right over the 'coal face' gigging 'entry level' of musicianship which must be, after all, the apprenticeship for any musician or entertainer.

Most music industry books seem to concentrate on the 'upper' end of the industry with regards to recording, publishing deals and touring etc.

That's fine, and that information may be needed at some point, but let's consider the entry level with regards to pub/club gigging, rehearsing, auditions, equipment, agents, basic management, stage craft, etiquette and, of course, basic musicianship. Purchasing equipment alone could fill a book, after all it is one of the most expensive areas of being involved in starting up in the entertainments industry.

As I explained before, this book concentrates on the up and coming musician/artist that may need simple, realistic, no-nonsense advice on the 'coal face' entry level guide to working as a gigging musician.

Personally, I can't remember when I didn't play guitar. I have played for most of my life.

Even now when I pick up my guitar and play, it's like opening a door into another world. I sometimes wonder if people think that after all these years I don't appreciate being able to play an instrument, and that somehow it may have become boring or that I take it for granted, but that is not the case. I love playing now more than ever and certainly as much as my first early years, when every new chord learnt gave me a new road to go down and gave me another week to practise new songs I could add to my list.

All through my life I have been surrounded by music and singing. When I was growing up in Liverpool in the sixties there always seemed to be a party going on in my house where my dad would pick up his guitar and sing for hours and hours. Obviously, I was only young (born

1960) but I can remember how exciting it was in those days with the Beatles and all the Mersey-beat stuff going on.

It obviously had my dad singing like mad and everyone seemed hooked, including me.

It seemed natural to join in and start 'drumming' on the arm of the 'couch', and I realised that even at that age I really loved people applauding and showing appreciation. I loved the fact that people clapped as my dad finished each song and wouldn't let him stop. I often fell asleep and woke up hours later in bed to hear him still singing.

He loved it that much, he once told me he was dying for a pee for hours, but I knew he didn't want to stop singing in case people went home.

I suppose it was then that I fell in love with being a part of the entertainment rather than watching somebody else providing it.

You could say it all became an addiction. I have obviously gained a great understanding for young up-and-coming musicians and the fact that they can find great escapism through music and entertaining, just as I did all those years ago.

It wasn't long until I realised the guitar would make a better instrument than the arm of a couch, and the fact that there was always a guitar handy helped. I would sit in the bedroom for hours on end, fascinated by the wonderful sound a simple chord would make.

Within a few years I could play well enough to do a few tunes myself so my mum and dad bought me my first guitar.

Although I am self taught I learned at a very early stage to pick up on any bits and bobs of information that I could. I would always, without shame, ask another guitarist or musician to show me something I didn't already know.

I would spend every waking minute learning the riff or chord or whatever that I had been shown. I often fell asleep with a guitar on my lap or next to me in bed.

Fortunately, a very good friend and work partner of my fathers, Bobby Arnold (who I would also have the great pleasure to work with in the future, as a roofing partner and also evenings in the same band), also taught me some great chords, shortcuts, riffs and tips. He also suggested I dropped my plectrum/pick and started using my fingers which I can never thank him enough for, as it's a far more satisfying playing style.

I also studied my dad's style of playing at every opportunity—and believe me there were lots of them. Just like me now, he couldn't walk past a guitar without picking it up and playing (he still can't). My dad

(Roy) is the old school-type player—although not technically brilliant, he can play just about any song ever written at the drop of a hat (or request) and he must know hundreds of songs—the amazing thing is that he remembers all the words too—a wonderful skill in itself.

For the grand sum of £8.00, I now owned my very own 'Kay' electric guitar, bought from a friend at school, who explained that he needed the money to buy the new 'Supertramp' album.

As my dad realised I was progressing well, he waited until my 16th birthday and took me to 'Moran Sound' in Breck Road, Liverpool and bought me my first 'serious' guitar, a real 'Fender Telecaster'.

That was it, other local musicians would suddenly think, "wow, he must be good—he's got a 'Fender'".

In the evening, myself and a few friends would often meet in a field near my house and we would swap chords and riffs and even simple strumming techniques, anything at all that sounded good and improved our repertoire.

It wasn't long until I received my first offer to join my first band. After a year of rehearsing in a cold damp scouts hut on the edge of an industrial estate in a place called Kirkby, just outside Liverpool, we turned into a great little outfit covering everything from The Beatles, The Eagles, Status Quo and later Thin Lizzy and also writing a few of our own to test our skills.

That was almost 30 years ago and believe me, it does actually feel like it was almost '30 years ago'. I started playing as most people do because I enjoyed it, in fact I loved it. Music soon became the biggest thing in my life.

It's a shame really that although you start playing an instrument because you enjoy it, the better you get and the more you improve, you inevitably drift into that scenario where it becomes a job. This wasn't something you even considered and would actually have been the last thing on our mind when you played your first few chords. Although it has to be said, any scraps of money you can then earn can be reinvested in better equipment and therefore improve your overall sound.

The biggest barrier in starting off as a gigging musician must be the lack of decent equipment that's needed to put a show across.

For most young musicians I meet nowadays generally or via my job as a Music Industry Consultant, it's obvious that the biggest struggle they face isn't a lack of talent, but simply having no decent equipment in order to gig, in order to showcase and also nurture that talent.

Unfortunately it's the 'vicious circle' scenario in which you need gigs to earn money to purchase equipment, but you can't do the gigs because you have no equipment to do one in the first place.

Imagine how many talented people are out there who may just have gone all the way, but for this one reason alone probably packed in at the very first hurdle without even doing their first gig.

Throughout this book I have tried wherever possible to give tips, pointers, guidance and advice on how to make this scenario seem less of a barrier. Obviously I have also pointed out ways in which you can certainly save money in the early years, which is, after all, the time you will need most help.

I only wish someone could have helped me more when I was starting out as a musician. I learned the hard way, like most musicians I know. I simply picked up scraps of knowledge and advice through the early years 'on the road'.

Though I am a guitarist, I have always sang and also done sessions in other bands on keyboards, banjo, bass, basic sound engineering, lighting and roadying.

I have also written songs all my life and although nothing quite shook the world, I did manage to gain considerable air play with the release of three singles and an album, all penned by myself.

I have learned the fact that there certainly is luck involved at the higher end of the market regarding original music bands and also the ' it's not what you know, it's who you know' scenario that is endemic throughout the industry. In fact, if you think of it, it's natural to any kind of industry and is born due to the networking process

I know wonderfully talented people who will never, for one reason or another, hit the dizzy heights of stardom. These musicians could wipe the floor with some of today's so-called 'pop stars'. Pop stars my a..e—most of them are manufactured tosh and I really can't believe the status and lifestyle these people enjoy. But you have to remember it's not their fault, they are merely the cogs in a well oiled machine that is the music industry.

Although I admit that this book is mainly seen through the eyes of a guitarist/vocalist, I would like to think it covers any form of gigging musician, whether that be a solo performer, duo, trio, band, singer, guitarist, drummer, saxophonist, 'settee arm percussionist' or whatever. Starting off in the industry is a steep up-hill climb, so it helps (to say the very least) to have some basic relative knowledge, and then hopefully the climb will be easier.

I make no apologies as to the nature of my usage of wording and my sense of humour, (I am after all a Liverpool lad), and the fact that long fancy words like anti-establishmentarianism have been kept to a minimum. I have kept it simple and easy to read. There are enough books covering the higher end of the industry so this book aims to help young, or maybe the 'not so young', looking to start out as a performing artist.

Although I love apple crumble, I could imagine living without it.

The same applies to lemon and sugar pancakes, or even my favourite shirt.

What I can't possibly imagine is life without music.

Did you know that a baby is very likely to have a favourite piece of music the moment it is born.

Music is important to us in many ways and can be responsible for a variety of emotions ranging from utter peace and calm, to exhilarating joy.

It's from the heart and it's merely my opinion.

So how can a musician have a bank balance of one million pounds after ten years in the industry?

Simple…he starts with two million.

chapter 1
starting off

It's quite amazing how many people have a guitar on the top of their wardrobe or in a junk room thrown on top of a pile of boxes.

Usually there is a string missing or a broken tuning peg, or it's so out of tune that it's simply been a case of neglect or 'can't be bothered'.

Just as a rough guess, there must be one in every four houses, so that works out at around two million guitars/instruments lying idle.

Chances are there will be one in your house.

Very few of us manage to get over that first hurdle and we all agree that it's the sore finger—tips that seem to put most of us off, followed by the tuning problems, and then simply finding time for quality practise.

The majority of us who do manage to get through these early barriers and learn a few simple chords or scales still seem to give up when we fall into a 'rut'.

A 'rut' can be one way of describing that period in your learning when you simply cannot learn anything new, as it's either too difficult or there is no one there to show you how to go about it. Don't give up. Get the guitar off the wardrobe and put some new strings on it. It doesn't take that long and for the sake of a fiver you could be on your way to becoming the next 'Eagles'. If you can manage to learn something new, it's amazing the way that one new thing can expand into another branch of ideas and skills on your instrument.

Other more common barriers include obtaining a decent guitar or instrument to play on, but even that's not really an excuse as there are instruments at every price level, particularly now that they are mass produced in China and Korea amongst other places.

And, of course, the internet has placed a million shops on our doorstep.

After all that is said, very few of us get through all the barriers and ruts and go on to be able to play well enough to entertain people. Even fewer musicians reach the goal of being able to earn money doing something they love. Of course not everyone wants to earn money from playing an instrument, but there are worse ways of earning a living.

Taken a step further, it's amazing how many barriers a musician has to pass before they can start to be rewarded for all those years of struggling, learning, rehearsing and amassing the equipment needed to perform live and actually begin to turn the situation round into a profit. I firmly believe (depending on what route you take) that any musician does not actually balance the books until the third or even fourth year of gigging. It all depends on the regularity and pay (if any) from the gigs.

The above also covers other instruments and also vocalists, though it should be noted that most musicians nowadays are expected to sing, therefore doubling their work load.

The following chapters are there to give an honest insight as to what to expect on the long, long road to becoming a semi/pro musician or performing artist.

Although the book is mainly aimed at starters to intermediate performers in the industry, it will in some places offer a more advanced insight into aspects of the music industry that many of you may never have had the good fortune to reach.

Throughout the book there are quotes and sections that have been written by guests and may offer a different perspective in order to give a broader range of advice.

Some guests have been to the very top of the ladder, some are simply gigging musicians in some shape or form. I have the same respect for all of them, no matter what range of success they may have achieved. After all what is success? To me success is learning an instrument well enough to truly entertain other people and even more importantly to entertain yourself with years of enjoyment and pleasure, regardless of the fact that you may never reach number one in the national charts.

Throughout the book I will be covering both the 'original songwriters' side of the industry and also the covers side, both differing in their routes. Solo work (covers and original) and band work (covers and original) will be included, and I will be starting from scratch as regards my advice.

"Most Artists will never really ask themselves 'why Gig'? What is the purpose of gigging, who is it for and is anyone actually interested in your band? There are several reasons for gigging/performance, one being money(!!) self gratification (ego), and the opportunity to show your mum and friends that all that prancing around the bedroom with a microphone substitute (hair brush) was not just day-dreaming and time wasted, but a realistic attempt to have an alternative career to the perceived norm!

There's nowt wrong with being a secretary or bricklayer, but for some of us the idea of going on stage to bare our souls to the world, can be the most nerve wracking and poignant moments of our lives".

—Keith Mullin, The Farm

chapter 2
how to form a band

Ok, so we all have to start off somewhere. There are no definitive rules or directions, but if you go about it the right way there are definitely some short cuts.

Firstly, it can take years for a musician to gain the confidence and basic musicianship needed to even consider joining a band and then find a suitable band they would be happy to be a part of.

Sometimes it just happens naturally, in my case it did and I am sure for most musicians it's a similar story.

As you already know, I hung about in my local park or street corner and would often take my guitar with me to show my friends what I had managed to learn that week.

The first few brave moments playing in front of your mates always start off with a tune on the one string (in my days 'Caroline' by Status Quo) then moving on to two fingered 'power chords' to do a rendition of 'Smoke on the water'. When you see the 'wow' on your friends faces it really encourages you. You gradually develop your repertoire into full chord tunes and then, without even realising it, you are jamming with your friends who have now had a word with their parents and have an instrument of their very own.

It's even more simple if you are surrounded by other musicians. For example at school, college or university it's very hard not to be. Every other student plays a few basic chords and it's always deemed 'cool' to look like your in with the local band.

Many well known bands started off this way and it's probably the most common scenario for producing bands/acts. A good recent example would have to be the band 'Keane', with the three members of the band all attending the same public school. This route is ideal as long as you are all studying at the same place. You have plenty of time to write, rehearse and talk about other aspects of your band's future. It's also a great way to really get to know each other's personalities and share ideas.

But what happens if you have left school or college and you only then start to consider forming a band or going solo?

Let's cover the band for now and we can consider solo work later as it's a completely different scenario.

A band is a group of people that get together to play their instruments and/or sing together, but if the band are short of a drummer, for example, and they don't actually know one, how do they find one?

And vice versa. Let's turn the situation around and say there will be a suitable drummer somewhere but how does he find the band?

Depending on where that drummer is based and actually lives will certainly have a big effect on his or her chances of finding a suitable band or act that may require his or her skills as a musician.

On my travels over the years I have met countless musicians of every calibre and skill level who are having big problems actually finding like—minded musicians with the possibility to audition, never mind getting to the position of actually joining them.

It's always the small towns set out from the big cities that are going to be the problem areas, due to the simple fact that there will obviously be less of a music scene going on, which is also going to effect a musicians 'networking' skills.

Apart from deciding to actually move base, which in a lot of cases is just not an option depending on your status, and of course your willingness to venture further afield, there are some ways you can enhance your chances of finding a suitable outcome.

You have to consider the two options:
a. **Wait around for several years until you find an advert or meet somebody requiring your services with a view to auditioning.**
b. **Advertise and market yourself and your skills in local press etc.**

So let's go into both options in more detail with some useful pointers and tips.

The first option is and always will be the very lazy option.

I know of many musicians, some quite talented, that wait around for months and in some cases years before they join up with other musicians, simply because they can't be bothered with a spot of advertising, marketing or networking their skills. I meet them everyday through my job and I find it extremely hard to understand how they can go for years without actually gigging or in some cases without even rehearsing. They seem to think that if they wait long enough a suitable band will walk into their living room and ask them to join. Even good old Frank Sinatra had to put up a card in his local grocery store window to find the musicians he would start his career with.

Crooner/vocalist available
male 20 years old
own microphone
willing to travel
ring Frank

It seems crazy. Why spend all of those years singing or learning an instrument and then hide your skills and waste valuable time doing nothing.

Let's look at the second option regarding advertising and marketing your skills.

There will always be a local paper in your area with a classified section in which, for a small fee, you can place an advert. Some regional papers actually advertise free of charge and sometimes these can actually be a better choice as they may have a bigger catchment area. If you have no transport and are just starting off, it may be a good idea to look for musicians in your local area, but if you feel you need to cast the net a bit further and you can afford to jump a few buses or a train, you may meet some musicians you can really work with.

If you are paying per word obviously you need to keep the advert short and to the point.

EXAMPLE

Male rock Guitarist
22 years old ring
Joe on…

That will do for now, but consider the papers like 'The Loot' where you can advertise free, you can now expand the advert to include more info about yourself, your skills and also what type of outfit you are actually looking for. It's very important that you are honest with regard to your skills as a musician. For example, don't put in your advert that you can blow 'Eddie Van Halen' off the stage. Chances are you will get plenty of replies but when you are at the auditions, struggling to play a simple barre chord, you will not only raise a few eyebrows, but you will also get plenty of rejections.

It's much easier to be honest and then, if anything, pleasantly surprise the other musicians you meet.

GOOD EXAMPLE

22 year old male rock guitarist, B/vocals, Good equipment, own transport. Only gigged at college campus but keen to join other musicians to write material and gig, influences inc Keane, The Eagles, Neil Young etc (don't mind doing some covers) based Liverpool—Merseyside area, ring Joe after 6.00pm on 0000111 or email joeytwangs.com…

GOOD EXAMPLE

Very experienced 23 year old female classically trained violinist plus vocals, looking to start or join a Corrs tribute band. No transport but great gear. Carlisle area. Please ring or leave a message on…or email…

BAD EXAMPLE

Drummer ready to go on tour. Likes dancing, cooking, and long walks in the sun. Can borrow some gear but only on Tuesdays and the odd Thursday. email www.bashdemskins.com

The two good examples give all the information the band or reader would need to know at a glance, obviously they will still need to audition you but at least they have a rough idea of your skill level and what you are looking for as regards some compatibility.

To put the advert the other way around from the bands perspective, it should look something like this;

GOOD EXAMPLE

South East based country band 'The Slam Dunkers' seek bass player (any age or sex) must be experienced and willing to work throughout Europe and UK. Transport not essential but pro minded is. Please email all details or leave message. ph…or email www.slamdunk.com

BAD EXAMPLE

Anyone out there wanna give the industry a big kick up the khyber, if so we'll meet you outside McDoodles at nine bells. Bring some money and any recent issues of the 'Viz' and anyone's number who owns a really big van. No cowboy hats or coffin dodgers.

REAL SAMPLES

> *"I remember putting a beer mat in my local shop window with the words* **'John seeks band to join'** *and six weeks later some geezer rang me from the salvation army asking what instrument I played".*
>
> **—B. Stapleton**

> *"I put an advert in the Liverpool echo* **'mega guitarist with boss gear seeks loud band with attitude problems'.** *A band rang and we arranged to meet for an audition. As I walked into the rehearsal room 'a little bit late' one of the band recognised me and I overheard him make a comment on me being a c…p guitarist, which dented my confidence somewhat as it was basically true. I'm 6ft 3" and 16 stone, that's what I meant by 'mega'. I didn't get the job, I remember telling my mates it was down to me turning up late".*
>
> **—A. Woodcock**

These samples are perfect. At a glance you can see the information, or lack of it, and therefore understand why mix ups and confusion can cause both parties wasted time.

Make the advert clear and informative, practise writing it down on paper and imagine you were reading it yourself.

chapter 3
the audition

Ok, so you have been brave enough to answer your first advert.

'POP ROCK BAND SEEKS A…

There are certain things you need to consider before you arrange your audition date, depending on whether you actually know the people you are about to meet.

If they have previous knowledge of your skills you would assume that you have a good chance of a successful outcome (**maybe you've been 'head hunted'**). The band would not waste time with you if they knew beforehand that you wouldn't be suitable. That prior knowledge of another musician can be put down to your **networking skills** and/or the fact that word has got out that you are a good musician.

If you happen to live in a small town it's common for every musician to know each other. If however you live in a big city, you may have to work much harder to get your name about. It's the 'big fish in a small pond', 'small fish in a big pond' syndrome.

Let's consider that the band you are auditioning with has no previous knowledge of you or your skills as a musician.

How are you going to impress them? Taking a photograph of your good looking sister might help but let's look at some other points.

*****Find out as much as possible about the band prior to the actual audition.**

You can make a great impression on a band if you ask some simple questions before you physically meet. Remember, although they are auditioning you, you in turn should be 'checking them out', after all they may not be up to your standard.

It's also a good 'ice breaker', getting to know each other before you actually meet.

TIP: Learn the basics of another instrument, like percussion or mouth organ, it's a great way to impress people with little effort, but don't let it be to the detriment of your main instrument.

*Ask if it's possible for you to attend one of their rehearsals or, even better, an actual gig to get an idea of their 'set'. This way you are going to get the chance to see what you are up against; are they the right band for you? Have you got the skills needed to join the band? Further questions can be asked at the actual audition, but the important info regarding compatibility may have already been answered.

If you can't manage this there are other things you can do.

*Ask for any recordings of the bands material or even better a recent video. Whether they are doing original songs or covers, you have a chance to learn the songs beforehand and impress the band at the audition when you know the songs as well as they do. You won't be expected to know all the songs but you could tell the band which songs you have learned.

If none of these are possible and your audition is the first time you have met the band, consider these things.

*Arrive early First impressions are crucial. Being late on your first meeting could give the impression that you will always be late. It's also unprofessional.

If you want to be anywhere on time you have to get their ten minutes early!

*Be honest, polite and confident, ask questions and enquire as to the bands aims and future ambitions. Don't however come across as over confident and cocky, you could make them feel awkward.

*Your musicianship will obviously be the most important thing at the audition, however **your personality** is more important than you could imagine. If a band are looking for someone to spend a good proportion of their life with, as regards rolling round the back of rusty transit van dodging mic stands and runaway speakers, and doing all the other common things a band has to do together, they are going to consider you as a person as well as a performer. In other words you are going to have to fit in **socially as well as musically**.

Fact: Most bands split up due to it's members not getting on together. It's actually quite unusual for musicianship to cause a band split, and that is endemic throughout the industry at any level. Think of any of the great legendary bands and you will find it was always a rift or clash of personalities that split them up.

Therefore, being able to 'get on' with each other and gain a rapport with the other band members may be just as important as your musicianship.

Initially though, it will be your music skills they will notice first, after all, that is why they are auditioning you in the first place.

So to cover both of these hurdles you should be polite, look confident and play to your best ability, which under the strange conditions and the fact you may be very nervous is probably easier said than done.

FROM THE BANDS PERSPECTIVE

Try to find out anything about the person auditioning before the actual audition.

The band should make the person auditioning feel as comfortable as possible with some friendly chat before any music is played.

Wherever possible the band should choose three or four songs and supply a recording of those songs prior to the person auditioning, preferably with enough time for the person to learn the material.

Under no circumstances should a band judge somebody by looks alone. Some of the greatest musicians and front-men are not what you would call perfect to look at.

> *"I remember when he first walked in, we all stared at him and thought he'd walked into the wrong room. I remember thinking 'I wouldn't argue with him'. He was massive and ugly. He introduced himself and he was our sixth person on the list. He explained he had learned a couple of the songs on the list and we started playing one of the songs. He started singing and I remember we were all 'gob smacked'. He had the voice of an angel. Needless to say we took him on straight away".*
>
> **—J. Travis**

Ok, so you got the job, well done. It was all worth it, but don't let your efforts end there. If you like the band and want to try go places with them, it's important not to rest on your efforts. They'll be keeping an eye on your input and musicianship as the months go along. Keep up the good work and become a solid member, someone they simply could not do without.

Ok, so you didn't get the job. Don't be too disheartened, you gave it your best shot. Lots of established stars had knock backs before becoming respected as musicians.

Think of the reasons you may not have impressed enough at that particular audition.

Maybe you didn't fit in because of your looks or your personality, maybe it was your lack of quality equipment or the fact that you have no transport. Don't be afraid to ask if they haven't already told you. You may not be in a financial position to go out and purchase a car and better equipment, but if it's your skills as a musician that caused them to turn you down, that can be remedied by personal practise.

chapter 4
personal stuff

PRACTISE

How often have you heard the words 'naturally talented' and thought to yourself that the person with the 'natural talent' just woke up one day, bought a set of golf clubs and turned 'pro' two months later. Or the person bought a guitar and two months later did a one hour solo session on Jazz FM. What I am getting at here is that, yes, there are naturally gifted people, but they have usually practised 24/7 and put their heart and soul into becoming that 'naturally talented' person. Obviously some people have to work harder than others, but one thing is for sure—we all have to practise. It's an extremely rare phenomenon for somebody to become a genius on their instrument without practising.

(But there is the odd one)

> *"Mummy, Mummy, can I have a new pair of trainers when I've finished this symphony"*
> **—Wolfgang Amadeus Mozart, aged 8**

Forget it, it just doesn't happen like this. Mozart was a born genius, an absolute prodigy. History, however, tells us that even he had to practise sometimes!

Before long you are going to realise that personal practise will be the backbone of your career, or at least as a performer no matter what instrument you play. If you are quite happy to be one of the performers who just wants to plod along and not improve on your technical skills such as phrasing, dynamics, interpretation of a piece of music and the art of actually putting a piece of music across to an audience, that's up to you. But it's much more rewarding (with the added advantage of possibly earning some money doing something you enjoy) if you can keep improving.

"Talent is no substitute for hard work" (my ex boss!)

Before you start your practising you need to consider what you actually need to practise.

GUITAR

If we are talking about guitar, for example, you should start with the simple things first.

Most guitarists like to by-pass the boring stuff and learn a 'Jimmy Hendrix' riff. The problem is that when it comes to creating and improvising pieces, it just doesn't happen because the 'Jimmy Hendrix' riff only works with the song it was created for. It may influence your playing style if that's how you want to sound, but that's about it. On a daily basis I meet guitarists who can play hundreds of parts of songs but no whole songs. That's ok to impress your mates and people walking past in guitar shops but as far as gigging is concerned you need to do some back—tracking.

With any instrument it's important you make sure you are doing the basic things right before moving on to more advanced stuff.

Rhythm guitar technique and 'chordal' stuff for example is very underrated and misunderstood by a lot of up and coming guitarists, who tend to look at super-speed emotionless guitar solos as the way to impress all who dare to get in the way. Of course, lead guitar playing has a very important roll to play in modern guitar playing but learning good rhythm techniques and chordal work will actually make your lead playing even more admirable. A mixture of the two 'rhythm and lead' with the right phrasing is actually akin to playing piano on a guitar (think Mark Knoffler, Albert Lee, Chet Atkins) should be your ultimate target. That is of course my own opinion, but any experienced guitarist will back me up as to it being a style of playing you would be extremely proud of.

Experimenting with chords and chordal extensions alone can really improve your skills and technique as a guitarist.

What is a chord? Just in case you are just starting off, let's explain exactly what a chord is. Without going into to much theory, a chord is basically two or more notes that when played together sound good (you can do the same and come up with a dissonant—bad sounding chord—but what's the point, unless you are writing a piece of music for a horror film). It's as simple as that. Although you will come across numerous books with the standard chord shapes shown, it's important to remember that after you have learned the basic chords you can add or take away notes and experiment to make new chords. Don't worry about the name of them for now, if the chord sounds good and you can write or whistle a melody over it that's fine for now. In reality you could write a hit album with chords you don't even know the name of. Who cares! If it sounds good, use it.

TIP: Some simple basic chords sound great when played at a different position up the neck.

Dropping your pic/plectrum now and then and playing finger-style or finger-picking can also open up some new variations on your playing, although it should be noted that finger style guitar is in a different league to plectrum work so can usually be much more difficult to learn. The use of a plectrum or fingers may also be attributed to what style or genre of music you are playing at any given time. For example, the usual may be (although not always);

Rock = plectrum
Pop = plectrum
Punk = plectrum or anything at hand!
Soul/funk music = plectrum
Reggae = plectrum
Country = finger style/plectrum (sometimes together)
Folk = finger style
Classical = fingers
Jazz = depends on the type and player
Jazz/ragtime = finger style
Gypsy Jazz = extremely heavy gauge plectrums

Again, this would obviously be taken from a mean average of players as there will always be musicians doing their own thing, depending a lot on how they first started playing and whether that came via formal tuition or basically learning by ear (or vinyl, 'parrot fashion'!) There is certainly no wrong way. I wouldn't look at someone funny if they used a plectrum to do all the above styles, though it would be almost impossible to do the classical and jazz/ragtime stuff. Some musicians have been known to use their nose and even their tongue, it's not recommended!

It wouldn't be a bad idea to look at the different genres of music and decide which one you would like to start improving on. (I am under the assumption you can already play the odd chord or two.)

Remember, it's important to learn as many styles as possible, but that may take you years of practise.

If you are looking at the Pop/Rock route, then using finger-style is not really your first priority. Your first priority should be learning to use different rhythms and play in time as it would usually be a band you will be playing with if you are thinking of taking this route. Playing a guitar on your own and playing with a drummer and bass player (a basic rhythm section) are two completely different things.

Apologies if you are past this level but if you are at this stage and you have never actually played with a band you should look at practising to a metronome or a click track. You can use a metronome to practise both lead guitar and rhythm. A metronome is a device that creates a click with perfect timing not unlike a loud ticking of a clock. The speed of the click however, unlike a clock, can be adjusted to suit using a 'beats per minute' (BPM) dial. You can then choose a speed to practise to.

Pick four chords, for example;

C/A minor/F/G/(all in the Key of C) and play a four bar loop or turn around.

Start at say 60 BPM (a clocks speed) and play each chord four times on the click or beat.

This is also a good time to practise counting bars, or at least getting some idea of how a four beats to the bar (4/4) count would work.

Try this counting system—**1** 2 3 4—**2** 2 3 4—**3** 2 3 4—**4** 2 3 4—**5** 2 3 4—**6** 2 3 4 etc.

(Try tapping your foot, it helps to keep in time.)

Working out the chords to a song This will be very important if a band hand you a recording of any music (covers or original) that they would like you to learn.

After you have practised this for a while and your timing is improving, play to a piece of music or song. Try to find the chords used in the song or piece of music and play along as if you were playing with a band. If you can't quite work out the chords, try and find the bass notes on the thick E string. If you can find these notes, you then need to work out the full chords.

The full chords will usually be 'major' chords or 'minor' chords. Hopefully you should know your barre chords, but if not, it's time for you to learn them. There are many books and guitar magazines you can buy that will take you through the myriad of chords and chord extensions. But for now the important chords to learn are your 'F major' barre chord and 'F minor' barre chord. Once you have learned these two chords you can move them up the arm and play all the major and minor chords.

Once you have the chordal work sorted and a good rhythm technique, you can then start with some lead guitar practising. Again, there are plenty of books, magazines and DVDs you can purchase that will show you all the different scales and then it's basically up to you to learn them. Put some time aside everyday and practise scales, there are different scales depending on what type of music you are looking to play.

WHAT IS A SCALE?

A **scale** is nothing more than a clever and melodic way to travel from **octave** to **octave**. **(C to C for example.)**

The **chromatic scale** is the scale that includes every note in an octave.

Octaves are equally divided into twelve notes.

Every other scale (there are hundreds of them) is constructed by selecting only certain notes from the **chromatic scale**.

Two scales are distinguished from one another by:

* The number of notes they have.

* The distance between their degrees measured by '**Tones' and 'Semitones'**.

* **A Tone** or ' full/whole step' is **two notes** up or down (two frets on a guitar or two keys on a piano—any colour) in other words it's a two note gap. If you raise the key by a full tone you would move up two frets and vice versa.

* **A Semitone** or 'half step' is **one note** up or down (one fret on a guitar and one key on a piano.)

A tone and a half would be three notes etc:

Simple scales to consider are the **pentatonic scales**, the minor usually used for blues style playing (with added notes) but both can be used with most forms of music. The pentatonic scale is probably the most common scale. There are two types of pentatonic scales, one major and one minor, both consists of five notes (one octave) but more notes will be added if played in modal or two octaves form.

(Hopefully you know guitar tab numbers represent fret position, strings are named.)

(All scales shown over two octaves)

(Bass guitar players can use all these scales on the E-A-D-G for four string bass)

34 THE ART OF GIGGING

(A major pentatonic) Starting on the route note A

```
Thin   E  |---------------------------------------------------5----7----
       B  |---------------------------------------------5----7-----------
       G  |---------------------------------------4----6------------------
       D  |---------------------------------4----7------------------------
       A  |--------------------------4----7-------------------------------
Thick  E  |--5----7-------------------------------------------------------
Fingering  1----3    1----4    1----4    1----3    1----3    1----3
```

Below the boxes notes are numbered to correspond with fingering. (I am also presuming you know from palm face it's thumb then first, second, third, fourth—it ends there unless you are a very lucky person and have extra fingers.

(A minor pentatonic) Starting on the route note A (* The basic 'blues' scale)

```
Thin   E  |----------------------------------------------------5----8---
       B  |---------------------------------------------5----8-----------
       G  |---------------------------------------5----7-----------------
       D  |---------------------------------5----7------------------------
       A  |--------------------------5---7--------------------------------
Thick  E  |--5----8-------------------------------------------------------
Fingering  1----4    1---3     1----3    1----3    1----4    1----4
```

* If we add these two new notes it starts to sound 'bluesy'

```
Thin   E  |----------------------------------------------------5----8--
       B  |----------------------------------------------5----8----------
       G  |----------------------------------------5--7--**8**-----------
       D  |---------------------------------5---7-------------------------
       A  |--------------------------5--**6**--7---------------------------
       E  |--5----8-------------------------------------------------------
Fingering  1----4    1--2--3    1---3    1--3--4   1----4    1----4
```

(These notes are sometimes referred to as the 'blue notes')
(Another example with more added ' blue notes')

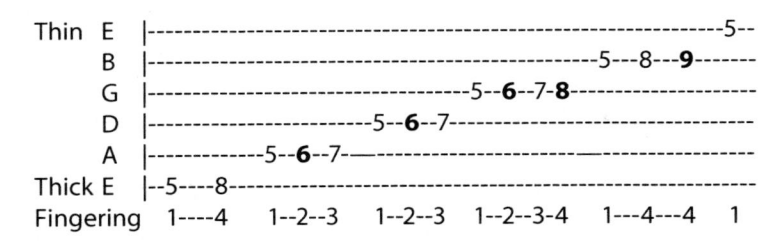

```
Thin    E   |-----------------------------------------------------------5--
        B   |--------------------------------------------------5---8---9-------
        G   |-----------------------------------------5--6--7-8--------------------
        D   |-----------------------------5--6--7----------------------------
        A   |-------------5--6--7---------------------------------------------
Thick   E   |--5----8---------------------------------------------------------
Fingering   1----4      1--2--3    1--2--3   1--2--3-4    1---4---4    1
```

'Blue notes' can also be referred to as passing notes. It's up to you to create melodic 'licks' using the notes available in the basic scale and also using some or all of the 'blue notes'.

Practise playing each scale forwards and backwards at different speeds, until you can play them without thinking or looking (by now you should recognise any mistakes by ear).

Whilst practising scales or chord work be careful not to continue playing if you have pain in your wrists or fingers (do not play through the pain barrier !), take regular rests.

> "Learn all playing styles. Just because you are a rocker now doesn't mean you won't be a country fan in a few years time".
>
> **—Bobby Arnold**

Survival is the ability to evolve and adapt.

After you have mastered the pentatonic scales, you should then lock yourself in the bedroom for a couple of months, take the phone of the hook and concentrate on perfecting the full '**Major scale**' system.

Played on its own, the major scale is actually quite boring and has a pretty uninteresting sound. It is not that exciting to play, and, as it stands, not too useful in a soloing format (though it sounds quite useful when played over Jazz chords). Most people will add in passing tones to create a more melodic effect and some may also rely on the many modal solutions it can give. However, the major scale is the building block from which everything comes, and by applying some simple principles it can become the most powerful reference tool at our disposal for any type of music situation.

To fully access the vast potential of this scale, you must be able to play it in all positions up and down the neck.

When practising, **listen** to the notes while you play them. Try to become familiar with the overall sound of the major scale, to the point where you can instantly recognise the scale just by hearing it. (This isn't as difficult as it may sound as every major scale sounds more or less the same, regardless of what the root note is. After practising for just a short while, you'll understand what I am getting at.)

MAJOR SCALE AND THE 'MODAL SYSTEM'

Without trying to blind you with science, every 'Major' scale has seven degrees (notes). Each of the seven degrees can be used as a starting point for a scale. These scales are known as 'modes' and they each have a classical Greek name. It's an ancient system still used today. It was first developed by the church in Middle Ages. The major scale or **'doh ray me fah soh lah te doh**' as you may know it, is simply the **'Ionion**' mode:

The 'modes' consist of notes played from different points of the scale (**'Doh'** for example being the first and so on). Every mode has a series of fixed intervals, with the first note of the scale acting as the 'principal' or 'root' note for both melody and harmony. Each of the seven modal scales has it's own recognisable sound and character and can be used to improvise over most styles.

MODAL DEGREES

The pattern of modes on each degree of the major scale is repeated in all twelve major keys.

If we pick 'C major' for example, the modes are
(All scales are shown over two octaves)

C—**Ionion**—This is commonly referred to as the major scale. Standard major harmony is based on this scale. (C to C)

```
Thin   E   |------------------------------------------------------------7--8--
       B   |--------------------------------------------------------8--10------------
       G   |-----------------------------------------------7--9--10----------------------
       D   |-------------------------------------7--9--10------------------------------------
       A   |------------7--8--10------------------------------------------------------
Thick  E   |---8--10-----------------------------------------------------------------
Fingering  2---4   1--2---4   1--3---4   1--3---4   2---4   1--2
```

The correct fingering at this stage is essential. It's imperative that correct 'fretted' fingering is used for a number of reasons. One being to avoid lazy fingers, another being that it's the most economical use of the fingers. Scales and lead solos are much easier and smoother if correct fingering is used, especially when more advance scales (and speed) come into the equation. (Overlapping fourths, for example, would be extremely difficult with incorrect fingering).

D—Dorian—The Dorian mode is a minor scale. This is one of the most widely used melodic scales. (D to D) Here is the way I prefer to play it;

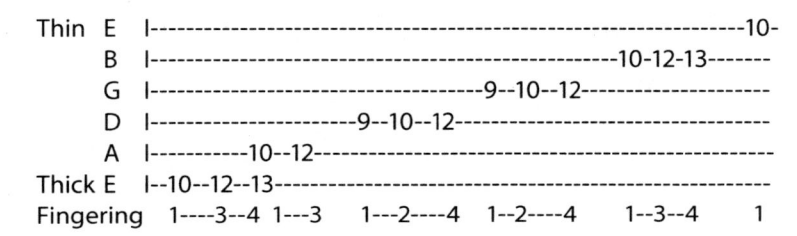

```
Thin   E   |----------------------------------------------------------------10-
       B   |-----------------------------------------------------10-12-13-------
       G   |----------------------------------------9--10--12--------------------
       D   |-----------------------9--10--12-------------------------------------
       A   |-----------10--12----------------------------------------------------
Thick  E   |--10--12--13---------------------------------------------------------
Fingering  1----3--4  1---3      1---2----4   1--2----4   1--3--4      1
```

E—Phrygian—This is another minor scale with a very distinctive 'Spanishy' sound. (E to E)

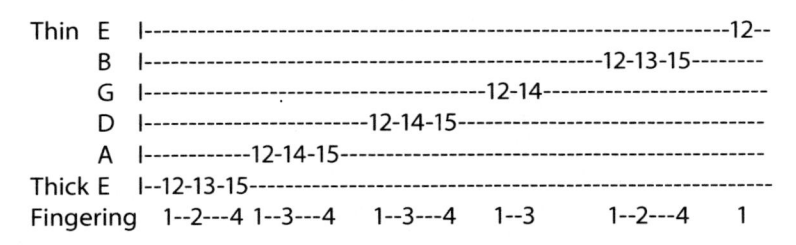

```
Thin   E   |----------------------------------------------------------------12--
       B   |-----------------------------------------------------12-13-15--------
       G   |----------------------------------------12-14------------------------
       D   |------------------------12-14-15-------------------------------------
       A   |------------12-14-15-------------------------------------------------
Thick  E   |--12-13-15-----------------------------------------------------------
Fingering  1--2---4  1--3---4    1--3---4     1--3          1--2---4    1
```

F—Lydian—This is a major scale with an unusual melodic flavour. Again very similar to the last Phrygian scale but starting and ending on the F note (F to F)

```
Thin   E   |--------------------------------------------------------------12--13-
       B   |-----------------------------------------------------12-13-15-----------
       G   |----------------------------------------12-14----------------------------
       D   |------------------------12-14-15-----------------------------------------
       A   |---------12-14-15--------------------------------------------------------
Thick  E   |13-15--------------------------------------------------------------------
Fingering  2---4    1---3--4    1---3---4    1--3         1--2---4    1---2
```

G—Mixolydian—This major scale is used in all types of music. This scale is representing the high G at 15th position on the fret board, it can also be played exactly the same at the low G position starting at 3--5 on the Thick E (G to G)

High G Mixolydian

```
Thin    E   |------------------------------------------------------------15-
        B   |-----------------------------------------------------15-17-18--------
        G   |----------------------------------------------14-16-17----------------
        D   |--------------------------------------14-15-17------------------------
        A   |---------------14-15-17-----------------------------------------------
Thick   E   |-15-17----------------------------------------------------------------
Fingering   2--4        1--2--4     1--2---4    1--3--4     1---3---4     1
```

Low G Mixolydian

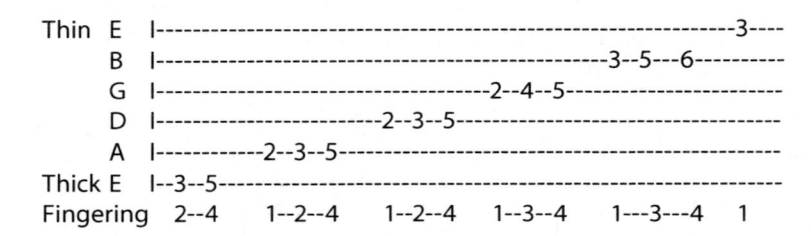

```
Thin    E   |-------------------------------------------------------------3----
        B   |---------------------------------------------------3--5---6----------
        G   |-------------------------------------------2--4--5-------------------
        D   |-----------------------------------2--3--5---------------------------
        A   |---------------2--3--5-----------------------------------------------
Thick   E   |--3--5----------------------------------------------------------------
Fingering   2--4        1--2--4     1--2--4     1--3--4     1---3---4     1
```

A—Aeolian—This scale is usually referred to as the minor scale. It is used as a relative minor scale to the major. In other words if you played the C Major and the C Aeolian, it would be the major and minor scale of C. (A to A)

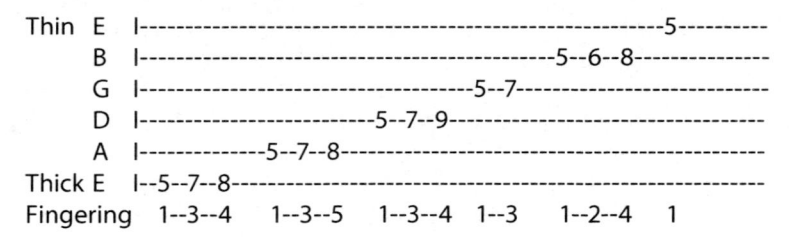

```
Thin    E   |-----------------------------------------------------5----------
        B   |-------------------------------------------5--6--8---------------
        G   |-----------------------------------5--7--------------------------
        D   |-------------------------5--7--9---------------------------------
        A   |---------------5--7--8-------------------------------------------
Thick   E   |--5--7--8---------------------------------------------------------
Fingering   1--3--4     1--3--5     1--3--4     1--3    1--2--4     1
```

B—Locrian—This scale is the odd one out as it's a diminished mode (all the others are major or minor). If you look carefully it's basically the C Ionion scale but starts on the B (B to B)

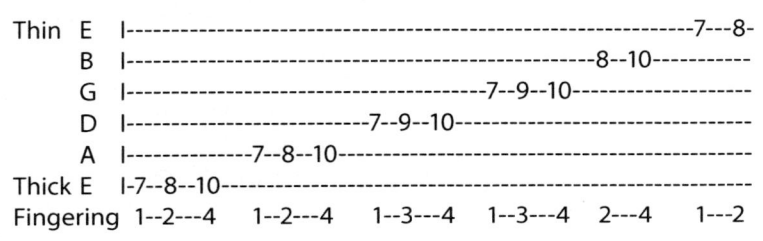

```
Thin    E  |------------------------------------------------------------7---8-
        B  |--------------------------------------------------8--10-----------
        G  |-------------------------------------------7--9--10---------------
        D  |-----------------------------------7--9--10-----------------------
        A  |---------------------------7--8--10-------------------------------
Thick   E  |-7--8--10---------------------------------------------------------
Fingering  1--2---4    1--2---4    1--3---4    1--3---4    2---4    1---2
```

When you have mastered all the scales above, consider playing them in different positions like starting from the route note on the A string or D or G. All the above scales have been shown over two octaves. If you play one octave of each scale, there will be several places to play the scale on your instrument. It should be pointed out at this stage that the first three scales above being 'Ionion, Dorian, and Phrygian played over two octaves would be sufficient to cover most solos and they all actually incorporate the other four scales within them. But if you have the time, why not learn them all. Although we have used the key of C as the sample key, it's important to remember that it would only be a case of moving fret position to alter the key, the same patterns would continue.

As an example below is the 'major' Ionion scale in 'A' (two octaves)

```
Thin    E  |-----------------------------------------------------------4--5---
        B  |---------------------------------------------------5--7-----------
        G  |-------------------------------------------4--6--7----------------
        D  |-------------------------4--6--7----------------------------------
        A  |------------4--5--7-----------------------------------------------
Thick   E  |--5---7-----------------------------------------------------------
Fingering  2---4    1--2--4    1--3---4    1--3---4    2---4    1--2
```

Note: It's exactly like the 'C' ionion but it's played at the 'A' route position at it's route note. Even the fingering is identical. To play the same scale in 'G' we would take it down another two frets (a full tone) etc. Similarly the Dorian scale would start on the second note, etc.

Remember all the scales in the key of 'C' Major can be played over any chord in the key of 'C' Major.

There are basically 28 Chords in any given key, 14 of which are commonly used. In each there are only 3 basic chords types (three x Major chords, three x Minor chords and one x diminished). The seven x basic chords are in column one below.

The basic chords can be extended by using a 7th, 9th, or 11th. There are a multitude of different ways to analyse the 28 chords in each Key, which creates the illusion that 1000's of chords exist, but there are in fact only 28 real chords in each Key. Here are the 28 Chords that are in "C" (remember, you can move any chord up 12 frets and it will be the same chord played in a different octave).

Depending on what type of music you are playing at any given time will command the use of the chords in one of the columns below. Modern pop music would usually be covered in column one and two. Jazz styles could use all four columns. For now don't waste time on columns three and four but instead use any available practise time on columns one and two, there's plenty of potential with those fourteen chords. In future, if you feel the need to move onto higher chord extensions like 9's and 11's, that's fine.

Column (2) below is the basic chord structure for learning jazz modes. The great thing about these chords is the ability to make a simple major scale sound 'jazzy' and very melodic when really it's actually the chordal work itself that does the trick.

As an example, if you can get someone to play Cmajor 7 to Dminor 7 to Eminor 7 (which is the **I II III** of the Key) and you play the C ionion scale over it, you will be pleasantly surprised at the result. (Remember, playing the scale on it's own is, as we have mentioned before, quite uninteresting and boring.)

The effect is that you are playing a really jazzy piece but it's the underlying chords that give it the flavour. Looking at the roman numerals for the key chord positions below, it's important to understand that a song could be written in a *I—VI—IV—V—*(1—6—4—5) pattern which is a very common song writing chord structure/sequence.

Examples—Dream Dream—The Everley Brothers, Everyday—Buddy Holly, Love is all around—Reg Presley + Wet Wet Wet.

Rock and roll and blues usually use the *I—IV—V* of the key, so in the key of C the chords would be Cmajor—Fmajor—Gmajor which when played over twelve bars creates 'twelve bar rock'.

Any of the scales below can be played over any chord structure in any order in the key of C major.

Column (2)—in brackets and 'key' chord number and matching scales

I	II	III	IV	V	VI	VII
Cmajor 7	Dminor 7	Eminor 7	Fmajor 7	Gmajor 7	Aminor 7	B* dim
Ionion	Dorian	Phrygian	Lydian	Mixolydia	Aeolian	Locrian

Column 1	(2)	3	4
I C major	C major 7th	C major 9th	C major 11th
II D minor	D minor 7th	D minor 9th	D minor 11th
III E minor	E minor 7th	E minor 9th	E minor 11th
IV F major	F major 7th	F major 9th	F major 11th
V G major	G major 7th	G major 9th	G major 11th
V1 A minor	A minor 7th	A minor 9th	A minor 11th
V11 B * diminished	B * dim 7th	B *dim 9th	B *dim 11th

* diminished = minor 7 flat5

Note = 7 basic Chords (major, minor and 1 x *diminished) x 4 extensions (basic chord, 7th, 9th, 11th)

Any song written in the Key of "C" will use only the above chords, unless the piece of music changes to another Key. Don't forget there are twelve keys, being

E—F—F#—G—G#—A—A#—B—C—C#—D—D# and back to E

It's important to learn the chords in one key first. You should learn the chord progression in your head first—practising on paper can sometimes be more efficient than practising on the guitar. Write the chords down on a piece of paper as if you are doing lines for being naughty at school. (It should soon sink in!)

Think!

The *I—IV—V* (1, 4, 5) modes are always Major chords.

The *II—III—VI* (2, 3, 6) modes are always Minor chords.

The *VII* (7) mode is always a diminished chord.

Another way to remember is **M m m M M m D**

There are many more scales and modes and they can be found in many formats in books and even on the internet. I have simply covered the most common and what I would consider the most useful. I personally do a lot of George Benson, Larry Carlton type stuff and a lot of Chet Atkins solo material, so the modal system together with octave and 'overlapping fourths' is crucial to my style of playing.

When you have learned some scales and exercises and created

some very hard skin or segs on the tips of your fingers, it's time to learn where to apply these scales or lead runs. The way you will have practised so far will unfortunately have been very methodical.

Learning and playing an instrument and creating melodies is not a science, it's an art form, so it's time to experiment and become an artist!

What you are going to have to do now is understand how phrasing, timing and 'feel'—along with some other characteristics of lead guitar playing like string bending, vibrato, use of dynamics, etc, can to be added to the equation. The notes on their own are like bricks to a house; you're going to need the carpets and curtains and all the frilly bits to finish the job properly.

The notes and scales you will have learned so far are all the notes you can use within a certain key. The problem now is to be able to create harmonious and melodic groups of notes or 'licks' by using the notes in different order, patterns, length, and speed.

In other words, you need to start experimenting with parts of the scales alongside different types of backing to see what sounds good with certain chordal work or genre of music.

It would be a really good idea to use some sort of backing track that you could practise to. There are some superb 'backing tracks' on CDs that come free with magazines—they usually have different styles of music including rock, blues, jazz, classical & country etc.

TIP: Practise using one solitary note and see what you can get out of that one note. Play it hard, soft, let it ring, hit it short, miss the note (as in a pause), use vibrato by wobbling your finger, bend it, damp the note by placing your strumming hand on the actual strings—it takes some practise but is a great way to change tone and volume—slide to it from one note below etc. Do whatever you want but try not to use another note (do the same thing with two notes then three etc). What should happen is you will find ways of making even them few notes sound interesting, then, when you add more notes you'll soon realise it's not the amount of notes you use or the speed, it's the way you play them and the melodies, textures and phrasing you can create from them. Obviously you can add speed and other advanced methods of playing later, then you can mix it all together.

Remember the length and speed of a solo is not as important as the melody of a solo, if you think of any of the great guitar solo's in classic songs they are usually a melody within themselves.

You can also jam along with a friend whenever that is possible but if you are going to be practising everyday you may find your CD player could be more reliable. If you fall into the trap of having to rely on using other musicians for your personal practise it could lead to you skipping what should become your regular sessions.

Further things to consider would have to be improving your theory (reading music etc).

Sometimes it's actually easier learning music theory in reverse. For example when you have mastered the C Ionion scale in tab form, look at the scale written in music notation and theory. The ability to read music is a very useful skill if you ever consider teaching an instrument and also for certain types of session work.

TIP: The majority of us who do manage to get through the early barriers and learn a few simple chords still seem to give up when we fall into a 'rut'.

Never be too proud to ask another musician to show you a new thing, however small. It's incredible how much mileage you can get out of one quick lesson, and it could pull you out of the 'rut'.

> "Standing on the set of Top of the Pops, resplendent in tight satin stage suit that showcased my wedding tackle in much more graphic detail than I realised at the time, it was hard to believe that I had finally achieved a childhood ambition. Most people assume a band or artist breaking into the charts for the first time are newcomers, but it is rarely the case. What they fail to see are the years of graft needed to get there.
>
> Shortly after buying my first saxophone, I blagged myself into a celebrity opening night in my hometown Leicester. I spied Rod Stewart's guitarist, Jim Cregan, propping up the bar with partner Linda Lewis, a hit artist in her own right. I picked my moment and nervously sidled up to them. I asked for advice on how to succeed in the music business and I was shocked by the answer which was blunt and succinct. It was some of the best advice I ever got.
>
> **"Practise like ***k !!"**
>
> As I practised my sax at home, I was reduced to blowing into my bedroom wardrobe to deaden the noise. It was still very loud. We lived in a terraced house and the old lady next door would bang on the wall in an increasingly frenetic fashion as I tooted away. It wouldn't have been so bad but the poor old dear had no sense of

rhythm! Eventually they put her in a home, not all my fault I hope.

After all these years, my advice to any aspiring musicians is, practise long and hard and prepare for disappointments. Persevere, and have belief in your ability, because all musicians that go on to make it will have had contracts dangled in front of them, only to ultimately have seen them snatched away. I have always maintained that the music industry consists of 90% disappointment and 10% exhilarating highs".

—John Barrow (Fun Boy Three & Black Gorrilla)

VOCALS

If you don't sing already, start learning now as it's **very** important. As musicians get better and better, sometimes the only difference between two musicians is their ability to sing or harmonise. This is particularly relevant with covers/tribute bands although new original bands like McFly, for example, use Beatle type 3/4 part harmonies. If you add to that the sheer number of girl/boy 'vocal only' bands with 3/4 part harmonies that have become so much a part of modern music then you can understand what I am getting at. At the moment there are two x four piece 'a capella' (without accompaniment) bands in the charts, one of them at number one in the album charts (April 05).

Through experience I would actually go so far as to say the ability to sing and harmonise may even get the weaker musician into the band if the superior musician has a weaker voice. Up to 80-90% of adverts for musicians for covers/tribute bands ask for vocals.

Most top covers/tribute bands have members who all have the ability to sing.

Most singers start of with a weak voice but it's no coincidence that most older musicians have a great voice, due simply to the fact that they started singing years ago and their voice has developed.

Some people, however, are obviously naturally gifted and have a great voice from the first time they sing, but even that voice improves over the years and will last the distance if developed correctly by some formal tuition.

Some formal tuition is advised if you can afford it but I believe regular singing will always improve a voice (as long as you are not shouting and yelling). I personally know hundreds of singers in the industry, most of whom have never had any formal vocal tuition whatsoever and yet have wonderful voices (that's not to say they wouldn't be even better if they would have had some formal training). My voice certainly improved after having some formal tuition although I had already been singing for 20 years before the tuition. It's the breathing technique and pitching practise (singing scales) that helps you to hold a note and pitch even higher and more importantly in tune. Scale work may be boring, but done the right way, with the right exercises it should result in very quick development of your voice. By 'scale work' what I mean is to practise singing along with one octave of the 'major' scale (and others) used earlier in the guitar practise section. Breathing technique and practising scales will be very beneficial to anyone and if you are just starting to sing it will be a really important introduction. For guitarists, there's the added bonus of being able to practise their guitar scales alongside vocal scales 'killing two birds with one stone'. Another added bonus is the ability for a guitarist to be able to 'scat' sing over any given scale, George Benson style. (Scat singing is vocal improvisation using sounds other than words—barra—bah—bah—bah—bah—da—da—da—da, etc.)

I first got into this form of playing and singing after catching the band 'Colonel Bagshot' in Liverpool around 1980. 'Art Caravan', the guitarist, would sing scat alongside his lead guitar rock solo's and it sounded magical. George Benson uses it to great effect alongside Jazz scales.

Besides lots of good practise, one of the most important aspects of good singing is the ability to control your breathing properly so it is used to maximum effect when you are actually singing, whether that be lead or harmony vocals. Before we go any further, I am not a vocal/singing teacher but I have had some tuition in order to be able to teach basic singing in schools.

We all have a diaphragm which is basically a breathing device. The diaphragm is a muscle system surrounding the lungs and is situated beneath the ribs around the stomach area. Most people breath very shallow and only actually use the top half of the lungs—breathing correctly uses the whole of the lungs so that more air is available. The singer then uses the natural action of the muscles (diaphragm and abdominal's) surrounding the lungs to control the amount of air that is exhaled when singing a note. It doesn't sound very rock-n-roll, but it does improve your singing. Better then to take a few pro lessons from a vocal coach even if it's just half-a-dozen to improve your breathing. After all is said and done, you don't need 'grade 8' to sing pop songs. If you simply can't afford lessons, just sing, it's better than nothing. As mentioned previously, 95% of the singers I know have never had any formal tuition whatsoever, and boy can some of them sing!

VOCAL HARMONY

Vocal Harmony is the result when two or more notes are sung at the same time. The combinations of notes that develop could be referred to as vocal 'chords'. In other words you are creating chords but using vocals instead of an instrument. Often harmony is used to support a melody or melodies and can certainly turn a mediocre song into a great song. Some bands rely heavily on vocal harmonies to create a certain style or sound. (The Bee Gees would be a good example. Their songs just wouldn't sound the same without their high pitched *falsetto harmonies).

*Falsetto = high voice forced beyond natural range.

Harmony, often used in Western music and other music forms, is the practice of singing in parts, where each person has a part (often of different pitches) and sings that part. The sounds become blended together, though of different pitch, to give a uniform, beautiful sound (if in tune!). Harmony usually has four sets of pitches: soprano being the highest, alto, tenor and bass (lowest). The highest voices are usually—although not always—for female singers and the lowest for male singers. The band Queen made full use of the entire vocal range in many of their greatest hits. It should be pointed out however that three singers of the same vocal range, ie, three tenor singers, could still sing three different notes within their vocal range and create a harmony and so on.

Other well known bands that have used multiple harmonies to great effect are (amongst countless others) 'The Beatles', 'The Eagles', 'The Hollies', 'Abba' and almost all of the well known black groups of the 50s, 60s and 70s like The Drifters, The Temptations, The Four Tops, etc.

Two part harmony specialists would have to include 'Simon and Garfunkel', 'The Everley Brothers' and so on. They are probably all before your time but their songs have all been re-released and covered by new artists over the years with the same harmonies used.

Most recently the so called 'boy bands' and the aforementioned 'McFly' have jumped onto the bandwagon and have realised the importance of harmony within songs.

It's a good idea to listen to the artists mentioned and practise singing in different pitches to get an idea of how harmony actually works. If you play an instrument it's not too difficult to work out which note sounds good with another note—pick out the individual notes within a chord. Taking that a step further if you played an open C chord, the three basic harmony notes would be the low C 'route note', the E note, the open G note and a further high C could be added as an octave harmony. That works out as the route note 1st + 3rd + 5th + octave note of the major C scale. If needed, more complex harmonies can be added once you have mastered the basic harmony notes, although it's quite unusual in most popular music to move away from the obvious harmonies. If you get the chance and want to hear some really unusual harmonies take a listen to Crosby, Stills & Nash's 'Lay me down' who add some very tasty and unusual vocal chord harmonies into their songs by adding extra harmony note extensions like 9s and 11s, etc.

MICROPHONE TECHNIQUE

You would not believe the amount of times I have heard the words "you turned the mic down when I sang my song" from a friend, relative or punter who has perhaps jumped up to do a song at a gig or a party. Besides the fact that you are being accused of cheating, it is also ignorant. If that person were to jump in a Formula One car, would they expect to do a lap as fast as Michael Schumacker?…I very much doubt it!

Another example is when the best man starts his well rehearsed speech at the wedding, only to frustrate everyone by resting the mic on or near his 'beer belly', therefore causing the 'well rehearsed' speech to be unheard, or at best 'sound muffled'.

Basically the persons in question do not know how to use a microphone and/or know how to project their voice into it.

That may be okay for somebody who only uses a microphone once or twice in their life, but there are many vocalists who also have bad microphone technique when singing, therefore putting across a weaker sound and performance.

If you are just starting off and you have access to a basic PA system you can practise your singing (and talking) whilst holding the microphone at different positions. Also, experiment using the mic—and voice projection—at different volume levels.

Important points to remember are **feedback**—caused when a microphone is pointed at a speaker, and **distortion/feedback** caused by having the volume too high.

A microphone will work best at a certain distance from your mouth.

This may sound obvious but it really is amazing how many people use a mic incorrectly by having it either too far from the mouth (very common) or too near (less common). Ideally a microphone should be around one inch from your mouth. If it's much further away than this it will lose volume, sometimes to the point where vocals will not be heard over any music, or at least the sound may be muffled and distant. It's slightly different if you are playing a guitar/instrument whilst singing, as the mic will be on a stand and I find (amongst others) that a microphone should be sound-checked with your lips almost touching the mic itself—that way you can gauge distance better whilst playing an instrument.

Practise with your equipment as the position will also depend on the type of microphone you use and your PA system. Another thing to consider is vocal dynamics when using the microphone—experiment with distance with regard to notes you may want to sound louder and vice-versa.

Remember, microphones can be used effectively to enhance as well as hide a singer's faults.

Vocal effects are important and are usually Reverb and Delay—sometimes known as echo. Reverb gives the effect of a singer singing in a large hall, delay gives a repeat of the note sang and can make the vocal sound warmer and add depth.

A mixture of the two can result in a very warm, attractive sound that can sit well in the mix of the music. Again, experimenting with effects is important—too much effect and it could sound muddy and too distant; not enough and the vocal could sound dry and harsh.

Remember, the more effect/s you add to a mic, the more it will sit into the mix. In other words, in most cases effects can create less volume for the vocals in the overall mix, so it's important to consider this when doing a sound-check without effects and then adding them later—best to sound check both with and without.

BUSKING

BUSKING UK

For the totally non-conformist amongst you, consider busking. It may not be a suitable route into opera singing but it will certainly improve your voice, confidence and playing ability. It's also a good way of meeting other musicians with the added bonus that if you are good, you could make some money.

Busking is not illegal, although some town councils require a license to busk. In some cases you have to actually audition (honestly!) in order to show you have the necessary skills to entertain people—after all, they don't want someone twanging away on a one stringed banjo howling like a wounded wolf, chasing people away from their beloved town centre.

Buskers can often be offered work from the general public, and in some cases (believe it or not) one or two famous names have been 'discovered' by record company A&R men who may have simply been passing them by on a street corner or railway station whilst they played.

SOME EXAMPLES—AMONGST MANY

Discovered busking with her younger sisters in the streets of her home-town Christchurch, New Zealand, the still teenage Hayley Westenra has now secured a U.S $4.5 million, five album contract in recognition of her simply beautiful voice.

Mercury Music Prize winner 'Badly Drawn Boy' A.K.A Damen Gough was also discovered this way.

Standing on a corner may not be some people's idea of making a living, but many entertainers have supplemented their income and education by doing just that. Earnings can vary from a bag of soggy crisps tossed into your cap in the middle of an extremely rough, one-stringed rendition of American Pie, to as much as £30 plus per hour (if it's a much better rendition!).

Of course money isn't everything…busking, as we mentioned before, can also be a useful way to practice your art, and if you write original material, sell your CDs.

If you want to sell CDs of your music whilst busking on the streets, you will need to pay for a Street Trader's Licence or Street Trading Permit from the local authority which varies in cost from council to council. It's not a bad deal and the cost will be covered if you sell one or two CDs.

Liverpool city council are introducing around eight fixed sites for buskers—to start late 2005—buskers have the chance to audition and if they are accepted, they will pay £100 which will include a buskers license and public liability insurance.

When music is played in public, the owner of the copyright is entitled, by law, to payment from the music user. The Performing Right Society is an organisation that collects and distributes this money (known as 'royalties') to it's members (this will be the owner of the copyright—usually the composer or their publisher). This means that buskers who perform cover versions of popular songs are required to pay royalties to PRS, but on the up side, if you are performing your own original works and you are actually a member of PRS you may be entitled to receive royalties! (Information courtesy of Performing Right Society.)

"Take a sad faced skinny dog with you—it works great. I actually trained my dog to look sad, it was really very happy. I earned over £10 an hour with the dog whereas before I had the dog with me, I was only making around a tenner a day. Some people were also leaving tins of dog food and biscuits so Rex was also very happy with

me busking, in fact he used to run around the guitar case all excited at the same time every day just before we would set off. Sometimes he was that excited he would be practically peeing on my guitar case. I have a mate in Spain who does it with a couple of puppies and he earns a fortune. He's now packed in doing the time share stuff to breed dogs cos he needs a constant supply of puppies".

—**L Johnson**

(Erm… please check with your local RSPCA branch before breeding sad faced dogs in order to boost any earnings from busking!)

This was a real statement from a busker in Liverpool on 4 April 2005.

BUSKING ABROAD

If you can manage to leave your dog with your auntie Joan for a couple of months you could also consider busking abroad. If you do it right you can pay for your trip and you may even earn enough to buy your dog a new collar. You can set your own hours, work wherever you want, meet lots of interesting people and top up your tan.

Personally speaking, although I have never actually done out-and-out busking abroad, taking a guitar with you when on holiday can lead to various rewards other than the obvious one—coins tossed into your hat.

Music is a common language, it doesn't matter whether people speak Arabic, French, Turkish, etc,—wherever you are in the world people love to hear a guitar or any instrument played well. I have on many occasions received many offers like cheap holidays, clothing, food, beer and hotel accommodation in return for playing my guitar. Anything played on a nylon strung classical guitar sounds simply wonderful when played outdoors on a balcony or terrace and although I do it for my own enjoyment, (I have never been abroad without a guitar in my life), it's a great way to showcase your talent (sometimes it's called posing) to people passing by. The people passing can also include hotel management, bar owners, etc, who more often than not tend to ask you to do some playing at their place in return for whatever you can manage to wangle. I don't really bother with money changing hands as it starts to become more of a chore and more formal—after all I am on holiday—but as I mentioned before, there are other forms of reward that can be just as beneficial as currency.

"Be open to receive offerings other than money. I've been pampered by an endless stream of pizza, coffee, gelato, free rides, and even job offers. Busking in out-of-the-way places can lead to interesting conversations that sometimes end in invitations. Be flexible. Not only will your talents keep your belly full, they'll take you where tourists rarely get to go".

—J Bear

"I dressed up as a woman and although I looked quite ugly, my takings doubled in one fell swoop. In between songs I would take the tennis balls out of the bra and do some one arm juggling. I packed it in though, after somebody stole my bag with my 'male' clothing in and I had to walk around Paris for two days with a dress on".

—I. Wilson (ex cross—dressing street busker)

"Sometimes I wish that I had listened to my father when he told me to go and get a proper job. I mean, busking in Eastern Europe during January/February isn't everyone's idea of a cosy career. It's not just the snow and frostbite that you have to look forward to but the aggressive tramps, alcoholics, beggars, hooligans and drunken tourists play their parts as well. There's also the impossibility of trying to pack away your mic, amp, lead, guitar and microphone stand in 20 seconds every time you see a policeman coming your way. Yes, you certainly attract a s..t load of unwanted attention! All this to contend with whilst being shat on by black-headed gulls and pigeons. Being a bricklayer would have been a less complicated career option. Not as interesting though!

—Andrew Woodcroft (serial European busker)

w: www.vocalist.org.uk a superb comprehensive website covering anything to do with vocals, singing, busking etc.

L to R—Myself, Alex McKecknie, my dad (Roy) & Brian Vance (at the back—with the real guitar!) doing some stuff in Turkey (April 2005) Four guitars, four voices and a few local percussive instruments thrown in for good measure, then add a big log fire and a few beers…happy days!!

Now and then you've just got to get away and enjoy doing a gig for the sheer pleasure of it (and maybe some free beer). After all, that's why we all started off playing in the first place—for a bit of fun. Music is so much more enjoyable when it's free and easy and even better if it's spontaneous—playing when you feel like.

NETWORKING

To simplify the term 'networking', it basically means making other people aware of what you do and what skills you may have, whether that's executed via personal contact, word of mouth, or both.

It's also important that there is then some contact information available, like a phone or mobile number, email, contact address, or even better a business/personal card containing all the above details to follow up that personal contact and make the networking process complete.

It makes sense that if you meet a fellow musician, or somebody associated with the industry at a pub, club, gig, studio, on the golf course, wherever, and discuss common music related subjects that you have contact details or the meeting may have been a waste of time.

Though networking may be thought of as something to be associated with the higher end of the industry, it can certainly help any up and coming musician/band as regards finding a drummer/guitarist/agent/manager/producer or sound engineer for example. Or looking at it the other way around, making other musicians/the general public aware that you are available as one of the above.

We could liken it to the domino effect in that it's cyclical. In other words the information you gave to one person, is then naturally, via normal human behaviour, (conversation or gossip!) passed to another person and so on.

Another way of looking at it in a non musical scenario could be;

You need a tiler to tile your bathroom, so you put the word out in your local pub,

an hour later the phone goes and somebody gives you the name and number of a good local tiler. The tiler's info, name and contact (and the fact that he's a good tiler) has been passed around naturally via a network of people.

It doesn't help to be shy, particularly in the music industry, as it decreases your chances of entering the networking system which in turn decreases your chances of meeting the right people who could further your career.

In fact, it doesn't help in any section of the entertainments industry to be shy or introvert. It's usually the more flamboyant personalities and characters that seem to get to the top of the ladder.

Imagine your name is John Begliano and you could well be one of the finest guitarists in your location. The problem is that you have never really told anybody you played an instrument or sang—maybe your mum and dad and your uncle Eric know, but nobody besides them has any idea that you are a musician.

Or your name is Joe Dunn, an average guitarist but everybody knows you and the fact that you play a guitar.

Chances are Joe Dunn will get more work, more conversation coverage, gain more contacts in the local music scene, more success, simply because of a simple thing called 'networking'.

John is a shy, introvert character but a great musician and could well join any band he chooses if he had better communication and interpersonal skills.

The problem is nobody knows of him or his skills as a musician and therefore he may never be part of the local music scene.

Joe would always be involved in some shape or form for the simple fact that every local musician knows of him.

Ever heard the saying 'it's not what you know, it's who you know'? Get used to it, you will hear it very often throughout your life as it's a very true and realistic phrase.

Contact cards are not expensive, costing anywhere around £30 to £200 per 100 depending on the quality. You can even buy them from vending machines at supermarkets or railway stations. The card can give essential information about your skills and even more important—a contact number.

We have all met people in our lives and lost touch, afterwards regretting we never made more effort to get some sort of contact details.

If you are considering having some cards printed, a really good tip is to do a few 'dummy runs' on blank cards as it's too late to change them once they have gone to print stage. The card needs to give clear details of 'your skills', your contact numbers including phone, mobile, fax, email, and in some cases office or home address.

The networking process never ends. Only this week I received an email from a promoter—a Mr. Joe West—from New York asking if I could help a young lady from Manchester with some gigs. He got my contact details from a friend of a friend.

We talked and he has now offered his services as a promoter for any of my student bands who fancy a few gigs in New York. (Come to think of it, I wouldn't mind some myself!) I have now given his contact numbers and e-mail to 'The Mags', a Liverpool band who will be over there (Manhattan—New York) recording anyway and hope to do some business and a possible tour via Joe.

You need to consider not only the people you have already met but also the kind of music industry people you need to meet to cover all bases.

It's good to know mainstream musicians like guitarists and drummers, etc. but when your career is moving along nicely, you also need to get some other names and contacts in your little red book. (These contacts may not be needed until you are a little further on in your career.)

Do you know any producers, promoters, sound—engineers, managers, agents, A&R, music journalists, etc? If not, it's time to get out there and meet some.

"Where am I going to find these people?" I hear you say.

Gigs, events, venues, rehearsal rooms, pubs, clubs, studios, colleges, social events, charity shows, open mic nights, concerts, music shops, classified's in the local press like the Loot, The Stage, NME, Melody Maker, you could even meet someone in your local launderette, (we all need clean clothes!)—basically anywhere.

TIP: Try your best to be polite to everybody you meet in the local music scene/industry, (in fact, everyone). It's amazing how often people move around and change jobs within the industry.

The spotty lad sorting the coffee and biscuits and mopping the floor in your local recording studio may one day be the head of A&R at a major label.

This scenario happens more frequently than you would imagine.

In fact, making the coffee is usually a good way, if not the only way into some music industry/studio jobs.

chapter 5
solo performers/covers

This chapter will cover the basic requirements and criteria for a solo performer on the pub or club and also the function/'covers' circuit. It's all very realistic advice and though it's not my aim to put you off pursuing a career in the entertainments industry as a solo artist, I believe some realistic advice as to your chances of succeeding and earning a living from the above should be considered.

Becoming a solo performer is one of the most difficult areas in the industry, particularly the covers circuit where you will normally be travelling on your own, sometimes long distances to find the work, performing on your own and playing to a room full of strangers on a weekly basis.

So let us presume that you may have decided that you would like to try to enter the entertainments industry as a solo performer for a number of reasons which could possibly be any of the following;

a) **You are naturally talented and you know or think it's the natural thing to do.**

You will have to consider that most singers starting of in the industry are unfortunately under the illusion that they may be more talented than they actually are. That's not being cruel, it's just realism.

If, for example, it's your mother or father or maybe your granny telling you you are the next best thing since Doris Day, then it may be a good idea to look for a more professional opinion. By a professional opinion I mean somebody you can approach who has been there and done it (not Simon Cowell!) like singers or other artists and entertainers, preferably with some sort of success as regards making some money in the game.

Attend some local gigs and approach the artist in their break and ask for a few moments of their time. Explain what you are looking to do and they should give you some tips, after all, they have all been in your position.

> **b. You have performed at a local Karaoke for years and though you know there is work to be done, you think life would be easier if you could hand in your notice and stop packing shelves for a living.**

Consider that since the emergence of Karaoke (if you are under 20 years old you have probably not known a time when it wasn't around), countless young people have been given the chance too use a microphone for the first time in their lives. Having had no previous experience whatever in the entertainments industry, they can now have a go at singing to an audience. That's fine but if there's no pay and it's all a bit of fun, there's no comeback, no judgment—therefore it's very unlikely anybody is going to make the comment that you are not good enough. Maybe you are!

> **c. You have tried to find other musicians to work with without success.**

Have you tried hard enough? If it's the only reason you are going it solo your venture may not last long. Unless you are totally 100% sure that solo work is your best option you will not enjoy it one bit. If you can't find a band, consider finding one more person and becoming a duo. You will then have some company, some help and support with equipment and obviously another musician on stage to help put the show across. Duos have a lot going for them, there is plenty of work and it's just a better situation all round. Although there is a sliding pay scale regarding the number of people as an entertainment 'unit', it shouldn't be a big loss adding one more person to form a duo.

Just to explain that payment structure a bit more, let's do an example.
- **Average solo act Saturday night = £150**
- **Average duo Saturday night = £250 after agent's fee = £125.00 each member**
- **Average three piece band Saturday night = £300 after agent's fee = £100.00 each member**
- **Average four piece band Saturday night = £350.00 after agent's fee = £87.50 each member**

- **Average five piece band Saturday night = £400.00 after agent's fee = £.80.00 each member**
- **Average eight piece soul band band = £500 after agent's fee = £62.50**

To put that in simple terms acts are not paid per person—if they were, I am sure there wouldn't be many solo acts about.

All venues, clubs and pubs have a budget for acts and entertainment, it has no minimum but for obvious reasons there is a maximum they can afford to pay.

d. You have realised that there is a large market in the pub/club scene for solo acts.

You are right, there is a massive market for solo work, especially if you are prepared to do some travelling. A solo act can work almost anywhere, from Cruise ships to domestic parties. Logistically speaking you could tour the world with equipment that would fit in a suitcase without actually playing the same venue twice.

e. You have auditioned for bands or other musicians to work with, but failed to make an impression.

It's important that you analyse the reasons other musicians did not actually take you on. It could be that you simply didn't fit in in some way, but it may be that you need to work on a few things. Always ask what the problem was—good honest feedback is essential. You can then work on any obvious problems.

f. You would simply prefer to work alone.

Go for it, but consider a trial period, then if things don't work out as you would have liked, you can reconsider your options.

If I haven't put you off by now—which I haven't meant to do, I have simply been realistic—and you really think you have got something you can sell to an audience read on.

The three obvious things you are going to need to start off are talent, some equipment and a good song repertoire. Later on you may need an agent or a manager and some transport but let's look at how you can build up to that scenario.

Let's presume you are starting from complete scratch.

The first things you will have to consider are your songs and show material; your repertoire.

You will need a minimum of one hour, thirty minutes (90 minutes) of music and songs which is more often than not the usual stage time (per gig) you will be expected to perform.

That should cover the usual pub/club criteria of two x forty-five minute sets or a support slot of approximately one hour.

It should be noted however that private functions like weddings, birthdays, corporate events, charity shows etc, can be negotiated with the customer though one hour thirty minutes is still the minimum amount of finished material you should have for your own benefit. That is certainly the case if you are working via an agency. (See agents.)

If you are the sole act for the night it is an almost certainty you will be asked to do two x forty-five minute sets, though if you are appearing with another act you may just be asked to do a one hour spot.

It should also be noted that work abroad can be very different as regards actual time on stage, where you can expect to do longer sets, or shorter, depending on the place you are working. (See working abroad.)

TIP: If you are doing a function find the name of the person/s the event is for. Then write the names down somewhere close to hand.

TIP: Remember when booking a gig to ask what time the second set is before you discuss a fee. It is very common for artists/bands to have to hang around for hours after they initially expected to. An average gig should be looked on as arriving around 7.00ish and ending around 12.00ish. Anything either side of these times should be pointed out at the time of booking. Ten minutes here or there is expected and is not really a problem, but private parties can run right through the night. It is not acceptable to be expected to continue without prior agreed payment for any extra time.

> "To gain valuable live gigging experience offer to do friends or relatives for expenses only. If people walk out after the first song, keep the set short. Don't be a fool though, if you start getting work from people in the audience that have seen you and enjoyed you, consider a higher fee".
>
> **—D. Brown (vocals—'Simply Fred')**

There are two kinds of mainstream 'solo' acts and obviously this chapter does not cover speciality acts such as fire eating, comedians, jugglers or sword swallowers etc.

a, So we have '**Self contained**' in which the 'act' provides all their own equipment including a 'PA' (public address system, the 'sound system'—the speakers you sing and play through), a microphone, all leads, and possibly some lighting (lighting is not classed as a necessity though it will certainly enhance the show). And of course if you are not actually playing an instrument, your own backing be it on 'Mini Disc', DAT (digital audio tape), CD, or audio tape will be required.

The latter two CD and audio tapes are **NOT recommended** as both are prone to jumping and snagging. (The future may be MP3 players).

Mini Disc players can now be purchased very cheaply for around £80-£150 depending on the make/brand and they are superb, as are 'DAT' players. Most artists are opting for mini disc players simply for their ease of use and their digital sound quality and if looked after and cased properly they will also last for years. Some mini disc players actually have the capacity to change the key of any given track which can be very useful if say, for example, the track is in too high a key/pitch or vice versa.

b, Non self contained. The self contained artist usually uses the pub/clubs PA sound system and may also use the resident duo/band if he/she provides music scores, commonly referred to as the 'dots'.

Although this is still happening throughout the UK and should continue for the foreseeable future it is a dying art as more and more pub/clubs are opting for the digital backing track revolution.

The booking agent/promoter should have prior knowledge that the artist is actually non self contained, in order to liaise with the pub/club to confirm the venue has the necessary equipment/resources.

This is where my argument kicks in regarding the use of your own equipment as it's so much more comfortable using your own sound that you are used to, and it's very hard to look 100% confident when using unfamiliar, antiquated, equipment.

My advice to anybody is to consider using your own equipment whenever and wherever possible in order to have a sound you are familiar with. Some venues have equipment that really should have been binned a long time ago, and it will certainly not do any justice to your show.

A decent start up 'PA' and microphone can actually cost less than you would imagine if you were to consider second-hand equipment. It's VERY important to always take someone with you who knows about musical equipment and also to ask the seller to give you a run through and a sound test.

Check if the equipment is in reasonable condition.

Check the speakers at all volumes to check signs of distortion (speakers can weaken over the years and can become brittle and possibly rip).

Check all inputs, some may not be working.

As I mentioned before if you take someone (an experienced musician) with you they should know what to look for.

You can also consider a new system in which case you would have a guarantee and also the advantage of the retailers back up. There are some very good entry/mid level PAs.

(See PA systems in equipment.)

Another thing to consider is power. It doesn't make sense to purchase a system that may be suitable for small pubs if there is a chance you may move on to larger venues. It would mean you starting all over again and 'buying twice'. Anything less than 300 watts per side is going to cause you problems in most average sized venues.

TIP: Take a sink, some soap, a toilet and a mirror with you to the gig! Most changing rooms are utterly dreadful and are not fit for a dog (even in some well known venues and theatres) reminding you if you needed it, that the job isn't as glamorous as you first thought! (Just warning you what to expect.)

Pub/club booking agents can usually be found in the yellow pages, for example under 'Entertainment Agencies' (see agents) or by asking fellow artists who they work for. Expect to do an unpaid showcase audition or if you can provide some evidence of past experience, a low paid 'gig' in which the agent should try to come along, or at least receive feedback from the venue.

NB. Venue usually pays artist in cash (after the gig) unless a 'cheque' payment has been agreed beforehand. The artist/act then pays the agent (15%). There is a difference between agents and managers and this will be explained in a later chapter, but for now note that an agent's fee is usually 15% and a manager's fee is usually 20%.

Rates for solo acts/artists are not set and can range from around £80.00 to as much as £2,000.00 (starting off expect around £80.00 to £150.00 Saturday night) depending obviously on demand and quality of the artist and their repertoire, and especially any TV, radio, press coverage. A useful tip though—a solo singer/musician with a great sound and great stage presence can be regarded as a better act than a superior singer with a bad sound and bad stage presence.

The punters love to see confidence and a good stage presence, and it often overrides talent. When the two are mixed it goes without saying that the artist will usually be asked back, and usually for a higher fee.

A good example of the above is the emergence of Karaoke. The public seem to think anyone with the confidence to get up and sing is a star, even if they sound awful. It's a fact that sometimes the worse the singer is, the more applause they receive.

I personally think the emergence of Karaoke has done some serious damage to 'live music' venues. In the early nineties at least half of all live pub venues cancelled live bands and introduced Karaoke nights.

Don't get me wrong, Karaoke will always be a good way to find the really good singers that would sound good in any circumstances. It's also a good stepping stone for young up and coming talented youngsters who may never have been spotted if it wasn't for the emergence of Karaoke.

It should be noted however that singing on a Karaoke is a far different world than getting up and singing professionally in a controlled environment for almost two hours with people expecting you to be good and professional. I suppose you could liken the situation to a pub footballer evolving into a pro footballer.

You are there watching your local pub team and Tommy scores a goal. The guy next to you comments that 'Tommy is a great footballer'—well he may be a decent pub footballer but would he ever be able to cut it as a pro footballer? Probably not.

It's not always that dramatic a situation for the reason that Karaoke is also a magnet for some very good singers who may simply be after some prize money. And taking that a step further, an inexperienced singer can use the Karaoke as a kind of rehearsal/practice situation, therefore collating as much experience and repertoire as regards songs and material as possible, before then considering moving on into a semi-pro situation.

It is also an ideal situation to gain confidence regarding stage presence and patter. Even working with musical equipment, holding and using a microphone is good experience.

If you are unsure of your talent and don't quite have the nerve (and you won't be the only one), try doing a few unpaid gigs for your friends' birthdays, weddings and so on and see how you get on. Don't be afraid to accept some criticism, it may help.

For instance, choice of songs at particular venues and parties is an art in itself. In other words, it's not a good idea to sing Tammy Wynett's D.I.V.O.R.C.E at a wedding!

Always remember to ask the approximate time you can be expected to finish. There are many times when the night feels like it has gone on forever. It's no fun hanging around two or three hours to do your second spot, especially if you have only charged the normal rate.

TIP: Buy the best equipment you can afford and always look your best. Try to wear something you normally would not wear, something elegant and try to smile—the audience will appreciate the effort. Remember the covers side of the music industry is a very difficult and sometimes harsh environment so it's good to have some friendly faces around.

Going back to song material. It's important to choose your material carefully and it should reflect the type of venue and gigs you will be performing in, and also your voice.

If, for example, you will be doing the obvious 'Cabaret' circuit then you will need very commercial material, songs everybody will know, hits, standards, a good mixture of popular songs with approximately 50% of the songs as possible second half 'dance' material.

Ballads are very nice but venues like to hear some faster music for people to dance to later on in the evening.

TIP: Make sure you know the next song coming up or use a set listing. After all a four beat intro by the drummer probably relates to 99.9% of your songs.

After taking into consideration all of the above, the financial aspect may resolve the final decision.

I know for a fact that there are numerous bands that have split up due to this potential money earning situation.

It has happened to me personally on more than one occasion with singers leaving to pursue solo/duo work in order to earn some decent income.

One particular band I played in in the early eighties had that many overheads at gigs, including PA hire, four roadies, two lighting engineers, a manager etc, that it was quite impossible to make a profit. Unfortunately our singer started doing some local pub gigs and realised that *that* circuit was where the golden nugget lay.

The pubs couldn't afford the full show with all the outlay so they got the singer (with backing tracks).

The exact situation (different vocalist) happened again almost 10 years later.

The bands I am talking about could not be classed as unsuccessful, quite the opposite. They were both signed (the first to a major) but unfortunately we were not making a profit, or at least not making enough money to keep everyone happy.

If a person is gigging simply for the monetary reward, then it's going to happen all too often.

INLAND REVENUE

Unfortunately we all have to pay taxes on moneys earned.

Although a good accountant charges you money to sort your finances they should be able to save you much more than they cost, and they can certainly keep all financial issues above board and lawful. You could possibly do your own accounts using something like a

'Simplex D' accounts book which is basically like an earnings income/outgoing diary system. Every penny going in or out in any given week is accounted by filling in the weekly chart. Every receipt should be kept and dated within the book and then it becomes much easier to fill in a tax form.

It should be noted, however, that even using this method it is still very complicated knowing what you can and cannot claim for. Therefore I would strongly recommend an accountant—preferably experienced in music related accounts—although a good accountant should know what they can claim for regardless of the trade. As we said before receipts are very important (do not throw them away). They can offset income as regards out-going expenses. Receipts should be kept for everything you purchase from petrol, to hair cuts. Yes, even hair cuts—we have to look good on stage if we are in the entertainment industry! Your accountant will then do all they can (within reason) to keep your bill as minimal as possible within the tax laws. Don't forget even the accountants fee is deductible to a certain percentage. So for example if they are saving you a couple of grand a year it has to be worth their fee. Accountants fees are also accountable!

GIGGING ABROAD COVERS

The UK as we know is starting to decline as regards venues for both original music and covers/cabaret music, and has been gradually doing so since the 70s.

(It should be noted however that there will always be work available for the best acts, if they are willing to travel around the UK.)

Therefore it may be an idea to consider spreading your wings and possibly working abroad.

With the EU now making Europe a more 'user friendly' prospect as regards to working abroad, it could add up to a good move.

Unlike the UK situation, venues are increasing abroad as more and more people take holidays overseas. In fact more and more people, including musicians, are actually opting for a life away from the UK, particularly in the likes of Spain, Greece, etc.

Conditions differ outside of the UK as regards the money you can earn per gig, time on stage per gig, and other aspects of the industry.

As a rough guide though, using Spain for example.

Hotel work can be harder than the UK with up to three sets of fifty minutes or even more.

Bars however tend to have shorter sets and time on stage, and can be negotiable between the artist and the venue. Don't expect more money abroad though, as it's a fact that the UK is one of the biggest payers for entertainment throughout Europe and that would also cover larger, more well known hotel chains.

Typical holiday entertainment hot spots like Benidorm, for example, have a massive market for solo, duo acts and DJs, and in fact one venue may employ up to four or five different acts per night, every night. Acts are paid between £40—£100 for the forty/fifty minute set, depending on their crowd pulling powers. You simply do your set and move on to the next venue booked—it's possible to do two or three a night, seven nights a week if you can hack it. In fact there is a strong case that you could actually live out there and never be short of work.

It has to be noted that this work is not really suitable for bands with full kit including drums, amplification etc, or at least if there is work for such acts, don't be expecting to make much (if any) money, unless you work for a good hotel chain via a good agent and have a rolling residency—in other words you play the same gig at the same hotels on a regular night.

Another main difference between the UK and Spain is the fact that in Spain they will always have a public address system (PA) the artist can use and it is expected that the artist will use it, whilst in the UK we are mainly expected to be self contained and use our own PA systems (though not at all venues.)

It's always useful to have a good agent to work through but if you are confident, a quick audition is all that is required from the management of most venues (although without an agent it's not always guaranteed you will be paid the amount agreed, in fact it's not even guaranteed you will be paid at all, agent or not!)

Work abroad can be affected by season although there will always be some work, even in mid winter with the mild climate.

If you can also put over some DJ skills then that becomes another area where working abroad can be lucrative, especially in the younger more modern resorts such as Ayia Napa in Cyprus or Faliraki in Rhodes where young people gather and party every night of the week to the latest dance music.

Beware though, work outside the UK can pose potential problems, not least the tax issues.

> "I got to Benidorm at 6.00pm (bearing in mind that I had never set foot there before and knew nobody). I was singing on a stage at 6.20pm—it was all a bit surreal. For that forty minute spot I received £60.00, an hour

later I was on another stage at another venue, another forty minutes later I had another £60.00 in my hand. It became very tempting to stay over there. Sun, sand and as much work as I could handle. One night I did three gigs at £60.00 each. It was only three years earlier I was in a freezing cold garage spraying cars".

—C. Gibson

AGENTS, COVERS CIRCUIT

BOOKING AGENTS COVERS CLUB/PUB/FUNCTION WORK:

It's more simple than you would think to find an agent but maybe not so simple to find a good agent and to then impress them enough to receive work via their agency.

HOW DO YOU FIND AN AGENT?

Agents can be found in various places, usually under the heading 'Entertainment Agencies'.

In your local Yellow Pages for example, you will find a listing of local agencies and they usually stress which kinds of entertainment or entertainers they provide, though most will cover anything from solo acts, duos, trios, bands, also function disco's and speciality acts, impressionist's, singing dogs etc.

Another place to find agents is to go on the internet to

'The Agents' Association of Great Britain'—www.agents-uk.com

They have a listing of all members in the UK and their website allows you to find local agents and it also lists the acts they currently have on their books.

All contact numbers and website and email addresses for each agent are included.

It's obviously also used by people who may be searching for an act for a function or corporate event/show which they may be holding.

Agents also advertise in local papers or other publications and are constantly looking for good new acts/artists/bands of any genre/description.

They can then promote the band to the club/pub circuit that they may have on their books for certain months of the year.

Agents usually hold 'showcase nights'. These nights are there to give any new acts/artist's/bands an opportunity to show their talents and more importantly show what they can do as regards entertaining an audience.

The act/artist/band will usually be asked to do around 20—30 minutes and give the broadest example of their repertoire.

The agent holding the showcase will usually invite concert secretary's and promoters plus of course the general public and will hope some of the acts may impress them enough to then book the artists via their agency.

A 'self contained act' (a band using their own equipment) will be expected to use all their own equipment inclusive of a 'PA' (public address) system and all back line including amps, drums etc (unless otherwise instructed).

Some acts are not expected to be self contained and will then be able to use the club/pub 'PA' system, as well as backing from the resident band/duo (although as we mentioned earlier in the book this is becoming more and more rare due to the emergence of 'digital backing tracks'.)

Members of the public will of course be welcome and the agent will evaluate any response/feedback from the audience, whether that be a good or bad comment.

An act may be asked back to have another go two or three times over the year if they were not quite "up to it" on the first show, (obviously to see if any improvement has taken place).

This is a common scenario due to acts/bands not knowing quite what they are getting into. They should then (hopefully) at least receive some good and realistic advice from the agent on how they can improve themselves and/or their show.

It's not rude to ask if expenses for travelling will be paid, though this should be discussed before-hand, so as not to cause embarrassment to both parties on the evening of the event.

If an artist/act/band do the business and impress, the agent will already have an idea of a fee he/she could put the artist/s out for on the circuit. Though there may be some 'testers' before anything major, the agent can, and will, then evaluate any feedback from the artists shows.

The agent will charge 15% (sometimes—but rarely—negotiable) unless you sign a management contract with them in which case you could then pay up to 20%.

You DO NOT have to sign an agreement with an agent.

But if you find a good agent, and that agent gets you good regular work and good money then it might be worth considering. It's very important to remember that if you receive a gig from an agent then you are getting 85% of something. If you try and then fail to get a gig yourself you will receive the grand sum of 0% of nothing! In other words, better having 85% from £100 gig = £85 in your pocket than 0% of no gig = £0.

For established acts, 'The Stage' publication is also very useful and provides info on good established agents who can provide work throughout the UK and Europe, (and even worldwide in some cases).

Some of them can (and usually do) sub-contract you (split commission) to other agents throughout the UK/Europe/World.

It is always very important to use a recognised agent and be extra vigilant when taking work abroad—ask to speak to people who have used the agent before, for example. Never accept work abroad from someone who has simply handed you a card at a gig without checking out their credentials. Anyone can have cards printed.

I know of a five piece band who once travelled to Spain to find the venue they were booked to play in had been shut down, no compensation was ever paid. I know of a duo that got to another resort to start work and the stage had not been built.

It should be noted that when working abroad or taking more 'up market' work that contracts would be required. That is obviously in your own interest, as well as the interests of the venue and booking agent.

> "We paid for our own air-fares after the agent told us we would be reimbursed on arrival by the guy who would be sent to meet us. No one turned up to meet us. Luckily we knew someone out there and we were working after a few days anyway, but it could have been a nightmare."
>
> **—H Joyce.**

OTHER ROUTES

CONSIDER OTHER FORMS OF INCOME ALONGSIDE GIGGING

It's very important for any musician starting off in the industry to at least consider other 'non musical' career options (whether it be full time or part time) to run in conjunction with their early musical career. Consider the fact that your postman may have better musical equipment than you do and could well be a better musician than you—just because he/she is delivering post doesn't mean he/she is not a great musician.

Somewhere along the line that person may well have realised that a guaranteed income would be the best way to purchase equipment (and pay the bills), therefore giving him/her a better chance of improving their musical career.

Although I was in a band from a very young age, I also served an apprenticeship as a floor-layer/roofer by trade (a very hard job) and because of that income I could always afford the best possible equipment money could buy.

Being a gigging musician is always going to be a good secondary income but as I already mentioned before, it's extremely hard relying on it as your main source of income.

Of the hundreds of musicians I know personally, only a few have been able to live solely off the income from gigging alone—so if we consider these musicians who range from the club/pub circuit guitarist/singer, to some that have enjoyed hits in the charts, then it's the broadest possible spectrum of musician that we are considering.

I know of some musicians that can gig five, six or even seven nights a week and yet are still having to set the alarm clock to do a day job.

This situation is not good for your health, but unfortunately gigging is not a lucrative income unless you are fortunate enough to secure a job with a very successful tribute/covers band, or a band who's gigging includes doing the holiday circuit playing their old top ten hits to the holiday makers.

There is nothing wrong with this but expect to live out of a suitcase, eat pizza's three times a day and end up slightly mad.

I did the holiday circuit myself many, many years ago and ended up with a strange facial expression which is not dissimilar to the vacant look on a young Koala bear.

To put it in simple terms, it's important to at least consider other ways of earning an income other than just gigging.

If you can play an instrument good enough to entertain people, you could consider peripatetic teaching in schools, youth clubs, community centres or private tuition.

To become a private instrumental teacher you do not have to have formal qualifications though it is almost essential for school based teaching for obvious reasons. The rates you will be paid by a school will be determined by any teaching qualifications you may have.

Some musicians can charge a school for half/full day specialist instrumental seminars. In fact this is becoming more and more popular, due to the school music curriculum changing dramatically over the last ten years to a more, shall we say, informal music educational system with the emphasis being on more creativity, performance and composition.

School music lessons twenty years ago seemed to encompass Handels fireworks music and how many fillings he had, what he ate for his breakfast, etc. It now tends to lean towards a more practical, performance and composition based outcome.

PC based technology and recording is also another field of peripatetic music teaching and is in high demand in most schools.

The experience of working with young musicians in schools is very rewarding and gave me a fantastic insight into how we view music as a child. It was always a great pleasure to see smiling faces as they learned a simple way to create music on any instrument.

Private tuition ranges from anything from £10 to as much as £50 per hour, obviously again depending on the qualifications or experience the teacher has and also the type of music being taught (jazz and classical tuition tend to be more expensive). If you need to brush up on your skills and in particular your theory—to be able to teach music exam grades—you may have to have to consider further education for yourself and possibly taking some sort of exam. Playing music and teaching music are two different things—it's amazing how much you may know, but getting that across to somebody else is another thing.

You could also consider writing for music production libraries but do not expect to earn a living from it unless you take it very seriously and find a good library that's willing to take your work (more on that in another chapter).

For now, look on it as a hobby, then if you are one of the lucky chosen few who's piece or sample may be used in a film or television advert—happy days!

For us older statesmen, we can consider using our skills and music industry experience to become a manager or agent ourselves, or even a compere/MC, (if you can stand the thought of being in the same place night after night after so many years of moving around).

Providing you have enough contacts and are a very skilful player, you could also become a session player, also known on the circuit as a 'dep'. To move into session work you need to consider the following pointers.

You will have to be a seriously good player, preferably with music reading skills although that can depend on the type of work you are offered or are looking for—I know many great players that cannot read music—but better still if you can learn to. You will need good reliable equipment and transport. It goes without saying that you will need to be completely professional and competent. There are session agencies that will take you on if you send them a CV and/or some recordings of your skills, be honest about your skills and remember to mention other instruments you may play as that versatility may just get you the job. Whenever possible try to get a tape or recording of the type of music you are expected to play.

BASIC SONGWRITING

Again this subject could fill another book, but we can look at the very basics and later move on to more advanced stuff, and some tips you may be able to use.

Although I will be assuming that the reader has some basic knowledge of an instrument, I will also cover vocalists with no instrumental knowledge.

To me, songwriting is a skill or talent that comes naturally. Writing simple songs is not too difficult, writing a great melody however, is much harder.

I think if you try too hard to create melody it can make the process more difficult, in other words if you force a tune or melody it's not going to work, or at least the finished song may end up with a 'factory finish'. The main point to songwriting melody is to simply play an instrument (solo or ensemble), or if you don't play an instrument, sing your lyrics and wait for that magic moment when something jumps out, almost as if you are an aerial picking up radio waves. You have to be completely receptive and open.

Anyway, that's all a bit heavy—let's get back to the basics!

I personally believe some of us have a natural ability to create great melodies within a song, therefore making the song stand out from the many others, but that's only my opinion.

There must be thousands of songs written every year using the same basic chord patterns, but only some manage to 'hook you'.

It's a fact, however, that there will be thousands of good songs out there, written by unknown artists and writers that unfortunately will never even be heard due to the nature of the industry, bad luck, no commercial back-up, no air—play, or perhaps a combination of the lot. People often say that a great song will always succeed, sorry, to me that is simply utter tosh. There must be hundreds of thousands of great songs that will never receive the recognition they deserve.

As I said before lyrics, and melodies can come naturally, even accidentally. However there are certain methods and chord structures that can make song writing an easier task.

That includes both the instrumental part of the song and the lyric.

Most people have their own way of creating a song, whether that be music first, then the lyric, or lyrics first then music added, or simply a combination of both. People talk about 'inspiration' when writing songs and of course that may account for the reason you want to write a particular type of song. But a song can also be created by complete accident or chance in a spontaneous moment. In other words great songs can sometimes simply come from an idea you have had, or a particular chord you have strummed or something someone has said that may just give birth to the beginning of a song. It's a well known fact that if you put a band in a rehearsal situation and leave them to experiment, they will find and create songs by simply playing instruments and picking up on musical ideas. Obviously the ideas then need to be fattened up and rearranged in order to develop the end product.

Lets start with lyrics and some very basic possible ways of making the important start of the lyric.

I personally, as others may well do, usually pick up on a phrase, name or title that you come across in everyday life.

That title or phrase could then, and often does, become the subject of the song. So there we are on our way to a song, although there is obviously a lot more to do to it, it can be a launch pad.

I then wait until the mood arises and the song normally develops naturally.

That title or phrase could be picked up in a conversation or whilst watching the television, reading a newspaper or even reading a book.

If you have never written a song before, this technique usually works.

It certainly did when I introduced it at the school I worked at to improve lyrical composition skills and my own children now use it.

Pick up a novel or book you have lying around—it has to be a fiction novel, maybe a Catherine Cookson book or something of that type.

Open the book, flick through it and pick a page at random.

Now without purposely looking, scroll your finger down and stop.

Take a look at the line of the book you have stopped at.

(I am doing it now as I write this book—here's the line I just stopped at…

'He turned to me, he narrowed his eyes, 'Why are we in New York?' he said.

Now look at that line and you can use any part or all of the line as a title.

Obviously *you* are not in school and you can continue until something more interesting as a title comes along, though I must admit if you had to use it (which you would have had to do in my school lesson), there is an obvious title there—not including the obvious one sang by old blue eyes—' He turned to me'/'She turned to me', (changing 'sexes' pronouns he/she is allowed).

Just as an experiment, lets try and knock up some basic lyrics with that title. I am doing this **'real time'** and will stop only for very short pauses.

She turned to me
She turned to me, and tried to smile
But I couldn't see the pain inside
Then all at once I realised
The love we had, had gone and died
What can I do—my life has gone
I thought she was the only one
I'll try my best to walk away
knowing that the pain is here to stay

As you can see, in a couple of minutes it's actually starting to sound very like the beginnings of a song, simply because of the lyric around the title and the choice of words that can naturally flow from a title.

Ok, so it's just a very simple unfinished lyric, but it proves a point in that a title can give you a head start.

Incidentally, if I was serious about finishing these lyrics I would work on each line and try to improve the phrasing of wording, etc.

I would also delve into my backlog of tunes and melodies which are already stored in my memory or recordings from previous bouts of songwriting.

This is just one of the many different ways a song lyric can be born. A lyric can come from any source—something you hear in a conversation, something you read, something emotive that's happened to you can all create a lyrical idea.

Another important tip is to look back at the lyric and analyse it see if there are better words to use—there usually are a few changes that will improve the wording of the song. It wouldn't actually take that long to consider every single word you use.

A song can be written in an hour, a month or a year.

Here's one I spent a little more time on around the late 80s. My publisher asked me to come up with something for a holiday company regarding summer holidays. I picked up a travel brochure for some inspiration and the words **'Got to get away'** jumped out from the front page.

So with a little bit of imagination I came up with this lyric;

Caught in a heatwave

*It's over one hundred degrees
But I ain't complaining
It's probably raining back home
Don't want to go back
I could stay here for the rest of my life
Blue sea and sand
Girls getting tanned by my side
(Chorus)*
Got to get away *from it all sometime
Got to get away from it all sometime
Tropical island,
Somewhere in the middle of June,
Temperatures rising—it's not surprising at all.
Don't want to go back,
I could stay here for the rest of my life
Blue sea and sand
Girls getting tanned by my side
(Repeat Chorus)*

A very simple song which, along with the music, captures a summer holiday theme. I remember hearing the song being played months later and thinking of my next holiday, so it obviously worked!

Another very important point to remember is the lyrics do not have to make sense. Many lyrics have been written that do not actually tell the full story, therefore leaving the listener to form their own interpretation of the song. To put that another way is to say a lyric can merely suggest something and then leave the listener to form their own conclusion which could be quite different from another persons perspective of the lyric.

If you look at the famous songwriters throughout the years you will see countless lyrics that can be interpretated in different ways.

So let's stick with this for now and consider the fact that you may not play an instrument.

You would have to try to create a melody in your head that may fit the lyrics in order to be able to complete the lyric.

It's not necessary to consider a melody line yet, as you could simply write the lyric in poetry form and add the music or melody later.

It's at this point we should consider the fact that it would obviously be much easier to write songs and lyrics if you learn the basics of any instrument (preferably guitar or keyboards/piano).

With four or five basic chords you would then be able to create a tune or melody as well as the lyric, even if you have a melody it would be easier if you could put that alongside some chords.

It's remarkable how many melodies can be derived from five or six chords, you could actually do a very simple version of most songs with six chords, and taking it a step further if you learned seven chords—in the same key—you would be able to do a simple version of almost every song ever written.

We will cover the term 'Key' later.

This is all very basic advice and should help you start to be able to write simple lyrics and melodies. Nobody can teach someone how to write great songs, that is something that comes naturally.

Some people have the natural ability to create wonderful melody lines even if its just backed up by a few simple chords.

It has to be said though, that the better a musician you are, the easier the songwriting process should be, in that the more you play and the different chord structures and chord extensions you use can give more artistic freedom and create more chances for a melody to be born.

Let's go back to the simple chords you could learn, and explain the meaning of the musical term 'Key' in simple form.

When I am explaining this term to anybody, I always use another word as an example to try to get the meaning across. The word I use is "family".

So for example, if we say Key=Family, I can try and explain from there. Chords in a same key could be then likened to chords in the same family in that they belong together, they sound good together and they are related to each other.

Again keeping it simple, if we point out all chords are named after the first seven letters of the alphabet A to G, (there are many extensions to the chords but don't worry about that for now).

Let's now pick a 'key' and look at the chords in that key.

I am choosing the key of G as it's a good key as regards most people's vocal range and more importantly also has some of the easier chords involved.

Before we go any further, lets remember we are not talking about learning a guitar the way you would normally learn if you wanted to be an out and out guitarist, we are simply looking at chords you could learn in order to assist you as a songwriter.

So lets look at the chords involved in some common keys, starting with

the key of G
G—A minor—B minor—C—D—E minor—F sharp diminished

The chords in the key of C
C—D minor—E minor—F—G—A minor—B diminished

The chords in the key of A

A—B minor—C sharp minor—D—E—F sharp minor—G sharp diminished

As you can see there are actually just seven chords to learn in any given key.

Even if you have never played a guitar or instrument before it shouldn't take you too long to learn these chords. If for example you had a guitar lesson for each chord including a simple strumming technique, it's got to be worth it for the simple reason that you could then add chords and melody to your lyrics or songs.

Once you have learned the chords, you can then start to write simple tunes using the chords in any order, as many, or as few as you like.

As an example, two chords can make equally as good a song as seven can.

'Eleanor Rigby' by The Beatles uses two chords (in the key of C) being C and E-minor,

'Yesterday', again by The Beatles uses six chords. They are both equally wonderful songs. Going back to arriving at songs by accident, 'Yesterday' started out as 'scrambled eggs'! Late one night Paul stumbled across a nice melody and simply used these words until he had time to write better lyrics.

The use of a 'capo' (a device you place on the guitar neck) can be used to higher or lower the 'key' in which you are playing, you simply continue to use the same chords but the 'capo', which acts like an extra finger, changes the key. If for example you learn a C and place the capo on the second fret and play the C chord you would then be playing a D.

Ask your local music shop to show you how they work; they are priced from around £5 to £20.

It's a fact that someone with the basic knowledge and skill to play a few chords in any given key, could actually go on to write a hit album. If you look back at the 60's for example, the musicians may not have been technically brilliant, they just seemed to hit on a few good melodies. That is of course until The Beatles came along and added their own brand of writing that may never be surpassed.

The difference between The Beatles and other writers at the time was the simple fact that they weren't just great melody writers, they were also very underrated—superb musicians.

MORE ADVANCED TIPS

Biggest tip here has got to be to experiment. Go off the beaten track, get on the wrong train—it could take you to a different destination but it might be a nicer place. Experiment with chord extensions and relative bass notes as opposed to the obvious notes.

For example, try moving chords to different positions on the neck (like D or G for example) and you get some very interesting melodic results. There's also the ostinato effect in which a common theme or riff is repeated in a loop throughout a piece of music creating a possible hook. An ostinato could be a repeated bass line, a guitar riff loop, a repeated violin theme, in fact any instrument can create a common theme or riff running through a song or piece of music.

For purists, the term Ostinato

Ostinato = (Italian, literally 'persistent') as in basso ostinato meaning 'ground bass' (think bag pipes) a short, repeating pattern (melodic, harmonic, rhythmic, movement) which is intended to be performed together with a melody.

Melodic ostinato is a short, repeated melody pattern—or riff—which is intended to be performed together with another melody to produce harmony.

Harmonic ostinato is a short, repeated chordal accompaniment pattern which is intended to be performed along with a melody.

"A repeated riff or theme running through a song can make it instantly memorable, we did it quite often and it can give even an average song a better hook".

Sir Paul McCartney (Liverpool Institute for Performing Arts—'LIPA') 2003

Another form of ostinato is a constant bass staying on the one note whilst the song moves through various chords in the same key the bass is playing in. I make no apologies in using the Beatles songs again as examples, although 'Pink Floyd', 'Genesis' and more recently 'The New Radicals' and 'Snow Patrol' have all used it to great effect.

The Beatles 'Day Tripper' the common theme and hook is the guitar riff.

The Beatles 'I feel Fine' the common theme and hook is again the guitar riff.

The Beatles 'Blackbird' the common theme being the open G note throughout the guitar finger picking chordal work.

The Beatles 'Got to get you into my life' the common theme and hook is the bass line staying on a repeated note whilst the chords move around it (the bass note stays on the route note G whilst the chords played are the 1st (G chord) and 6th (F maj 7 or F) modes of the the key. The hook is the bass playing a G whilst the chord changes to an F maj 7, as G is related to F maj 7, this is why it sounds very catchy. Add to that great lyrics, harmonies and melody and you can understand why The Beatles songs have been covered by almost 80% of other artists at some time of their life. Earth Wind and Fire covered "Got to get you into my life".

Almost every classical composer has used ostinato to great effect at some time.

Some classical guitar pieces are played with a down tuned D (the normal thick E string tuned down to a D), therefore giving a continual accompaniment bass string drone throughout a piece—when played in the key of D.

Another idea is to use relative bass notes. If someone is playing a D chord for example, consider playing a relative note (a note in the same key but not the obvious D route note) like F sharp or G, C or E, in fact any note in the key of D played alongside the chord will make the chord sound more unusual and attractive. Guitarists should consider chords using this idea/method. A great example of a guitarist using this method would have to be the late Nick Drake who used superb chord work in writing songs.

By now you may have gathered that I am also an immense Chet Atkins fan. Chet Atkins would play both ostinato and relative bass lines and jazz ragtime runs alongside chordal work, therefore creating the illusion that two guitarists were playing at once (when in actual fact two pieces are being played at once with advanced finger style methods).

> "Songwriting is at it's best when the people are channels or transmitters, rather than consciously setting out to write a specific song. To write songs is to be in a state of grace."

–Peter Coyle (The Lotus Eaters)

It's early days yet, but an important thing to remember is that although songwriting is something we may start doing as a hobby or maybe as a bit of fun, if you are serious about it, it can in some cases lead to royalties for the writer of the lyrics and the song melody. (See MCPS/PRS.) But remember, for the thousands of songs that are written every single day, only a few are good enough to become hits and that is only if they have the chance to be heard by the right people. It's like a fish escaping through three nets and living to tell the tale. The first net is writing the hit song itself, the second is performing or recording it, the third is getting it aired to the right people who can then get it into the public domain.

But it can all depend on who you are writing the songs for. If you are simply writing for your own pleasure, that's fine and no one can tell you what you should be doing. You can get away with songs lasting ten minutes with two two-minute guitar solos and basically anything goes

If however it's A&R (record/publishing company personnel) or radio station producers/DJs you are targeting your songs at, then the ten minute songs need some serious editing. Such people are not interested in long drawn out songs or two minute guitar solo's. What they are looking for are short (around 3—4 minutes), strong, straight to the point catchy melodic songs—simple as that!

Sometimes writers, bands and artists just can not seem to settle on a style of music and this can become a problem with a set of songs that simply has no direction and can result in a 'mishmash' of a set.

If you just can't find a direction for your music, consider the artists and writers you may wish to be 'similar' to and that may 'influence' your writing.

The importance of influence can not be overstated. There is no harm whatsoever in your songwriting being influenced by your favourite artists or writers, after all the greatest and most popular writers in the world have all—in turn—been influenced by somebody (although it has to be said that sometimes they may not own up to it).

There is also the influence of a particular type or style of music. For example the Beatles were heavily influenced by skiffle music in their early days. The secret is not to be too set on an exact copy of the artist to the point were it's almost a form of ***plagiarism**. You need your own identity, there is nothing wrong with writing in a similar vein to another writer or artist (it's almost impossible not to sound like somebody), but copying and sounding too much like someone else can be looked on as cheating. There are however bands today who simply thrive on copying other successful bands to a fault, with no shame and they make a lot of money in the process.

***Plagiarism**—'taking ideas, parts of written works, song lyrics or pieces of music etc, from another writer or author and presenting them as one's own'. (see copyright).

Inspiration is another important word that comes to mind with songwriting. If something inspires you it gives you ideas and enthusiasm to do something other than just sitting around. If you have fallen into a rut with your songwriting or even playing your instrument, go and watch some other bands or listen to some of your dad's old albums. You may find the inspiration and influence you have been waiting for.

It may be difficult but if you can aspire to be different, you may just find a road no one has gone down. Use your imagination, be interesting—record companies, the media and the entertainments industry as a whole—just loves originality.

chapter 6
the road test

So you have practised until you consider yourself a decent musician. You have done a bit of 'networking' and successfully auditioned and joined a band and you are now ready to go 'on the road'. Well believe it or not, all of that may have been the easy bit!

If you are even considering starting up as a 'gigging' musician (going on the road), spend a couple of weeks or even months with a working act or band, preferably the latter.

Travel with them from the moment they leave for the gig. Don't just meet them at the gig, that's cheating. Jump in from the start. You should get an idea how long it can take to pick up band members and equipment with the added bonus of travelling in the back of a cramped van!

Were all members ready at their arranged pick up time?

It only takes one person to make everyone late, my bet is you will be late more often than you are on time. Lateness is a very ignorant but curable disease—alarm clocks and watches can help cure the person in question—although there may be some side effects like drowsiness and slurred speech.

Help with equipment (that's probably why they are letting you come along) but be very careful as it's very expensive stuff and usually very heavy. You should get an idea of moving equipment around, how awkward it can be and how it's loaded into the venue and unloaded. Loading tonnes of equipment into a van is also an art form in itself and sometimes has to be seen to be believed.

Observe any problems and discussions regarding how they are approaching the gig. Basically take in as much as possible, almost as if you are actually a band member. It's very surprising how much you learn from attending 'coal face' gigs from start to finish. Don't be afraid to ask questions if you need to; they had to start somewhere themselves!

Unfortunately most people just see the performance side of the industry but that is, after all, probably only a quarter of the night's work.

A gig starts the moment you leave the house until the moment you arrive home. An average 'local' gig could include; (all times approximate)

- 1 hour picking up band members and equipment from various addresses
- 1 hour travelling to the gig
- 1 hour to set up and sound check
- 2 x 45 minute sets (covers gig)
- 1 hour interval
- 1 hour taking gear down and loading van
- 1 hour travelling home
- 1 hour dropping off band members and equipment, total average gig 7-9 hrs.

Remember that includes only 1.5 hours of actual performance.

Your observations at the gigs should also include; (it will take more that one gig)

Do the band own their van or transport, is it a hire van, have they hired a roady with a van? Don't forget this is going to be an added expense when you are gigging. Most bands just about break even after paying out for transport.

Who (if anybody) is in charge of the situation? Do the band have a manager or a particular member running things, or is everyone chipping in?

Was the gig arranged by an agent, promoter or management? The gig must have come from somewhere—it's a good idea to start finding out how you can get gigs.

Did the band arrange the gig themselves and promote it? If so, how? Find out how they promoted the gig. Did they use tickets, flyers, posters, newspapers, their own website, etc.

Who is professional? That will become obvious as the night goes on.

Who is unprofessional? That will become blatantly obvious as the night goes on.

Sadly, it can take just one person to let the whole band down, just don't let it be you.

How do the band approach the venue's staff including promot-

er, or concert/booking secretary?** The first thing any band should do on arrival at a gig is to find someone in charge, (preferably the concert secretary or promoter), introduce themselves and the name of the band and confirm the gig is still actually on before unloading the van. (The band should have confirmed the gig beforehand but things can change on a daily basis.) The artists should be as polite and professional as possible to any staff at the venue. Care should be taken when loading in equipment and even more care should be taken as to where it is actually placed—the artists should not block emergency exits with equipment, not only is it dangerous they will be asked to move it.

How does the venue welcome the artist/s? There should be someone to meet the band on arrival to help with regard to the best place to load in, running order for the night and times. Changing room facilities (if any) and payment procedure should also be discussed. They should also be polite to the artists. All these points should be the same whether it's a working-men's club or a theatre gig. Whether it's 'The Rolling Stones' or a local up and coming band, promoters, agents and concert secretaries should treat musicians with respect.

Are any members holding up the others in any way? For example, has the guitarist decided to change his strings just before going on stage, therefore holding up the sound check? Has the drummer taken much too long to set up? Has somebody been on the phone to their boyfriend or girlfriend since they got there?

Every member of the band should be helping in equal measure.

The equipment used by each member. So far you may only have been rehearsing and may not have all the necessary equipment needed to do a full blown gig. Or maybe your equipment may not be up to the same standards as the band's. It's a good opportunity to listen to other musician's equipment. Check out their PA equipment, instruments, effects pedals, amplification, microphones, lighting effects, etc. Have you noticed any equipment that you didn't think of that your band would need to do a gig.

Any problems with equipment. Is anybody having a problem with their equipment? How do they go about fixing the problem? Do they have a tool kit for repairs? Is it a problem they had at the last gig that they could have sorted before this gig?

Do the band have any 'roadies'? Besides you, are there any other people helping with equipment or are they doing it themselves?

How does the band 'sound check'? Individually, collectively or both? Every act, artist or band of any level or size should have a sound check. Every venue has different acoustics and they obviously come in different sizes. How does the band go about the sound check, collectively or via each individual member or both? (It should be the latter; individual, then as an ensemble or 'full band').

Is there an off stage mixing desk? This may depend on how well the band are getting on in the industry. It will certainly improve the overall sound but an off stage mix usually means extra cost for outboard mixing desks, multi-core, cables, extra microphones for micing drums and amplification, and obviously a sound engineer to do the actual mix.

Health and safety issues, for example does the stage resemble a dish of spaghetti? Are speakers or lighting stands liable to trip people?

How do they manage the stage as regards who sets up where?

The bands/artists image/dress. Do they have a change of clothing or do they play in the same gear they turned up in? This could depend on the nature of the gig but even so it's always handy to have some change of clothing, even if it's just a clean T shirt. Gigging is a sweaty job.

Do they carry spares? For example, does the guitarist have a second guitar? You should always carry spares, even if it's a cheap spare to get you by till you can sort any problems like a snapped string for example.

Does the band/singer/artist look confident? Is anyone hiding behind equipment or speakers? This is an important point. I personally can't believe the amount of bands I see were either the guitarist or the bass player is almost hiding behind a speaker. It makes the whole band look unbalanced and also makes the musician look unconfident.

Is there an obvious weak member/s of the band? This may be hard to spot because you will be listening to an ensemble of instruments, unless it's blatantly obvious.

Is there an obvious strong member of the band? This would be much easier to spot. Talented people usually stand out and make the act work.

Observe stage presence and how the 'front man'/artist introduces songs and applies general banter with the audience between songs. Again another very important item. A gig is not just about the music alone, there has to be some communication between the band/artist and the audience at any level.

How long are the sets and times of the sets? Again this will depend on the nature of the gig and whether it's a pub or club, a function, or an original music only venue.

Is it a covers gig, or an original music gig, or a mixture?

Are they taking the audience into consideration with song material? This would not apply at an original music venue where you do your stuff and if the crowd don't like it, tough!

What songs work, what songs don't, does that bother the band? Mainly applies to covers, but if the band are doing some original material, is it going down well?

Is there any difference between first and second set as regards tempo? It's not just the dynamics of a song that's important, the dynamics—highs and lows—of the set can also make a big difference to the overall feel of the show.

How do the band evaluate the gig? That will happen on the journey home from the gig—usually under the influence of alcohol.

Did the band have any promotional literature/cards re future gigs/contact etc.?
If not they should have. Every gig is a fantastic promotional tool in itself. If people want to book the band or contact them there has to be some bumph to hand out. At every gig, if only two people decide to follow the band to their next gig, that will soon add up to a decent following. People who follow a band usually take friends who in turn may start following the band and so on.

Did the band enjoy the gig or was it a chore? Usually it's a bit of both, depending again on whether the place was a paid night at a working-men's club or a local 'with it' venue.

Did the band check the stage before leaving to check no equipment left behind? (Very important.) Equipment is very expensive and it's a pain travelling back to collect something the next day if you were gigging a couple of hundred miles away, especially if you didn't get home until all hours of the morning. An after gig stage check is essential.

How do you think they could improve any aspect of the gig? Think!

What have you learned from the experience? That should fill a book!

How will you change anything regarding your outlook to gigging taking all the above into consideration? You've got a lot to think about. Analyse **everything** you have observed, take note, and use it as a guide.

To get a true analysis of all the above points and general gigging and travelling with the band, you really could do with hooking up with the band over a month or two to see how they cope with all forthcoming situations, scenarios and problems.

You can not get a true reflection if you just attend the one gig, problems arise all the time but you have to physically be there to experience how the band copes with the situation.

These different situations that can arise are the things you simply can't teach someone how to cope with, it's something you learn whilst 'on the road' for a while.

If you do travel round with a band and you have not yet observed any problems, you have not been doing it long enough.

Tip: Wear gloves, not just to protect your hands from the cold, it also protects them from knocks. Strong shoes are recommended too.

"A friend of mine had been gigging for years when I decided to get into it. At the time I had a job in a wood suppliers and I was sick of it. I jumped in on one of the gigs, basically to get some idea of what to expect if I decided to start gigging myself.

'The gig was in Workington in Cumbria and I got picked up first around 3.00pm by John 'their roadie' who lived in the next street. We lived in a place called West Kirby on the Wirral in Merseyside. It was a Saturday night in October or November, early winter '81 or '82 and I remember it was absolutely freezing. As we picked up each member of the band I was relegated to the back of the van, which by now resembled a skip full of cold metal and plastic. All in all it took just over an hour to pick up four people and their equipment. It was nearly 4.30pm and we were now in Chester, further from Workington than we were an hour and a half earlier.

I remember thinking 'I'll ask them to drop me off' as we were going past my area on the way to the motorway, but I felt a bit stupid and decided to grin and bear it.

It must have taken another three and a half hours to get to the club, it was horrible. I couldn't believe it when we got there and this guy was 'tapping his watch' telling us we were late. I had never been so cold, the van's heater wasn't working and I couldn't feel my fingers or my feet. We all started loading the stuff in and the guy told us we would have to use another door as we were letting cold air into the concert room. I felt like telling him were to go, but the lads just got on with it so I followed suit. The place itself was a dump and I remember thinking 'what are they doing playing in a place like this?'. The changing room was an absolute pit, I wouldn't have expected a dog to use it. My mate's band were very good though and the night improved a bit, though the beer probably helped, I had to have a few drinks to numb the impending horror of the return journey. For all their efforts I think they got around £25 each after paying the roadie and the agent. Apparently the agent actually had a bigger share of the gig money than the band members. The journey home was even more horrendous, we had just started off and turned a corner when a mic-stand fell off some speakers and smacked me right in the kisser. I ended up with a cut lip and a cracked tooth. I finally got to bed around 5.00am.

Funnily enough it didn't actually put me off, though it made me realise it's a very hard slog. I continued going round with them for a couple of months. Having had the experience of going round with my mate's band gave me a great insight into what to expect. I started gigging myself in the mid 80s and lasted up until a few years ago but I had to continue my day job. It just gave me a bit of extra money, I couldn't live off the gigging alone. I just do a few acoustic gigs now with some mates in my local, it's much less stressful."

—D Stone.

chapter 7
rehearsals

The rehearsal process can be seen as the building blocks for any band
or artist of any genre. When you attend a gig, you have to consider the work that the band or performer will have done to get their act together. Although they may have only performed for an hour or so, they may have been practising and rehearsing for months to make the performance as impressive and 'tight' as possible.

A show or performance is usually rehearsed enough to gig when you are just starting to hate the sound of it (try not to go past that stage), but it's all worth it when you perform the rehearsed show with total confidence at a live gig in front of an audience.

Rehearsing is also a great opportunity to create new ideas for songs and try out new group equipment, PA systems for example. Any new personal equipment like amplifiers, effects pedals etc, should really be tested and tried pre-rehearsal, (can you get there half an hour earlier than the rest of the band?) as it can get in the way of your actual band practise which is what you should be doing at rehearsals.

In research for this chapter I shadowed a local band (name withheld for various reasons) and came up with this culmination of events (honestly).

Please note times are approximate and any details of events relating to other bands is purely coincidental. No animals were hurt or injured during the making of this report.

Rehearsal room booked for three hours Saturday afternoon from 4pm to 7pm.

The 'rehearsal' scenario went something like this……
4.00—a small dog walks past the drummer's house and sniffs a tree.
4.10—nothings happening, even the dog has gone.
4.20—bass player arrives at lead vocalist's house to pick him up, mum explains that he has just got in the bath and that he will follow him down to the rehearsal studios when he's dried and had something to eat.
4.25—bass player arrives and sets up his equipment, rest of band not arrived yet so he decides to go to the chip shop.
4.40—lead guitarist arrives with singer and sets up, guitarist starts playing some riffs and trying out the first of one of the 24 preset distortions.
4.50—drummer arrives and starts setting up his equipment.
Lead guitarist tries to find cause of loud humming, not noticing the fact that every knob on his amp is on 10.
4.55—rhythm guitarist arrives, sets up and also starts playing favourite riffs, also informs band he can't make following weeks rehearsal because he has an interview at a local children's fun pub to wear the Bonzo the bear costume, adding that he needs the money to buy the latest ZX5000+ multi effects pedal, explaining that it's even better than the lead guitarist's, having over 34 built in distortion effects, and 8 preset wah wah's.
5.10—bass player arrives back from chippy with wonderful aromas of salt and vinigared chips.
Vocalist asks were he got them because he too is now starving and sets off to chippy after band sorts out loose change to share a bag of chips.
5.20—drummer now set up ready, starts drumming and basically making lots of noise, (he has to play loud to be heard over the guitar amp).
5.25—the small dog returns to the tree and sniffs it again.
5.30—lead guitarist turns volume up so he can be heard over the noise of the drums, now also trying out number 4 of his pedals preset distortions
5.35 vocalist returns, band eat chips, vocalist is struggling with microphone feedback because of the extremely loud volume in the room.
Bass player, whilst still eating his last chips, uses spare hand to draw band's logo in black felt pen on the rehearsal room wall plus some general doodling.
5.40 drummer goes to toilet, just as lead guitarist's girlfriend arrives.
Rhythm guitarist still playing favourite riffs.
Drummer's mobile phone goes, the person ringing asks to speak to

'Bigsby', the nickname for the ex guitarist who left the previous month reason being he did not have enough time for his girlfriend due to having to rehearse every week.

Drummer struggles to hear but never-the-less carries on banging bass drum.

5.45—rhythm guitarist then actually asks everybody to be quiet while he plays a new song he has almost finished.

Bass player tries to tune bass and plays some possible bass lines over the chords.

Guitarist's girlfriend mentions the song is c…p and why don't they write some Shania Twain type songs.

Bass player agrees.

Vocalist disagrees.

Lead guitarist grunts and keeps playing riffs over discussion, now on number 11 of preset distortions

5.55—drummer returns from toilet and hasn't even heard the new song.

6.05—vocalist asks if the lead guitarist has any lyrics for the song.

Drummer asks 'what song?' and starts a drum solo.

6.10—mobile phone goes off and drummer talks to girl he met the night before.

The girlfriend of guitarist sits at drums and starts hitting bass drum pedal.

Rhythm guitarist now decided to ditch new song.

6.15—bass player goes to toilet, drummer starts doing 'Wipe Out' theme and some more general loud drum bashing.

Lead guitarist snaps a string whilst trying number 23 of presets.

6.20—vocalist tells band they have a possible gig the coming week but they need at least another 40 minutes of material.

6.25—bass player comes back from toilet and explains he has to get off at 6.45 because he is going to the cinema with his girlfriend, he didn't hear the fact that there may be a possible gig coming up.

6.30—lead guitarist now replaced string and starts to play extremely loud riff normally performed by Slash.

drummer joins in,

vocalist joins in,

Rhythm guitarist takes music magazine from guitar case and goes to toilet.

6.35—bass players girlfriend arrives.

Girlfriend mentions "Bigsby" (her brother) the ex guitarist has now decided he would like to rejoin the band.

Band look around make various grunting noises and then all gather to see her new tattoo and pierced tongue.

6.40—drummer starts setting down gear whilst inquiring how much it would cost to have his nose pierced.

6.45—bass player grunts and leaves.

6.50—lead guitarist and vocalist pack up and leave building, outside the vocalist asks lead guitarist the name of the new rhythm guitarist.

7.00—Rhythm guitarist comes back from toilet and starts playing his favourite riffs for ten more minutes and leaves.

Total time rehearsing = 22 minutes

Total time on toilet = 28 minutes

Total time wasted 2.5 hours

Yes, unfortunately it does sound like an episode from the Simpsons (I am thinking of sending a copy to the producer of the show) but it's not that far from the norm. I know I have been guilty of some of the above, time wasting or 'noodling' as it's sometimes known, but that was a long, long time ago.

If you add the fact that the rehearsal time has also been paid for by people who can't even get the money together for a bag of chips then you have to consider it a total and utter waste of time, money and electricity.

So let's look at rehearsing from a professional point of view, taking all the mistakes above into consideration. As we have already mentioned, it's absolutely vital for any band or artist to rehearse their set. The rehearsals should be treated almost as important as a gig itself, after all, everything you are rehearsing could one day be performed in front of a paying audience. It is also a very useful way for bands or acts to have the chance to 'gel' together and form a bond.

Firstly, why are the band rehearsing in the first place?

To hopefully take original song ideas they may have and experiment to develop and create complete songs, to a point where the songs could be performed with confidence to an audience.

Where covers are involved, it would be a case of each individual member learning their piece and then rehearsing it as a band ensemble to make it sound 'road worthy' and 'tight'.

There is more to rehearsing than just the technical performance. It's not just about learning the right chords and starting and ending at the same time, other things need to be taken into consideration.

Like;

The overall balance of the band as regards volumes of different instruments. This may alter at a real gig but you should start looking at levels and get used to a relative balance.

Dynamics within the songs. Songs sound much better when thought has gone into the highs and lows of the instruments or vocals. In other words a song may sound better with parts played softly and parts played with more vigour. Unfortunately most young bands and even some experienced bands tend to fight for the 'I want to be the loudest' prize. All that happens is each instrument is drowning out the other in a volume fighting frenzy, then the vocalist starts screaming to be heard—all adding up to quite the opposite of dynamics. Instruments have their place in a song and it's not a bad thing to lay off now and then and listen to the overall mix of each instrument. Consider there may be parts of a song that may even sound better without your instrument and vice—versa, there may be times when your instrument should have a more prominent sound.

If you think of a conductor—conducting a symphony, not only is he introducing instruments into the piece and keeping time, he is also controlling the dynamics (the highs and lows) of each set of instruments. One of the greatest modern popular musical examples of dynamics used within a song has to be Queen's Bohemian Rhapsody. The song travels from quiet lush piano and operatic vocals to full blown out-and-out rock, more opera, more rock and then fades back to serene piano to end. The dynamics cover not only differing volume but usage of different instruments to create a complete pop masterpiece and in my humble opinion one of the greatest pop rock songs ever recorded.

Timing. Every piece of music and song should sound 'tight' (all instruments should be in perfect time) at the start of the song, whilst the song is playing and at the very end of the song. Everybody should end on the same beat. Generally getting to know each other's playing styles and experimenting with sounds, vocals, harmonies and equipment will improve the tightness within a band. It's usually the drummer and bass player who control how tight a song can be. If you have a weak drummer or bass player the basic rhythm section of the band will not sound tight.

"So why would anyone want to get on stage and risk embarrassing themselves, actually letting your friends know that you may have a sensitive side? Standing there demanding the audiences attention, "look at me, I'm different and I have something to say.' Performance is risqué and requires a dedication to rehearsing; it's not just a career choice but more, a life choice, this is who I

am and this choice will help define the rest of my life.
You take on music for better, or for worse—its like a marriage".

—Keith Mullin, guitarist, The Farm

Your rehearsals should be a regular slot at a regular time of day so it becomes habitual—once or twice a week or even more—that a band puts aside to rehearse and this should be strictly adhered to.

If a certain member can't make a certain 'slot' per week then the other members should consider doing something like lyric writing or even learning new song arrangements etc. If a band or act cancelled a rehearsal every time a member could not make it, it could lead to laziness and dysfunction.

In fact it's a good measuring point of any band to find out who is really serious and who is not. If you have a constant weak member then it may be time to look for a new one.

Obviously sometimes someone may have strong commitments, like work or three children to pick up from school and cannot always make it, but you can usually tell when someone is just not truly committed.

Having said that, it's vitally important to have breaks from the rehearsal routine, the band should take a week off now and then just to recharge some brain cells. If you don't put aside some spare time to relax, band members may start looking at the whole idea of being a musician as a chore and that can cause big problems. Having a break can also create opportunities for some new ideas to develop.

Rehearsal rooms are expensive (unless you are using your dad's garage), therefore it's important that you get the gear set up as soon as possible.

It's also a good idea to practise your parts before you rehearse. In other words any solo parts or even harmonies that can be practised before the rehearsal. In fact, it's highly recommended that you run through harmonies and vocals acoustically, without the music to check if you are actually in tune. Try two parts before moving onto three and then four and so on. You should then find any weak link and work to remedy that.

Don't forget to 'recap' anything you have rehearsed, ideally each subsequent rehearsal should start by going over songs you rehearsed previously. It may sound a bit formal but you should knock up some sort of rehearsal schedule and stick to it.

If you are having problems with the logistics and cost of moving all of your equipment around, perhaps you can do some rehearsing without using your full kit. That could be a good idea, although it's imperative that you use all of your available equipment near to a gig in order to get the right sound balance and mix rehearsed.

After all that is said, you can actually over rehearse if the sessions are simply too long and everyone becomes tired of the noise, damp, cold, stress, and the general lack of comfort of a rehearsal room.

Rehearsal rooms are usually cold and clammy and have no seating, and it's hard work sitting on an amp for hours on end!

Some time should be set aside to have a discussion before the rehearsal, preferably separate from the rehearsal time booked.

There are countless things to talk about regarding the band's future and ambitions and the obvious things like song repertoire, funds, etc, but what usually happens is the band get to know each other's first names and it ends there; sometimes it doesn't even get that far.

Unplug the equipment and turn the drummer's stool upside down, otherwise it just never gets done.

So there you have it, enjoy your rehearsals but consider all the above and it should help you to get the maximum benefit from them.

> *"I remember turning up at the 'Fire-station' club in Liverpool. We'd been rehearsing for months to do a thirty minute support set. I was horrified when the 'bell rang' and we all looked at each other in complete horror when we realised we just weren't ready to do a show. We managed to 'wing' it by telling everyone we were a punk band, but it taught me a big lesson, rehearse your stuff properly".*
>
> **—A. Gormley**

> "I met this girl and started skipping the rehearsals. After about a month the band ditched me and got a new bass player. Just after that the girl dumped me too. The band went on to have two top ten hits. I remember watching them on 'Top of the Pops' thinking that could have been me up there, what a wally".
>
> **—P. Coughlin.**

THE ART OF GIGGING

> "I rehearsed for nearly six months with one band then we split up. I didn't even get to know the drummer's second name, I think it was down to a lack of communication" (you don't say!)
>
> —**D. Sayce**

After years of frustration and knock backs, Sir Paul finally gets to meet Mark Singleton (left) and Ramon 'Sugar' Deen. If only he had rehearsed more he could have retired by now!

And waiting patiently to get his chance to meet me! Sir George Martin (the fifth Beatle)

chapter 8
equipment

GUITARS

The guitar has established itself as the worlds most popular instrument of the 20th century.

SO, WHERE DO WE START?

Let's start with the different types of guitars available. Then we can talk about buying new or second-hand and then where we can buy them from, and also what to look out for when actually buying one. I will also be covering some highly recommended entry to mid level guitars at different price ranges. I will be using some other resources to gather some of the information although personally I have been playing now for around 35 years and have owned over 100 guitars.

I personally, currently use a Parker Fly Deluxe electric guitar (it weighs less than five pounds and sounds like god, which is very handy as I have had a back operation and have extreme problems using heavy guitars); a 50 year anniversary model American Fender Stratocaster electric guitar; a 25 year old Yamaha classical guitar; an Aria AK 30 CE (used for a throw—about and work, great though!); a 20 year old Yamaha steel strung FG 350 W—fabulous old steel strung acoustic with an adjustable bridge—which are quite rare these days (it's my dad's actually—I borrowed it for a week ten years ago!) and I am just in the process of purchasing a semi acoustic arch top guitar.

I am probably going to enjoy writing this chapter more than any other for the simple reason that I absolutely adore guitars.

SO WHAT WOULD WE CALL A BEGINNERS OR A STUDENTS GUITAR?

I have to laugh when guitars are recommended as student guitars, when actually most of them are not good at all to learn on. They are called student guitars basically because they are cheap and usually nasty.

With the odd exception, a cheap guitar is usually very difficult to play on because not too much attention has been put into the finished article, the strings are usually half an inch or more away from the fret-board and therefore cause various problems for the guitarist like blisters, sore fingers, sore wrists and even back problems caused by having to clamp the strings down to play a chord. What I am getting at here is if you are going to purchase any kind of guitar, make sure it's comfortable to play. If for example you are looking at a specific price range, you should always consider that for a few quid more you could buy a much better guitar to learn on.

I personally think a nylon strung classical is a good starter guitar. Why? Because nylon strings are easy on the fingers; it's also acoustic so no amp is needed; they have a wide arm for easy fingering and are also very portable. They are also very elegant to look at, robust and look wonderful as an ornament or piece of furniture. The most important thing is they have a nice sounding natural fat tone.

Classical guitars have an average price range of anything from £50 to £1,000 and over, for professional models.

For around the £100-£150 range you can get a decent model to learn on, and for that amount of money you can also add some on-board electric's (with the added ability to be able to play through an amplifier via a pickup system).

To lessen the chances of being sued by a guitar manufacturer I will only give positive feedback on guitars I have personally used, tested or come in contact with.

No guitar companies are sponsoring me (unfortunately) so most of the info is my personal opinion and a little help from my muso friends out there.

It's very important to note at this stage that a budget guitar 'set up' properly, can play as well (if not better) than a more expensive guitar that has not been 'set up'.

Set up: Every guitar (unless it's a hand built custom job) has a factory finish 'set up'.) Some music retailers can add ' added value' to the factory finished job by improving the way the guitar feels and plays, before selling it on to the public. A 'set up' usually involves improving the string height and intonation (the ability of the instrument to stay in tune at any position on the neck) and can dramatically improve the guitars overall feel and playability. Remember, though, the more expensive a guitar is usually means it's been made with superior materials and fittings than a cheaper guitar, therefore giving it a longer life span.

Lets look at the four different types of modern guitar.

THE CLASSICAL GUITAR—NYLON STRUNG

I will argue with anybody that a half decent classical guitar can be a lot of fun anywhere, anytime and anyplace. If we are talking 'entry level' you can use a classical guitar to play any type of music acoustically (including classical of course) and if looked after properly will give you years and years of pleasure. As I mentioned before I have a very old Yamaha G 228 and over the years it's basically become part of my body and a very close friend. It has a lovely warm tone and plays like a guitar that would cost three times the price, it has travelled the world with me and has entertained people in places such as America, Spain, Malta, Greece and Turkey. Another good thing about classical guitars is the tuning. On steel strung guitars any slight tuning problems stand out like a sore thumb, a nylon strung guitar has a much more tolerable sound, even if played slightly out of tune due to the warm soft, fat tone and sound of the nylon strings (nylon strings do not rust and very rarely snap). If you end up moving on to join a band, you are going to need an electric guitar but you should keep your classical guitar for practising and writing—and also a bit of fun.

WHAT CAN YOU GET FOR YOUR MONEY?

For around £100 you can have a new **Crafter JC45E classical electric**, for this price you can't complain and it's actually quite nice to play.

For around £120 you can own a brand new **Aria AK 30 CE.** For that price I would have to say that pound for pound this has to be complete bargain. Not only is it extremely nice to look at, it's also got a nice comfortable playing action, and to top it all it's got a built in PZP-5 Piezo pick-up together with a four band graphic 'eq' and volume, plus a battery-check light facility. That's a seriously good package for the price.

I use mine for my day job and I have to say it's superb. I don't think it will have the longevity of my old Yamaha and I certainly wouldn't recommend it for a solo concert at the Royal Albert Hall, but overall as a starter guitar, it's absolutely superb and gets a 9 out of 10 from me. (NB. Mine was set up free by the shop I purchased it from, being 'Frets' in Liverpool.) A set up is essential.

From the same company for around the £350 mark you can have yourself a brand new **Aria AC 25 CE**. Again it's a classical electric but has a much better build and construction materials than the AK series. This guitar scored straight 10's for performance and value from a review in 'What Guitar' magazine (09.04). (This is a seriously good magazine, and they obviously thought very highly of the guitar!)

Yamaha have some fine entry level classicals but you need to try a few as they have so many models at different prices. Another point to remember is that you can try a number of exact models but they will all feel slightly different.

If you are actually learning classical guitar and you are not too bothered about on—board electric's, a new model by **Fransisco Bros the B40 Classical** at around £240 received straight fives (maximum score) in a recent Guitarist magazine review.

Dream on
Gibson Chet Atkins Classical electric

THE ACOUSTIC GUITAR STEEL STRUNG

The good old acoustic has certainly been the most popular of all guitars over the years and is the most common type of guitar used for learning your first few chords and it's also a great guitar for writing songs. They are a little harder to look after than classical guitars as they are steel strung, and entry level acoustics are prone to tuning problems. However acoustics have moved on over the last few years and are now manufactured on a massive scale from all parts of the globe. (I'm surprised there isn't a factory on the moon knocking them out.) There's a massive range but we'll look at good entry/mid level models. It's hard choosing where to start from really, but lets start at around the £150 mark again. Remember second-hand guitars can sometimes play and feel better than new models but it's very difficult to advise on second-hand equipment at this price level, so let's look at some prices for new.

The **'Aria AW 75 QN'** is a good entry level acoustic guitar for around the £150 mark with a spruce top and mahogany neck (no electric's).

The **'Washburn WD 32 S'** is also the biz. I have always liked the finish of Washburn guitars and at around the £200 mark this model has the look and feel of a guitar twice the price. This acoustic has a spruce top, sapele back and sides, and a satin finish. The model I tested felt superb with it's factory set up. (No electric's.)

The 'AMI Cedar' (pronounced Amy) by 'Art Et Lutherie' from around £200 new is another superb acoustic earning rave reviews (What Guitar 09/04, plus my humble one!). It's a small three quarter sized bodied guitar with a very big sound. It has a cedar top and wild cherry back and sides. The guitar is not only very pretty to look at, but also has a superb tone. This style of guitar used to be called a Parlour guitar because of the size and weight. I was personally gob-smacked by the overall playability, sound and feel of the one I tested.

(Sheehan's Music, Leicester, 03/05, priced at £200 with a custom soft case). It played and felt rather like a Martin acoustic (a guitar pioneering giant). I would love one myself (I don't know how I left the shop without it!) but I would have to sneak it into the house! There are no electric's on this model but there is a classical version and more superb models that do have electric's.

The 'Crafter MD 80 12 EQ' is a very good twelve string electric acoustic. For around £280 you can own a beautiful solid spruce top, mahogany back and sides guitar with on-board electric's (tested 14/03/05.) Again a set up is essential.

If you run into some money, say £400-£1000, the choice becomes harder but check out some Takamines, Yamahas and Lakewoods.

Dream on!

If you run into some serious money or you sign to a major record company, for £1,000—£2,000 or over you can jump into fantasy land. Gibson, Breedlove, Taylor and Martin guitars are simply stunning. At this price range it's important that you consider the second-hand market as guitars this expensive lose money after the first retail sale, rather like a car does. The second-hand value however will usually hold level unless the instrument is damaged in any way (keep an eye on the kids !).

It should be pointed out again at this stage that the second-hand market in musical equipment is MASSIVE, the reason being that so many people treat musical equipment like a dog and basically don't want to know about the equipment a few months after Christmas.

THE SEMI ACOUSTIC 'ARCH TOP' GUITAR.

The distinctive warm tone and sound of archtop guitars has featured in many types of music, most notably early rock & roll, blues, Jazz, and early country styles. Their use today covers most styles and also the pop industry seems to have jumped on board too. What you get with an archtop semi acoustic is a bit of everything. You have an acoustic instrument you can hear unplugged (although it's much more muted than a normal acoustic), it can also be played as an out and out electric guitar. They are bigger than a normal electric and in some cases enormous (and heavy). However, the 'thinline' models like the Gibson ES335 are more comfortable to play and have in fact been widely copied and have also influenced many guitar companies. The real item may unfortunately be out of your price range at around £2,500 but let's look at some second-hand example prices and copies or other models you may be able to afford.

Peavey JF 1 (jazz fusion) at around £200. I really can't believe this is an entry level archtop (as regards price). Had a little play of one, not a bad sound and it looked absolutely stunning in the transparent red flame, especially considering the price. It's also received some great reviews on the internet—I may be investing in one myself!

Epiphone Sheraton (licensed by Gibson) The new price for this model comes in around the £400 mark. For that you can get a half decent copy of the original Gibson ES335. I had one for a while and although it was quite heavy, it was very very nice to play (if set up well by a pro, these guitars can fool you into thinking they are the real thing, the real Gibson sound however can not be copied). Second-hand you can find them from around the £200-250 mark. Epiphone along with other brands have a wide range of archtops—you would benefit from trying the different models if this is the type of guitar you are after.

Dream on!
Gibson, Gretsch and Heritage models.

THE SOLID BODY ELECTRIC GUITAR

Solid bodied instruments have dominated the electric guitar industry for just on forty years. The most popular instruments are either classic models that were first developed in the 1950's or models that have clearly been influenced by them. In other words we all know that Gibson and Fender models were the kings of the industry, but lots of other brands have kept to their basic design and simply added their own up to date features. Yet most guitarists still prefer the original design and models and they are still very well sought after, and in some instances are commanding several thousands of pounds. I have to mention PRS guitars who's models have now been around for twenty years (happy anniversary!) and have now become another roll model, and are now also being copied themselves.

Let's look at modern day guitars and prices.

This category is so vast that it's hard to know where start. To keep it slightly easier we will again start at entry level to mid level and I'll be asking quite a few muso friends to help, doing lot's of research (testing the actual guitars wherever possible—I love doing it so not a problem) and also using the net (and why not, it's an incredible resource). I will also be quoting some reviews from several high quality guitar magazines. All in all, that's not a bad collection of resources I can tap into, plus the fact that I must have personally owned around 100 different brands and models at some point over the last 35 years.

Total entry level. There are actually some good electric guitar and amp packages out there, but I think you really should look at spending any money you have on a guitar you are going to get some pleasure playing and consider an amp when you have learned a few chords and a tune (at least 'Smoke on the Water'!).

I have to start with the Chinese and Korean revolution. They are knocking out some serious copies and all new original models. There's a particular company (amongst many) called Shine guitars who are sending over some incredibly low budget guitars, but the strange thing is that the materials and finish are superb (for the price). I tried the **Shine telecaster model S1 30 blonde** at Back Alley Music, Warrington (18/03/05) and I have to say for £120 the guitar feels like the real thing, in fact it has an ash body and maple neck and also a good factory set up. Amazing for the price…www.saein.co.kr

At entry level for under £200 pounds you will have a hard time finding a better deal than the **Yamaha Pacifica 112.** As a Fender Strat copy at this price it's remarkably good. I owned one in the mid 1990's and although it was mainly used as a spare it always did the job when brought on as a reserve. But it's more than a super sub, it's actually a multi award winning entry/mid level guitar. I have seen them advertised second-hand for around the £100/£120 mark. That's seriously good value and it's a good, solid, alder—wood guitar with good quality fixtures and fittings so no hangs ups about it's strength.

And in the red corner! More than a bit of competition for the Yamaha Pacifica would have to be a standard **Squire Stratocaster** (not the cheaper affinity model, but the standard large head-stock model). This is another very good entry level guitar for less than £200 that should get you by until that first record deal! You can always change pick-ups quite easily with these models. Look out for the brand new **Squire Tele Custom II**—again at around £200—it's going to be a mover!

(**Squire guitars are licensed by Fender**)

For entry/mid range guitars around the £400 mark, try a Korean built **Washburn Idol W165** which is a superb bit of kit for the price (tested 17/03/05). It has a superb array of sounds plus added bits and bobs like the Buzz Feiten tuning system which keeps the guitar in perfect tune. The pickups are also seriously good and it feels expensive.

(Looks a bit gothic-y if you can put up with that, if you're into gothic your laughing!)

For the same price range (around £400) also consider the **Ibenez RG320FM,** another very good entry/mid level guitar with a good array of sounds and expensive feel. I have always liked Ibenez guitars, particularly the higher end models.

I have to give a mention to the standard **Epiphone Les Paul** range here (£180—£500). Some of them are superb and feel like the real thing (Gibson), but you need to test them yourself as there are so many models to choose from.

NB. When you get to the higher end of the Epiphone Les Paul range you should consider a real Gibson Les Paul second-hand model.

(Epiphone guitars are licensed by Gibson).

Second-hand has to be considered at this price range when you consider you could own a standard **American Fender Stratocaster or Telecaster for around the £300—£500 mark.** There are so many of them knocking around that the second-hand market is swimming with good models selling at half the new price. With the risk of being sued, I would have to say that it would be crazy to actually buy one new unless you have money to burn. Before you go out and start looking it's important to learn a little about the most famous guitars in the world (alongside Gibson). You simply have to own a Fender at sometime in your life (I have for the last 28 years, although I also own a Parker Fly Deluxe which can keep the strat 'on the bench'). There are literally hundreds of models to choose from and the same amount of differing prices. Don't think you have a bargain until you know the true value of the model you are buying. Buy a good guitar mag and there will be a list of all the models and prices. The above also applies to Gibson guitars.

The late great multi award winning guitarist Bobby Arnold 1947-2003. Bobby could get a tune out of a twig, so give him a Fender Strat and you have the ideal partnership! Not only was Bobby a great musician—he was also a lovely man.

If it's your birthday however and you are buying new, you should consider a real PRS guitar. The cheapest model in the PRS range is the PRS SE Soapbar at around £550. The guitar scored straight 10s for value and performance in a review from What Guitar magazine (09/04) magazine.

"However hard it is, try not to buy a guitar because of it's looks. A beautiful looking guitar can sometimes seduce the buyer into thinking it must sound equally as good as it looks—nonsense, some of the cheaper

brands work on the notion that looks alone will sell a guitar and cost—cut regarding sound, materials and playability".
  M Simpson
  TIP: Unknown brands may be cheap but will obviously be a lot harder to sell when upgrading or quitting, consider this when buying your instrument.

BASS GUITARS

What's the difference between a bass guitar and a normal guitar? A standard guitar has six strings and a standard bass guitar has four. The four strings on a standard bass guitar are the same as the lower four strings on a standard guitar and are in fact tuned exactly the same, albeit an octave lower (a standard guitar is tuned E-B-G-D-A-E, take away the two highest strings (the 1st and 2nd E + B) and we end up with G-D-A-E.(Note, there are two E strings on a standard guitar, one high and one low). (Also note—there are five and six string basses available—better to master the four string before moving on to one of these).

To play a standard guitar you need to learn chords, to play a bass guitar you need only to learn notes, and a bass also has less strings to get confused with.

Yes, you're right, a bass guitar is far easier to learn, probably around ten fold (like for like) depending at what level you want to play.

If we say that to become a decent blues guitarist it could take around ten years (completely from scratch), with the same amount of practise, to reach a similar level on a bass should take around one/two years. So if you are just starting off and you are still pondering which instrument to learn, you should consider this.

However, you will never enjoy a bass guitar like you can enjoy a standard guitar.

You can't, for example, take a bass to a party or sit on the balcony on holiday and play some tunes—it's just not that kind of instrument. NB. If you learn standard guitar playing, you are also learning bass guitar, but it doesn't work the other way around.

Bass guitars are very different from normal six string models. Besides the obvious things like the amount of strings and the sound, a bass guitar has a much lower register and frequency than a normal guitar. I personally think amplification has a stronger say in the overall sound. I have owned several bass guitars over the years and I have to say that unlike a guitar (which can sound quite identifiable whatever amp you play it through—within reason), a bass simply has to have good amplification. With bad amplification it will sound muddy and the notes become indefinable. Confused? So am I!

Taking all of the above into consideration and looking at entry level basses, I'll recommend a few starter basses but as soon as you can afford to upgrade, do so. My personal favourite (and numerous other musicians will back me up) is the good old standard **Fender Precision or Fender Jazz models** (around £800-£900 new). I also love the Ernie Ball Music Man basses (starting at around £600 new). For some reason Gibson have been very laid back in the bass guitar department.

Here are a few entry level models that feel good and look good. (Don't forget the sound will largely depend on your amplification).

Again starting at the £150 mark you can consider the **Squire Affinity Precision** copy, or for a little more, the Jazz copy (licensed by Fender). If you are considering moving up to the real Fender models, why not have a copy of it to get a rough feel of one!

The **Washburn XB100** is also good value for around the £150 mark.

The **Peavey BXP** has the looks and feel of a much more expensive model and
according to some research it also has a good set of pickups at around £160.

Moving up a little in price to around the £200 mark, the **Cort Action Bass** looks and feels great and I also managed to test one myself (08/03/05). However the guy in the shop plugged me into a £1,000 amp, so it's hard to say what it would sound like in normal conditions.

Move on to the mid level price of around £300-£500 and you enter the semi/pro level of guitars and there are some great models out there so go out and try some. Of the many I have tested over the last year or so there are a few I would personally recommend. The Korean built **Dean Edge Q4B** comes in at just over £500. It's a very expensive feeling bass guitar (it also comes in a five string model). The same company also do a semi—hollow body bass (Paul McCartney-style) called the Dean Rhapsody HB. In my notes, it says "22.9.04—approx £ 400, absolutely gorgeous, sounds great, plays brill, little bit of acoustic volume for off amp practise, recommend to anyone at any level". www.deanguitars.com

Warwick, Wal, Overwater and Status basses are the dream machines in the bass department and are something you *can* dream of. However Warwick have a budget series under the name of **Rockbass** and do some great mid level basses
for around £400. The basic series **Rockbass Corvette** had a superb review in Guitarist magazine.

There's a few for you to consider but why not spend a few weeks testing some yourself—there are much worse things to do with your time.

Remember not to be taken in by looks alone which happens all too often (I've done it myself). If you take your time, you should end up with a guitar that not only looks great but sounds and plays great too. If you are going to buy second-hand from any source, take an experienced guitarist with you.

If you are buying new, you simply have to get a copy of 'What Guitar', 'Total Guitar' 'Guitarist' or 'Guitar Player'. They have some serious dudes checking every available guitar and they also gather advice and guidance on other musical equipment, therefore doing all the hard work for you and narrowing the field.

Remember, if you can find a second-hand guitar at the right price (after a bit of haggling) you should then be in the position of being able to sell the instrument on in a few years time at roughly the same price, therefore having actually owned and used the guitar free of charge.

In this scenario, it's important to look after the instrument like it's one of your children.

I can honestly say I have never lost money on a guitar and in some cases have made a profit. Here is a good tip; whenever possible, visit the music store at a quiet time, especially if you are there with the cash to actually buy something. Don't be rushed and, I repeat, **do not judge the guitar or instrument on looks alone,** after all you wouldn't do that whilst choosing a member of the opposite sex would you!!

Guitar tuners You simply have to have one. They are cheap, easy to use and will tune your guitar to 'concert pitch'. I couldn't imagine not having one now. They are wonderful, especially in noisy dark places (like stages/venues) as they have LCD lights to tell you when the string is in tune. It's so important to have an instrument tuned well as it sounds dreadful if it's not in tune, and that in itself is an excuse to throw your guitar on top of the wardrobe. It's also important to note that although a guitar is in tune, it may not be in 'concert pitch'—this is a global tuning pitch in which all instruments are in tune with each other. To put that in simple terms it actually means that a guitar can be in tune with itself, but it does not mean it is in concert pitch.

To tune it to concert pitch is not a problem nowadays with the introduction of the new guitar tuners which work to a common 'concert pitch'. Again, there are hundreds of tuners ranging from £10-£100. I use the Boss TU 12 chromatic tuner. Most standard guitar tuners are fine with bass guitars—although there are tuners dedicated to bass guitar so ask when buying.

CAPO'S—WHAT IS A CAPO?

A Capo is a small device that acts like a clamp. You can move it up the guitar neck to clamp the strings at different fret positions—therefore changing the key and tone. You can then play the same chord structures you have learned anywhere on the neck.

If you are a learner, a capo is a good idea. Some guitarists are under the illusion that it's cheating. This is complete and utter tosh—ask The Eagles (Hotel California); George Harrison (Here Comes The Sun, Norwegian Wood, etc). A capo can be used to alter the tone of a guitar and also to change key especially if using open string chords. If you have a naff guitar it can also be used to make playing easier by lowering the string height.

Modern day bands, like Travis for example, use the Capo to great effect giving a mandolin-ish feel to the overall sound. A good one costs around £15 but they last forever (if you don't lose them).

Fran Heeley Cavern gig, Liverpool, October with a beautiful Guild 12 string plus his Capo at 2nd position.

Guitar cables/leads All hi-fi buffs know that cables and leads will certainly alter sound, and guitar leads make a difference too. Choose a good quality make—any with `Klotz' cable are especially good as this cable has a special construction which sounds great. Not too short or too long—about 8-10 ft is ideal. Whirlwind leads are also recommended—I have had one for 22 years and it's still going.

Plectrums (plecs, pics) Believe it or not, changing your plectrum can make a big difference to your sound, volume and tone. So before you borrow money from your local bank manager and change your amp, guitar or pedals, consider trying a new plectrum—it could save you a lot of money. Even the subtle difference of using a 'Jim Dunlop ' 0.88mm USA nylon plectrum can alter a volume by almost ten per—cent louder than a same brand of 0.73mm, if used with the same weight of hand. In my opinion (and I am not being sponsored!) these are the best 'plecs' on the market for regular guitar playing. Try to snap one! If you don't lose them—they last forever. It's important however to use a plectrum you are happy with, just buy one of each and try them all till you find one that suits your style of play. You may even find you start using different ones for different songs.

PICKS AND STRINGS BY BRIAN VANCE (BRIAN PLAYS GIPSY JAZZ STYLE GUITAR)

"The tone produced from a guitar is not only dependent upon the type of guitar or amplifier used. It is also dependent upon the type of strings and picks (plectrums) chosen. Many great players over the years have achieved part of their unique tone as a consequence of this fact. Examples of players doing this span the last few decades. For instance Brian May was famed for his warm fat rounded tones by playing his guitar with an old silver six-pence. Stevie Ray Vaughn got his deep blues tone by using very heavy gauge strings. The high E string was a 0.13 or a 0.14 instead of the normally used 0.9 and He had to tune his guitar a semi tone lower than normal to enable him to still bend the strings due to the high tension of using the heavier strings. Even as far back as the 1930s Django Reinhardt who was one of the most influential guitar players used a thick waist coat button for his pick. and used high tension strings (Argentine strings)

Picks bought off the shelf can vary in size and thickness and are normally made from plastic, celluloid or nylon. Generally speaking pick of thickness less than 0.04mm are considered thin; 0.04mm to 1.00mm are considered medium and those above this range are considered thick. Normally it's easier to strum a guitar with a thinner pick and play fast lead with a thick pick. It therefore follows that Jazz players normally favour very thick and small picks and use heavy gauge strings while blues and rock players tend to use middle of the road picks in shape and size with thinner strings which can be bent more easily. Acoustic on the other end can vary but most players normally use the larger thin picks or "finger picks" with heavy gauge strings (wound thirds).

Picks can also be custom or homemade. Picks made from coconut shells for instance produce a bright tone while picks made from graphite are more percussive. Most guitarists normally consider picks made from tortoise shell to give the best overall tone but these are rare to find now and often expensive due to current laws which prevent the use of such materials. In the case of strings, Bronze wound strings are warmer sounding on acoustics but sound a little thin on electric guitars where all steel wound strings are preferred. *An electric guitar's magnetic pickup can't always reproduce the tones from bronze strings.* It is up to the player to experiment with various combinations of not only guitars and amps but also picks and strings to get that unique tone. Remember the right combination of pick and strings can make an average sounding guitar sound great and a normal sounding player unique.

Some interesting Web sites were varieties of picks and strings can be obtained are as follows
- www.newstrings.co.uk
- www.acousticmusic.com
- www.wegenpicks.com

TIP: Don't throw away old credit cards—cut (or bend) off the corners and keep them in your guitar case as they make very good emergency plectrums—if you happen to forget the real ones. That may only happen once or twice a year but it's still worth it. I actually use a credit card 'plec' to create a particular sound.

Guitar stands You simply have to have one. They are not expensive and can save your guitar from nasty accidents. Most guitar 'injuries' are caused by guitars falling over when leaned against a wall, table, amp or whatever. There's a new stand now by Hercules (distributed by www.stringsandthings.com) which clamps the neck of your guitar as the weight of the guitar rests on the base. But even a basic model would suffice. Price range from £10—£50.

Guitar strings I have always used 9s/10s over the years (mainly 9s), but in my younger, leaner, chest—wig 'Thin—Lizzy' days, I even used 8s, although that gauge would not suit my playing style and sound now.

Clean your strings with a tissue after every gig as it removes the sweat and grease from the string and it keeps them sounding livelier and brighter for longer. Obviously they still need changing every so often, but for the sake of ten seconds it's well worth the effort.

Strings rust very easily and once rust is involved they will snap easily.

Next time you are in Liverpool, take a peek at 'Cy Tucker's' strings—

they are the perfect example of how strings should not be and they often have a distinct similarity to barbed wire!

The last time I used his Telecaster (when I got up and did a song with them) it felt like it had half a roast dinner on the fretboard.

Bass players, if you are really short of cash, boil your bass-guitar strings (it works, honest), also, be first out of the taxi and last into the pub (bass guitar strings are at least double/triple the price of other guitar strings).

Guitarists, if you are really really skint (no butter or cheese in the fridge, etc) but need spare strings, buy a half set, these being 1st, 2nd, and 3rd strings as they are usually the strings which will break first (unless there is something wrong with your guitar). If it's your birthday and there is some cash to spare, remember strings bought in bulk purchase can work out almost forty percent cheaper if you buy around ten packs.

If I have to visit my local guitar/music store for a set of electric guitar strings, it can cost anything from £6 to £7 a set, whereas if I buy ten sets from an internet source or a magazine, they can cost as little as £3.20 a set.

You should always trim the strings after you have re-strung your guitar. It's very common to cause injury to another musician or even yourself with strings protruding from your guitar head. I personally have had strings scratch my face just under my eye, and in my early years (which is when I learned my lesson) I almost poked my eye out.

Changing strings properly is essential and if done correctly will help keep your guitar in tune. There is nothing worse than an out of tune instrument—if you just change your strings without stretching them properly they will continue to 'slip', therefore causing the strings to almost constantly sound flat. First thing to do is remove the old strings. Now, whilst you have the chance, clean the guitar and the arm with a recognised guitar cleaner. (I have always used normal polish but there's bound to be someone out there telling me it's the wrong thing to do.) When the guitar is clean and you have changed it's nappy you can then fit the strings slack onto the guitar. Depending on whether you have locking or non-locking tuners will result in how many turns you need regarding the string in the tuners eye. I personally swear by locking tuners (you can have them fitted) but if you don't have them, consider at least two/three turns of string in each tuner eye. The thin E and B string may need an extra couple of turns, depending on the gauge of string (light gauges 8s and 9s need more turns/grip than 10s upwards, also classical and acoustic guitars will need more).

When all strings are on the guitar, it's time to start the stretch tuning system. Get used to it and practise it as it will improve your tuning no matter what guitar you are using. (Almost every up and coming guitarist I meet via my job has problems with guitar strings slipping out of tune—this problem dramatically improves when they use this method). So you tune each string to it's pitch with a tuner. You will notice as you return to the first string you tuned that it will have 'slipped' to a much flatter pitch. The reason it's slipped is because it has not been stretched. Lie the guitar down on something soft like your lap and use the weight of the guitar to stretch the string by tugging it half a dozen times and re-tuning it—until it eventually stops going flat. It can take as many as twenty stretches which works out at about a minute per string.

Repeat the process an hour later. That's not a lot of time to improve the tuning situation and it will save you time and cause less hassle in the future as you won't have to re-tune as much. Trim the excess of the strings. Keep your spare plectrum and strings on your amp or within easy reach at a gig.

Guitar straps—Buy a comfy one—guitars become very heavy on your shoulder after a while and that can actually cause serious back problems. **Strap-locks** are essential to stop the guitar strap from popping off the guitar. Without them, your guitar is only going to crash onto the hard floor (or your feet) and that could cause serious damage. Imagine it—a broken guitar and a broken toe—OUCH! If you move about a lot on stage they are absolutely essential. Only a month ago Brian Adams was performing an acoustic song on daytime television and guess what? Yes, his gorgeous Gibson J 200 acoustic went 'for a burton' on live television. Luckily enough he managed to catch it, but it proves my point, big time.

Guitar cases—a good solid case is essential for any instrument. Not only will it protect your instrument from knocks and falls, it is a good place for your instrument to stay over periods between playing. Good guitar cases are made with lush padded interiors to keep a guitar safe, in tune, and a reasonable temperature in extreme conditions—with the added bonus of a few places to store bits and bobs like leads, strings, plectrums, books, capo's, etc.

Purchasing equipment at your local music store

When purchasing any musical equipment, try your best never to pay the price on the ticket. Look at that price as a starting point—pretend you are in Turkey! (If you've never been to Turkey—they haggle!) If you are cheeky but very polite you will get the price down.

Start with the old 'how much for cash?' ploy (phony—but it always seems to work) and if you are a student, mention it.

By now the price should have come down a little but don't let it end there, try to squeeze that extra £5 or £10 out of the deal (after all, that money could be used for your only decent meal for weeks if you have been saving your money for equipment!).

If, for example, the salesperson says they can't possibly go any lower, call their bluff—you can always pop out for a long walk around the block and return later quoting the lowest price you managed to negotiate—before you went for the walk!

It hasn't ended yet—politely ask if a guitar strap, guitar cable, or a set of strings can be thrown in with the deal. You have to have good bargaining powers but it can save you a lot of money over the years.

Make sure you are always very polite and, if possible, humorous, and then thank the salesperson who sold you the item and try to remember their name for future reference. Next time the process should be a little easier if they know you are expecting some discount.

They really shouldn't mind, after all if you become a good customer and introduce friends and family to the shop, they (the shop) are going to make a great deal of money over the years.

If you have equipment to sell it's usually much more profitable to sell it privately. You may get some time-wasters but you will always get a better deal than doing a part exchange with a shop. A shop will only offer you the absolute rock bottom price.

So lets look at a possible scenario (I have used some of these, though not all in the one visit!).

You walk into the shop with a slight limp (sympathy vote), you look at the guitar or piece of equipment you are interested in and stand there gazing at it until a salesperson comes over. "How much is it please, I can't quite see, I am very upset because I have just had to have my dog put down" (more sympathy).

Salesman says "It's £199, sir", OK, pause…then you throw in the old 'how much for cash',… salesman; 'well, I suppose we could make it £190',

You thank him, but again mention "the vetinary fees I have just forked out for good old ' Fido'", (more sympathy) and offer him £160.

Salesman; "well, we can't really go any lower than £180". So you then ask if you can meet him halfway at £170. If he agrees, wait until it's being boxed then ask "Is there is a guitar strap included, and some plectrums?"

Don't forget to then ask his name and thank him, and tell him you were happy with the deal and as soon as you get over the sad loss of your dog you will be back in to have another look around and that you will also recommend the shop to friends and family.

So there you have it, you have lost an imaginary dog but gained a good friend and contact in a music shop, plus you have saved around £30 and have a new 2005 reg guitar strap. It's not always possible to get some discount if the price of the goods are already discounted and at the cheaper end of the market anyway, but there is certainly no harm in trying.

GUITAR AMPLIFICATION

There are simply too many makes of guitar amplification to mention all of them and then each make has it's own wide array of choices, so it's difficult to know where to start.

So lets start from a beginner's 'first amp' situation.

Most young musicians/guitarists tend not to have much cash and would therefore choose an amp by it's price, or maybe it's been a Christmas present and it's usually the most basic guitar amp, being five/ten watts; one speaker; no effects.

There's nothing wrong with this introduction to guitar amplification, and at the very least you can appreciate being able to drown out the sound of your sister's hair dryer!

The problem is, as your sister gets older and uses more powerful hair dryers, you realise you may need more power yourself. This is the time to start touring the local music shops for the power and sounds of a newer, more flexible sounding amp.

As we try out new amps, we realise we could seriously blow someone's head off and also add a few effects to the sound for good measure. This makes choosing an amp a matter of personal choice as there are so many.

The most common effect on a guitar amp is 'reverb' and it's still a 'must', even with all of the new effects pedals knocking around.

The next most common effect, which is now found on most models, is 'overdrive' which can come under a range of headings on the amp face. For example, it may also be called 'crunch', 'distortion', or a variety of other names—there's a new one every week.

On some amps, particularly Marshall, the overdrive can be a natural sound to the amp when using the master volume on high gain to create 'distortion' overdrive.

The first amp to hit the scene with a built-in effect other than spring-reverb or vibrato was the Roland JC120 in the mid 1970's which incorporated a 'Chorus' effect, sounding like a doubling of the notes resulting in the sound effect of two guitars playing, rather than one.

Today, with the advent of digital modelling continuing to gather pace, it seems guitar amplification has moved into the future. (Digital modelling basically means the ability for the amp to copy/assimilate the sound of another amp.) That's not to say the new digital revolution will be to everybody's taste but it now gives the musician a massive choice as to multi built-in effects, as well as tone and volume.

ENTRY/PRACTISE LEVEL

Marshall & Fender (amplification pioneering giants) have some seriously good entry level practise amps. If you are going to buy one, it's a good idea to have an amp with some built in effects for you to experiment with and have some fun.

For £50 you can own a new **Marshall MG10CD 10 Watt Combo** which is a very small amp you can carry anywhere, anytime. It's features include Twin channel—clean and overdrive, headphone socket for silent practise (keep the neighbours happy) and a CD input for jamming.

For around the £100 mark my choice has to be the Marshall **MG15DFX 15 Watt Combo.** My son actually owns one of these and it's quite superb with pro effects and a great, clean sound. Effects include digital reverb, chorus, flange and delay. If you are considering something louder for your first gigs, just double that price and for around £200 you can upgrade to a 50 watt model, being the **MG50DFX.** This model also has twin foot-switchable channels and the same effects set up as the other model.

Fender have similar spec entry level models, the cheapest with reverb effect being the **Fender Frontman 15R** at around £70. The amp also has clean and overdrive channels. For a little more (around £100) you can move up to the **Fender Bullet 15DSP** which houses sixteen digital effects.

A new amp, again by Fender, the **Fender G-DEC** (DEC—Digital Entertainments Centre) was launched at this years NAMM (North American Music Manufacturers) event. The amp has been described as a practise amp loaded with it's own backing tracks (or a karaoke amp!). For around £250 you could own a 15 watt amp that has built in adjustable bass guitar backing and drum loops, and countless other effects—fantastic for practising on your own with a pretend bass player and drummer (imagine it—no arguments or having to share your chips).

www.fender.com

If you get used to these makes, it would make sense to just upgrade to louder, more expensive models as you reach the point where your volume needs lifting. There are some seriously good amps out there and they all have a different character and, obviously, sound. It really depends on what kind of music(and guitar) you are playing at any given time that will determine what amp you will end up with.

As I mentioned earlier, you could even opt for the new digital modeling amps which create the effect that you have a number of amps at your disposal, when in reality it's just one amp doing impersonations of other amps.

For around the £250 mark, the **Line 6 Spider 11 112** does just that and it's also a 75 watt model so it's ready for the real gigs.

For around the same price (£250-ish), also consider the **Fender Princeton 65 DSP** (65 watts) or the **Crate GTX65** (65 watts) or the **Kustom Series 65** (65 watts). These three, plus the Marshall model mentioned earlier, are all very good amps at this price range and are very capable of entry/mid level gigging. (Don't forget that you can always mic an amp up through a PA system.)

How does volume work? Just in case you needed to know, it's very mathematical and has a lot to do with Decibels, but here's a very basic guide:

Does Wattage = Volume? Basically no, wattage is only half the equation. The other half, of course, is the speaker. But to understand these, you must first understand how sound/volume works. Like most things in nature, sound is logarithmic.

The mathematics are like this:
a) = 1 watt = Standard
b) = 2 watts = Twice the power but only slightly louder
c) = 10 watts = Twice as loud
d) = 100 watts = Four times as loud
e) = 1,000 watts = Eight times as loud

This contradicts everything you may have been told about loudspeakers, but it's the way physics work. Twice the input does not give you twice the output.

As you can see by the above, an amp with twice the wattage is not necessarily any louder than a smaller amp.

Fender's 50 watts may be 60 watts to Peavey, which might be only 30 watts to Mesa Boogie but 70 watts to Marshall. Then there's solid state amps vs. tube amps. While solid state amps have the same clean headroom as their tube equivalents, tube amps can be over-driven (used near full volume) fairly hard without sounding bad or distorted, whereas many solid state amps tend to clap out before they hit their maximum power rating. This is why you will often find that 200 watt tube will sound just as loud as a 500 watt solid state amp. The solid state amp might really only be putting out 300 watts before it begins to distort, and the 200 watt amp can really push out 300 watts without sounding bad.

Amps usually come into two categories—solid state and tube (lately, however, modeling amps have also come into the equation). What's the difference?

Solid state amps don't have tubes. Most amps currently sold for home use (either in receivers, integrated amps or separate amps) are solid state. There are various solid state amp designs, and there are various tube amp designs. Modeling amps do impersonations of the both amps.

WHICH ONE IS THE BEST FOR YOU?

The tube believer will prefer the sound of tubes and defend their corner to 'the last bell' and the solid state believer will do the same. It's all down to personal preference and your guitar can make a difference too. Listen and decide!

The main difference between solid state amps and tube amps are that the solid state amps are much more reliable (there isn't much to go wrong), much less expensive per watt, and generate less heat—and heat is the arch enemy of all electronics. Tube amps require occasional 'topping up' with the replacement of tubes, which can be very expensive—in some cases it could be cheaper to buy another amp.

A test between solid state amps, tube and modeling amps was done recently in America by ten very experienced musicians. The ten musicians involved were blindfolded and then had to listen to ten different amps. The amps were solid state, tube and modeling. The results were astonishing!

Every single tube amp was mistaken for a solid state amp, and every modeling amp was mistaken for a tube amp.

Considering some of the tube amps in question cost up to £1,500 and some of the modeling amps cost as little as £300, that's an amazing result.

There are also a number of effects pedals available with the same modeling functions on board. Below are some of the main players in this field.

Line 6 (www.line6.com)

Digital modeling amps, preamps and effects boxes including the AX2, Spider, Flextone and POD series (POD, POD Pro, and Bass POD), Distortion Modeler, Delay Modeler and Modulation Modeler.

Johnson (www.johnson-amp.com)

Tube Integrated Modeling amps which combine digital modeling and tube technology, including the Millennium Series, Marquis Series, Mirage Series.

DigiTech (www.digitech.com)

Johnson's sister company's RP2000 incorporates amp, cabinet, acoustic and pickup modeling technology, as well as a range of digital effects.

Crate (www.crateamps.com)

DX Series digital amps featuring digital modeling and built-in effects.

Pretty soon every amp company will have it's own modeling amp/effects series.

TIP: A torch is a very useful item to have in the back of your amp. **Do not** put drinks by electric's or on top of amps—it's almost inevitable that they will be knocked over and not only is it dangerous but it can also ruin your valuable equipment.

Effects pedals Sorry, I can't really help you here as there are literally thousands of them and it depends on which effects you would like. Best thing to do is take a flask of coffee, a few bags of crisps and a cushion and spend a few weeks trying out the many different types on offer. Don't forget, more and more amps have the basic effects you would need as a guitarist—so it all depends on how many sounds you actually want. Most common effects that would satisfy 95% of the usual guitarist's needs are usually distortion, delay, reverb and chorus. Digital effects use batteries or mains supply. If you use a mains supply pedal at around three times the price of a battery, you will save hundreds of pounds over the years.

THE PUBLIC ADDRESS (PA) SYSTEM

WHAT IS A 'PA'?

Your PA system is usually your most important piece of kit and can make all of the difference to your show. (If you don't know, it's the speakers you see either side of the stage.)

The PA you use will depend on what you can afford (though it should be noted that the better you sound the more work you should get, therefore it may be a case of ' speculate to accumulate').

The venues you play should also be taken into consideration when choosing your PA, but again it's better to have power to spare than have to struggle in the bigger venues.

PA' s come in all shapes and sizes and obviously different degrees of power and can range from vocal only (usually contained in one unit per side) to full range systems which can add up to two, three or even more units per side. In some cases full range units which can incorporate top, mid and bass can be housed in one cabinet per side.

What can you get for your money?

COMPLETE ENTRY LEVEL FOR PRACTISE, HOUSE PARTIES, SMALL GIGS, ETC

Kustom Profile 1—100W PA System For the remarkable price of around £270 this package includes a 100W mixer/amplifier plus two speakers. It also looks good, very portable, very easy to use and an ideal solution for practising or small acoustic gigs/open mics. There are 8 built in effects including 4 x reverbs—small room, large room, small hall, large hall, chorus, chorus reverb, slap back (delay) and echo. So it's also great to plug your semi acoustic in too (for an extra £100 it comes with stands and cases).

Peavey Escort 2000 We are not talking Wembley Arena here, we are talking about a first introduction to a PA system, and as such it's a revolution.

For under £400 you can purchase a PA system which includes;
- a two way speaker system
- a five-channel 150 watt stereo mixer amplifier.
- 4 x XLR mic inputs 2 x stereo line inputs.
- a high quality digital reverb (you will recognise that effect as the echo sound, plus the effect of singing in a hall)
- 2 x folding speaker stands.
- Microphone and cables supplied.
- (No van unfortunately !!)

Don't laugh—to top it all, it comes in a suitcase design with luggage style wheels. How good is that? You could jump on a bus to the gig, no road crew needed.

Shame on anyone who reads this and thinks it's a toy, it actually sounds quite good and for the entry-level price it's quite amazing. Everybody should have one!

As you progress, unfortunately you are going to need something with more power. The last PA may suffice for rehearsals/practise, etc, and small pubs but if you are looking to move onto bigger venues you are going to struggle with volume. If you overdrive (use on full volume) a PA amplifier it sounds terrible and will distort the sound coming out of the speakers.

Guitarists don't mind that problem and in fact some distortion is welcome, but it's completely different for vocals.

The next move up in volume should be in the range of around 300/500 watts per side for solo/duo work and maybe as high as 1000/2000 watts (1k) for bands. Again, it all depends on the size of the venue you play and what you are actually putting into the PA, and of course your ability to move it from A to B as regards transport.

There are numerous mid range PA specs and they come at different prices. The best thing you can do is to pop along to your local music venues (pubs and clubs) when they have acts on, and see what they are using. Take note that a PA system is a two part item—speakers plus an amp. One won't be any good without the other unless they are powered speakers (the amp is built in). Peavey, McGregor and Mackie do a good range of entry/mid level PAs or if you can afford a bit more, you should consider EVs, JBLs or Adlib Audio systems.

As you progress even further up the live performance ladder, you will find that the PA equipment which sufficed in your early years cannot cope with your desire to sound better, louder and possibly have control over your sound.

This is when you may decide that all vocals and instruments including drums would be better off being sound engineered (mixed) via further amplification, through microphones or DI boxes into and through a mixing desk.

This enables a sound engineer out front to listen to the balance of the whole band and use the mixing desk to adjust volumes, tones and effects where he/she deems necessary.

An example would be raising the guitar volume when the guitarist is doing a solo or adding more vocal volume or effects, etc., or taking effects off the main microphone whilst vocalist introduces songs, etc.

This luxury is particularly useful at larger pubs, clubs and other venues where the volume and sound has to be altered throughout the gig.

When a band or artist can simply not afford to purchase a decent PA system, hiring one would be the next best option and would also help in other ways.

For example, if you hire a PA it usually comes with one or two roadies and engineers included in the deal.

Hiring is very advisable for showcase gigs or concerts, album releases, etc when a good live sound production is obviously very important.

At bigger more important gigs like this, a fold back (monitor) system should also be included. This enables the band to have their own mini speakers facing them on stage in order to hear themselves, therefore giving them an idea of the balance of sound going out to the audience. NB. I used the word 'idea' of the balance of sound, as it's just that—you would never hear the exact same sound as the out front speakers, basically because of the different design of the speakers and amplification. Also you may want more vocals or guitar or even both in your personal monitor mix.

With a professional sound you can start to see the benefits of a good 'PA' and the improvement it could make to your band's chances of gigging more, or even being signed.

However, it must also be taken into consideration that a good 'PA' amplifies the whole band, so 'flat' notes and timing are also amplified—in fact everything is amplified. In a nutshell, you get out of a PA system only what you have the skills to put into it.

Hire PA's can cost around the £200—£400 mark for, say, a small PA = 1-2 K (K=thousand watts) and for that you should also have the pleasure of a sound engineer. For around double that figure you can include a fold-back system and maybe a second engineer. The fold-back itself can also be engineered from side-of-stage.

There are many packages and it is recommended that you find out in advance exactly what you are getting for your money. Most professional PA companies will send you a 'PA spec' which is a full list of the components, effects and personnel they will be supplying (is transport included?).

It goes without saying that there is no real ceiling to PA hire and most pro companies which hire pub/club 'PA's' usually have a system for every possible situation or occasion.

> *"As soon as a gig is over, pack away your guitar/instrument and effects pedals, they are usually the single most expensive pieces of equipment and certainly the most fragile. If you don't, they are liable to be damaged by other members of the band or roadies trouncing round the stage".*
>
> **—T Clare (roadie)**

When purchasing equipment consider the size as well as the sound. Equipment is expensive, but it's going to be even more expensive if you have to buy a bigger vehicle to get it around.

Transporting equipment Reliable transport is as important as reliable equipment.

It's common for a band to spend thousands of pounds on equipment and then spend £200 on a dilapidated converted milk float with a dodgy wheel and an oil leak, and then wonder why it breaks down half way to the gig!

Make sure at least one band member has a vehicle breakdown membership and a mobile phone.

Always get a contact number for the venue in case you are delayed (which is more common than you would expect).

Never presume you know where the gig is—relying on the public is not always recommended. Some years a friend asked for directions to a pub whilst in the Lake Districts (Cumbria), the answer from the man, after a pause, was "ooh, you don't want to be starting from here"!!??!.

A gig is stressful enough, so it makes good sense to be well prepared with reliable transport, a map and good directions before setting off.

Whenever possible, do not leave equipment in a van overnight. Apart from the obvious reason that the van could be stolen along with all your valuable equipment, it's not a good environment for electrical equipment in general, particularly in cold, damp conditions. If you have no choice then it's a good idea to have industry standard padlocks and engine cut out devices fitted. Even then you are still taking a risk. Whilst on the road, tie equipment down with bungee type ropes to stop it moving and causing possible damage.

Stage lighting Ok, maybe you are not Pink Floyd or Genesis but lights will always enhance the show and create an atmosphere. You can start off by hiring a basic rig until you can afford your own. The most basic rig you can hire would be a four x 1000 watts—parr 64 can lanterns per side = eight. They will do the trick until you are doing theatre size gigs. Hiring a lighting rig plus lighting engineer can cost anything from £100 to £200 depending on whether it's a pro company or a one man band outfit. If you manage to purchase your own lights, remember when setting them up that it's roughly 5 amps per 1000 watts of lights.

Strobe type lighting is now banned in a lot of venues so consider that fact before buying your lights. Second—hand lights can be a good idea and will save you money, but remember to have them checked by an electrician as the person you may have bought them off could have wired them wrong (which may be the reason they are selling them).

Casual roadies and equipment: It's great having some help taking your heavy equipment in and out of the gigs, but remember how expensive and delicate the equipment is in untrained hands. Experienced roadies are bad enough but if you give responsibility to friends—beware of possible breakages. Untrained and inexperienced roadies or helpers can actually be a hindrance and can certainly damage your finer equipment, rather like a Bull in a China shop. The amount of people I have seen over the years walking on to the stage to offer help only to step on a new pedal or cable and ruin it (even knocking a guitar over). If you are desperate for help, at least make sure all the cables and smalls are packed away before calling for assistance.

Roadying is an art in itself and has to be a learned skill like any other trade.

Maintenance Learn some basic maintenance jobs like soldering, wiring a plug, etc., but leave anything more complicated to professionals.

If you are very careful, soldering is something which can be done yourself (if you have been taught properly). You will find guitar cables and speaker cables sometimes fail due to simple 'dry joints'.

PAT Test From July 2002, every piece of electrical equipment taken into a venue has to have a 'PAT' (Portable Appliance Test) test sticker with a certification. It is also expected to be renewed annually. A PAT test sticker can only be applied to a piece of equipment that has been tested by an approved electrician.

VOCAL MICROPHONES

Most of your life, you've probably been prancing around the bedroom holding a hairbrush or an ice-cream cone pretending it's a microphone—well maybe it's time to get a real one!

Yes, you will need one of these to get yourself heard, after all—that's the name of the game. In order to get you voice across to the audience via a PA system, a good professional vocal microphone is essential (there are some very cheap vocal microphones but they are really only useful as a toy). We say vocal microphone for the simple reason that microphones can vary in build and design to suit different circumstances and some are also designed specifically for various studio usage and to mic up various instruments.

Without going into too much technical detail, there are basically two kinds of microphone you will come across as a vocalist/musician.

One is a condensor microphone which uses a battery as a power source, or the more common 'Dynamic' variety of which there are, again, different types.

The most popular option for a live performance vocal mic is one of the dynamic variety, rather than the condenser type, and in this field the most popular and commonly used has to be the good old Shure SM58. It's a good old tried and tested road worthy mic that just seems to eat up the gigs and hangs around long after the drummer has left and brought up a family and sent them off to university.

> *"I dropped my Shure SM58 down four flights of metal stairs whilst loading in at a gig—it didn't even have a dent on the cover, it worked as well, and I've still got it now, twelve years later and it's been dropped over a dozen times since."*
>
> **—T Spencer**

SM58s can be purchased for the measly price of around £69 (2005 prices) via some internet music stores, which is great value for money. If you buy one second hand you should clean the head by screwing it off and dipping it (and the foam) in TCP or something similar, or you can buy a brand new mic head for around £10.

Of late though, there is some stiff competition as more and more instrument manufacturers jump on the mic/technology band wagon.

Various magazines have done some road tests for some less-obvious mics over the last few years and a few contenders can be considered.

A budget mic for example for those musicians who can't quite afford the Shure mic would have to be the 'Apex 880' which retails at an amazing £29 and is certainly no toy. According to tests, it offers surprisingly good sound quality and build. Although some corners have been cut to take in cost, it is still a very professional sounding mic with a sturdy case and adequate finish.

For full specification and more info on the Apex 880—www.apex-electronics.com

Another 'newish' mic that has had very good test reports is the AKG D880 which is coming in at around the same price as the SM58. Again it's a very rugged mic and has very similar characteristics to the Shure.

Microphones are usually priced on a combination of factors, these usually being the mic's output sound, the mic's build quality and the mic's resistance to feedback.

Feedback comes in two types, positive and negative, but then you probably don't want to know about the negative one in this instance. Hold a microphone in front of the speakers from which the sound of the microphone is coming out of and you have a feedback loop. In this case it's positive because the sound coming out of the speakers will go into the microphone and adds to the sound coming out of the speakers which gets added to the sound going into the microphone, etc. Feedback very quickly becomes loud and can damage equipment unless properly tamed.

What is feedback? Basically it's a loop caused by audio or video signal being fed back into itself. In audio, the effect, manifested as an echo or loud horrible squeal, is caused when a microphone is aimed at a speaker, therefore picking up it's own signal. (I have actually heard a singer that creates a feedback type horrid squeal and that's before his equipment is even switched on!) If Tony Spencer is doing a gig on your local, consider renting a DVD and staying in.

You can always ask to test a mic but remember a music shop will not be the same environment as a pub or club venue. You will probably be using an unfamiliar PA system so it's quite pointless—better then to just take advice and recommendations.

DYNAMIC MICROPHONES

Dynamic microphones are the simplest and most rugged of all microphones—no power needed from batteries or any external sources. They generate their own signal with few moving parts. The two types are the moving coil, which works like a miniature loudspeaker in reverse, and the ribbon, which exhibits low mass similar to condensers but has lower output voltage.

PHANTOM POWER

Condenser microphones need a source of power to impress the charge on the capacitor. One of three methods is used. Either a battery will be inserted inside the microphone, a permanent charge is retained on the diaphragm or backplate thanks to some clever material scientist, or phantom power is used.

THE PROXIMITY EFFECT

Some microphones have a funny phenomenon called the Proximity Effect. This describes the increase in bass as the microphone moves nearer the sound source. Similarly, the further a cardioid microphone is from a source of sound, the more thin it will sound. Experienced vocalists, producers and even comedians have used this phenomenon to great effect, especially in simulating a punchy, 'live' effect by almost eating the microphone while singing or telling a joke! The proximity effect can also cause problems, especially when dealing with inexperienced speakers, as the tonal qualities of their voice will change as they moves their head or the microphone.

WIRELESS MICS

Think Karaoke, DJ and also stage performances. Wireless mics can be both convenient (no cables to trip over) and a pain in the butt (batteries running out in the middle of your first song, punch-line; interference from the taxi driving past). These mics are basically the same as ordinary microphones but house a transmitter and the most expensive source of power being a battery.

MICROPHONE STANDS (VOCALS)

You will need on of these and they come in two basic formats. There is a standard mic stand and a boom stand. The standard mic stand is a straight job with a base in tripod form or a discus type design, these will suit vocalists. If however you also play an instrument like a guitar, bass or keyboards—in particular—you will be much better off with a boom stand—which has an added arm that can be used to create some clearance for your instrument. Stands have improved recently and there are some good lightweight models on the market at around the £20 mark.

There are many other mic stands that serve a variety of purposes, mainly used for micing up drums, amplifiers etc.

KEYBOARDS

THE BORING STUFF BY NICK MURPHY

"Most keyboards have a way of backing up (saving) all the sounds. Do it. If ever the keyboard is damaged or stolen, you can get it replaced but not the sounds you had become so used to, laid out in an order that was second nature to you.

This is also true of any data, be it recorded music or computer information.

Make copies of everything you can and keep one set with you at the gig and another at home. It's boring but well worth it.

Keep your keyboards in a good strong road case, not the cardboard box it came in!

Get a keyboard stand which you are comfortable with. It needs to be adjustable, easy to set up, not too many separate pieces and roadworthy.

Read the manual. Modern keyboards are basically musical computers with black and white keys instead of alpha numeric ones. Many useful functions are hidden behind menus and sub menus which are impossible to find without referring to the manual. If you don't have one, most can be found on the internet or copies can be bought from the manufacturer.

Get a good sustain pedal. You will stand on it often. It will be placed on some less than sterile floors and be expected to work every time.

Carry at least one spare multi voltage power supply unit. If you don't need it someone else may do.

Carry a basic tool kit with cutters, pliers, soldering iron and solder, plastic tape, Philips screwdriver and a torch. A lot of small problems are easily fixed with the minimum of skill. NEVER work on any kit which is connected to the mains even if it is switched off. NEVER work on any mains related problems with your kit, even rewiring the plug, if you're not confident.

If you are working with more than one keyboard, work out and rehearse a contingency plan if one keyboard should fail. You will hear the difference but your audience should remain oblivious.

Keep a set of headphones in your kit. You can check sounds, run through a song that has just been put back in the set, or simply amuse yourself without bothering anyone or any outside noise bothering you.

A mic'd guitar amp fed through the mixing desk cannot compete with a better than CD quality stereo sample of symphony orchestra string section or a massive swirling bass synth patch. Always remember, less is more and stay in control of the awesome sound creating potential literally at your fingertips."

—**Nick Murphy—keyboards freelance 30yrs**

WHERE TO BUY

- www.mia.org.uk
  Music Industries Association—represents businesses selling instruments and associated equipment

Look for your local retailers, try www.yell.com.or try

- Digital Village—www.dv247.com
- Turnkey—www.turnkey.co.uk
- Thomann Musikhaus—www.netzmarkt.de/thomann/thoiw2_index.html
- Dolphin Music—www.dolphinmusic.co.uk
- Guitar, Amp & Keyboard Centre www.gak.co.uk
- Sound Control—www.soundcontrol.co.uk
- Academy of Sound—www.academyofsound.com
- Dawsons—www.dawsonsonline.com
- Red Submarine—www.sub.co.uk

SECOND-HAND SOURCES

- Loot—www.loot.co.uk
- Ebay (be careful when buying, ask an experienced musician to advise before parting with money.

ADMAG

See also magazines and private ads in newspapers

BOOKS AND MAGAZINES

- Guitarist—superb mag usually comes with free play—along CD
- What Guitar—superb buying guide including prices, specification's and recommendations
- Guitar Player
- Total guitar—as above
- Rhythm
- Keyboard Player (various)
- The Mix
- Making Music
- Sound on Sound—particularly good reviews for pro-audio equipment
- Classical Music
- The Singer
- Future music
- Computer Music
- www.sospubs.co.uk

MUSICAL EQUIPMENT INSURANCE

It really is a sensible thing to insure your equipment against loss or theft, after all it may have taken years to afford it. I know from personal experience how devastating it can be if your favourite guitar or piece of equipment is stolen.

On that occasion I was not insured. We had done a gig at a friend's party and I, foolishly (under the influence of too much free ale) decided to leave my guitar with our then roadie who decided to leave it in the van overnight; you can guess the rest.

That guitar was a 1970's Fender Telecaster, my first serious guitar and I still miss it now, twenty years later.

Since that happened all those years ago, I have never left any instrument in a van overnight, so I learned an expensive lesson, but at least, hopefully, it will never happen again.

Unfortunately, insurance is not free and it's yet another overhead for musicians but at the end of the day it's got to be money well spent.

If you are spending thousands on equipment, surely it's worth a little more to protect that investment.

There are specialist insurance companies who deal with musical equipment and it's good advice to use these companies rather than the usual insurance companies.

If the company you insure your equipment with does not have specialist cover for instruments/musical equipment, there will probably be so many restrictive clauses that it simply will not be a viable insurance, in other words it won't be worth the paper it is written on.

It's important also to declare exactly what you do with the equipment insured—it's no use saying it doesn't leave the house, for the simple reason that if it's stolen from a vehicle, what would it be doing in that vehicle if it 'supposedly' never left the house? The insurance company could use that discrepancy/reason for not paying out and deeming the claim void.

Below are some check points you should look at on a policy..

a, **Theft from vehicles/Transit cover**

Usually most insurance policies will cover equipment damaged in a collision/crash but cover against theft is a completely different scenario and can be much more problematic.

Therefore you should check if there are any stipulations in the policy, for example does the vehicle have to be alarmed, even immobilised, if left unattended.

b, **Old for New**

Make sure the policy has cover for replacement as new. The insurance company should reimburse you for full cost of replacement at the current price—you will not be able to replace a Gibson Les Paul, for example, at the 1970's price.

c, **Cost of hiring**

It's another part of the policy which is important if you have to hire equipment whilst your insurance claim is being processed as this can, and often does, take months.

d, **Do not under—insure your equipment.**

The Musicians Union has special rates for musician members which includes instrument and Public Liability Insurance. (see Musicians union)

The Public Liability Insurance, which again is essential and can cover against injury to a member of the audience through the band's negligence. It protects against legal action being taken but does not constitute an automatic payment.

MUSICGUARD—Insurance for musicians and their instruments. For online quotations

www.musicguard.co.uk

chapter 8
your first gigs

You can rehearse and practise forever, but nothing will ever take the place of a real gig, where people are watching you, judging you, analysing your songs, analysing you as a musician and probably even paying to see you (or at least the booker/management of the venue is paying you).

These are the things you can never experience from any amount of rehearsal.

(Rehearsing, however, is extremely important in the build-up to the 'real' gig.)

Obviously, it's very important to rehearse and tighten up your sound and musicianship, but being out there in the public domain is a very different experience.

Your first gigs will open your eyes to all manner of things you simply cannot experience in a garage, bedroom or rehearsal room situation. So far it's been very comfortable—easy, in fact, with only yourself and fellow band members to please. Your only feedback may have come from a few of your immediate family or friends who, realistically, are not always likely to tell you that your songs/show/repertoire is not quite ready.

What I am trying to get across here is that basically, to learn the trade you have to get out there in the big world and start doing real gigs. I meet so many singers, artists and bands who seem to rehearse for years but never actually get out and do it for real.

Like any trade, there has to be an apprenticeship which gives the student job experience. It's no different for a musician and the early pub/club gigs can and will be that apprenticeship.

Even top level education cannot substitute the real thing, I have met many young musicians who have attended college after college for music education of some form. I have even met musicians who have actually gained a 'Degree in Performing Arts' and yet have only ever done one or two gigs in the comfort of the university grounds.

That seems wrong to me. If that student had, for example, used a tenth of the time he/she spent studying on actual gigging, then he/she would be a much better performing artist.

If an advert in a local music shop/paper/publication asks for a bass guitarist for example, and two musicians turn up—one clutching a pile of qualifications, the other with none—it would not matter one iota. They would both be expected to audition and perform some material with the band. Whoever shows the greatest aptitude, experience and skill will secure the job—the paperwork will be totally irrelevant.

Qualifications are important, however, if that student is looking to going on to teach in some capacity.

Rehearsals do not bring out the adrenalin that real gigs do as there is little pressure and therefore no real, true 100% performance. Any musician, band, act, front man/person needs adrenalin to perform to their best ability. Adrenalin is not produced in any great supply at rehearsals.

SO HOW DO WE GET THOSE EARLY GIGS?

The most common early gigs and probably the easiest route towards the the higher level gigging, are usually friend's birthday parties or even charity gigs where you are surrounded by people and friends who aren't expecting perfection. And because it's not a high paid gig they would not be expecting the usual one and a half hours of music.

These gigs, as we have pointed out in another chapter, are useful for the simple reason that they give you a chance to 'test' your set/songs/repertoire without the worry of having to spend too long on stage.

If an agent and a proper fee were involved, you would be expected to do around one and a half hours which amounts to two sets of forty-five minutes, obviously depending on whether you are the only performers on the occasion

So if we look at the scenario that a friend is having a 21st birthday party in a local function room, you could then suggest doing, say, a thirty minute set or thereabouts for free, or maybe some expenses.

It's got to be a good idea all round as it gives you a chance to do a gig under less pressure than a paid gig, but more pressure than a rehearsal and also provides some live entertainment for the audience. Everyone's happy!

"If you are paid in beer, which is after all a regular form of currency in some venues and even more regular at friends parties, pace yourself. As you drink, lyrics and chords become harder to remember, you stagger about and the audience becomes more and more blared as the gig goes on, as does your guitar. You may even end up winking at the wrong girl or even worse playing the wrong solo to the wrong song...I've been there, done it."

—T Spencer (below average singer, great boozer)

Don't expect too much praise at your first few gigs and be wary that feedback from friends may hide some truths, but at least your show is now 'on the road', and it can only improve.

It's only natural that after the gig you will analyse your set, discuss what songs worked, what songs didn't work, what songs need working on, how the set sounded, volumes, mix, etc, even your position on stage can be considered.

Stage room It's first come first served as regards your gear on the stage. If you get there late you may find the DJ has taken up most of the room and this could seriously hamper your back flips and your Shadows dance routine!

Another thing that is immediately apparent during your first real gigs is the gap in-between songs.

At rehearsals, you end the song and usually the drummer hits a few beats whilst the guitarist tunes up; plays a few Beatles riffs, etc.

All of a sudden you now face an audience who expects some communication, patter—anything at all between songs.

This again is a part of gigging which can only come naturally and develops over the early years on the road, and which certainly does not come with rehearsing alone.

It's at this stage that an inexperienced band/act/artist can lose the audience by simply not getting a good rapport going.

Though it's not quite as important on the original circuit as the covers circuit, it is still very important to be able to communicate with an audience.

The atmosphere of any gig can be controlled by good banter and can then go on to enhance the whole show and it's also a way of jelling the songs/set together.

Don't ever be too proud to take note of things you have said that have worked and use them again. Don't forget; another night, another audience.

If you don't take notes and write down things that worked, you will forget them. Many people in the industry use prompts; bits of notes written down to help them remember items throughout a set.

Remembering lyrics is an art form in itself, again, it's a good idea to have lyric 'prompts'—parts of the songs—written down to help you remember lyrics. You could just write down the first line of each verse and the chorus or whatever helps.

As mentioned previously, other early gigs could include charity gigs. Again, because there is little money changing hands, people are willing to put up with a few bad/flat notes and bad timing here and there. Time on stage is also negotiable, with the organisers quite happy that you are actually helping them out. It's also nice to know you are raising money for a good cause by playing your set.

Approaching your local pub landlord and asking for some 'expenses only' gigs is a good idea. Most landlords may insist on a recent tape or video of the band performing, so it's important to consider taping a few rehearsals—even if it's only for that reason.

It's also important to inform the landlord/booker of what kind of material you perform and the length of your show, and also discuss 'where' in the pub you will be setting up (check for power points, access for equipment, amount of room for your back flips routine, etc).

If you are lucky enough to get a date for a gig in your diary, it then becomes a date you can aim for; a date when it's all got to come together; a target.

That is when you start to notice possible 'chinks in your armour'. In some cases your armour may be 'heavily dented'.

- **Is the band ready to gig?**
- **Are you as good as you thought you were?**
- **Do you have enough material?**
- **Is your material suitable for the venue?**
- **Do you have the equipment needed to put the show across?**
- **How will you get the equipment to the venue?**

You are about to face the biggest challenge of your musical career so far.

But surely that's got to be a good thing after months of rehearsals in a garage.

These are the very things I am trying to get across in the chapter regarding the difference between rehearsing and real gigs.

But isn't it great to now be able to start facing these hurdles and getting over t them one by one? There are bound to be some problems in the early days—there are problems starting up in any industry or business and the entertainments industry is no exception.

So now you have done a few entry level gigs and you may have the confidence to move on to some higher level gigs.

You can find local gigs/venues in any local paper or music mag circulation advertising the forthcoming gig guide, and obviously who's appearing on what date/night.

Try to attend a few gigs to get the feel of different venues and 'suss out' whether they could be suitable for your band.

Try to speak to a member of the band appearing and ask some questions regarding who is the promoter/booker. Ask if they are using their own equipment/PA or is the *backline/PA supplied.

*Backline = amplification provided for instruments usually behind the players on the stage.

It's probably best leaving it at that stage (unless, of course you have met a very kind musician who is prepared to talk all night!). You can find out the rest of the criteria and gig situation from the booker if you are fortunate enough to meet him/her.

Once you have decided a particular venue would be suitable for your band (you shouldn't be at all fussy at this stage of your career—a gig's a gig), on future visits you should take some band biog/bumph, including if possible any recent recordings, and a diary.

> "What impresses me about a band/artist? Basically, a degree of professionalism. I like to see them making an effort to find out as much about the gig as possible before the actual day of the gig. It makes my job so much easier to discuss things like 'set' times, back-line equipment they may need. Though we do supply almost all back-line equipment, the band may not know that and start to try to set up their own drum kit in a five minute changeover period. Set up/sound-check times, even simple things like making sure I have their name spelt right for flyers, marketing etc. There is nothing worse than a band turning up two minutes before they are due on stage, the only contact being a short phone call three months earlier. It can lead to chaos and all manner of problems. So yes, though it makes my job a little harder sorting these things before-hand, it certainly makes up for it on the night. I also like to see a band has rehearsed enough to put over a decent performance."

—Alex McKecknie: multi instrument, booker and entertainments manager at the world famous 'Cavern Club', Liverpool.

When you actually start doing the more well known gigs around your local town it's important to milk them for all they're worth as regards publicising. Also approaching local press and music journalists to invite them to the gigs. Hopefully they'll turn up and give the band a good review, (if you are receiving bad reviews—you really need to work harder on your set—but don't let it get you down too much, every band has 'teething' problems).

TIP: Look confident and don't stand at the back of the stage or hide behind speakers or curtains. An average musician with a confident stage presence can easily give the impression of being a much better musician, and vice-versa—a good musician is easily overlooked if he stands at the back or behind the speakers.

So maybe your mum and dad wanted you to become a veterinary surgeon or even a nuclear physicist. Still encourage them to attend your first gigs and even applaud. If one person claps you will find others will follow. It's called the domino effect.

It's amazing how your confidence grows if there is a ripple of applause and a show of appreciation after a song has ended. All of a sudden all the rehearsals in the cold, dark, damp garage will seem worthwhile and you will find that you will start the next song in a much more positive and confident manner.

TIP: Athletes and footballers warm up before they start and it's not a bad idea for musicians to do the same. Ok, so you don't start running around the venue and do thigh stretching exercises or press-ups, but you could do some breathing and vocal warm ups. Guitarists; playing some chords or simple scales can get you off to a better start. That actually doubles up as a guitar/equipment check—if there's a string due to break with the guitar lying idle between gigs—it may just snap in the warm up which is far better than during the actual gig itself.

Vocal warm ups are essential—if you think of how much your voice improves after two or three songs, it proves the point.

On the other hand, not doing light vocal warm ups and going straight into full blown vocals at full throttle can severely damage vocal chords.

THE GUEST LIST

You should always find out in advance who can come into the gig free of charge on a guest list. This would obviously include band members and 'proper' roadies (someone carrying a spare string may not be seen by the venue as a roadie!). If you turn up with your nan's neighbour, your auntie Lil, uncle Joe, five cousins and their friends, it can cause big problems. Particularly if the venue has sold tickets and has no seats left. In fact it's a serious problem if all involved have travelled a long distance only to be told they can not enter. Most times even offering to pay for your guests can not solve the problem for the simple reason that the club may be full as regards insurance regarding safety numbers, and also there may not be any physical room for more people, regardless of seating. This problem can arise at both social club level right through to concert venues.

You will need some kind of **business/contact details**—a card or a leaflet with the band's name and contact details on. If somebody enjoys a great night watching the band and wishes to hire you, finding half a fag packet with 'Dick Spanner and the Wheelie Bins' and a phone number scribbled on it won't look too impressive in the cold light of the next day.

It may not be the epitome of rock-n-roll but you should always carry a **pocket diary**. You never know when you will be offered a gig (or a date!) and remember it's very important to keep the other band members up to date too. Also remember to take the booker's contact details and confirm the gig after booking. If you start doing really well, you should have a dedicated diary just for gigs to avoid mix ups and double bookings.

TIP: **Venue address** Make sure you have the correct venue's address before setting off to the gig—there are around four thousand 'Dog and Gun' public houses in England.

TIP: **Spare tyre** Put the spare tyre somewhere you can reach it, not behind two tonnes of equipment (I learned the hard way).

The Geezer! Be polite 'just in case' but don't get too excited when a man with a nice Cartier suit offers your band £ 5,000 a night to do a world cruise gigging on his yacht. Chances are you will never see him again, and his suit is a Turkish fake. He or she will inevitably waste at least an hour or two of your precious 'after gig' time. If however he takes you to his yacht, be even more polite and consider the offer!

TIP: If you fall off the stage at a gig, try to give the impression you meant it—breath in deeply, try to ignore the pain and try your very best to convince the punters that it was part of the band's new show by jumping swiftly back onto the stage (all in the one movement if possible, and try to hide the blood!).

If you rehearse this procedure with the rest of the band it should all look quite good and could even become an important part of the act. I still think to this day that the Shadows dance routine started with a member of the band tripping over a guitar cable and the rest of the band just joined in to make it look like it was deliberate. The rest, as they say, is history.

STAGING YOUR OWN GIG/EVENT

There are various reasons why you may decide to put on your own gig. Perhaps as a fund raiser for a local charity or to give you a chance to promote your act and show everyone what you have been doing in the garage for the last two years. Whatever the reason, staging a successful gig/show can involve a lot of work and preparation.

To stage a successful gig you have to consider various pointers. For example marketing the gig via local press, band web-sites, mailing lists, posters and fliers. Timing is another important thing—don't book a venue for the Saturday coming up if the flyers can't be printed until the day before.

Putting a lot of effort into the organisation of the gig will help things run as smoothly as possible. It goes without saying that the more work you have done in advance, the better equipped you will be to deal with any unexpected problems which may arise on the day.

First things first:

When you first consider putting on your own gig (whether that be just your band performing alone or a number of bands) there are two main things to take care of;

a) **the venue** (whether that be indoor, outdoor, a local pub or a theatre)
b) **the band/s involved**

Both of these should be dealt with before making any other plans.

The most common reason for a band to put on their own organised gig is to showcase their own band. It's also a good chance to invite other local bands to perform at the gig, therefore giving each other's fans a chance to see what else is happening on the local scene. Although there is a lot of jealousy and competition between some bands, it's inevitable that they are going to end up on the same bill sooner or later so why not get it over with. It's actually a good idea to get a more established band than yourself in order to get some 'bums on seats'. People are more likely to come if there's a 'name' band on the bill (it would be a good idea if the band plays a similar genre of music as yourself). Hopefully their fans should give you a chance to show what your made of. There's also the added bonus of learning a few things from the more established band.

Ok, so now you have made the decision on which bands or artists are appearing, but what about the venue? The age group (is it for adults only, are children allowed, etc.) and also the amount of people you are expecting will have to be taken into consideration. If you are expecting under 18s to attend it's important to find somewhere which allows this age group as some licensed premises will not allow under 18s in their establishment, but some will providing they are accompanied by adults. Other places like youth clubs, community centres, village halls, school/college halls will obviously allow children. Remember, when starting off a small venue is much easier to fill, therefore creating an atmosphere and it also makes sense with regard to getting a good sound—large halls are notoriously difficult sound-wise and they tend to have bad acoustics. If it's a mainstream gig aimed at adults, try to find a recognised music venue in your area. If a place is associated with live music then you may also get some passing trade (punters just calling in to check out what's going on). How much the venue will actually cost can vary venue to venue depending on a number of factors. Some venues have full back-line (all guitar and bass amps—possibly drums and a PA) supplied, even an engineer, whereas some have nothing but a stage. Some venues will require a retainer (a guaranteed amount) that could come from door money and the band gets the rest of the money or an agreed percentage split. If you are expecting a lot of people, it's a good idea to have someone keeping an eye on the door takings. Make sure you understand your commitments before agreeing to use the venue. Most recognised venues have basic gig contracts.

TIP: Have a marker pen to mark people's hands if they have to leave the concert room for any reason, it may be that the venue has several rooms or toilets outside the actual concert room. It can be very difficult to know who has and hasn't paid when a place is busy, dark and very noisy.

ARTIST/BAND BIOG/PHOTO/WEBSITE

Somewhere along the line you will need a band biog including a photo in order to let people know your bands history so far, and to show possible customers and any press what you look and sound like. Eventually, your own website will have all the info needed but you need something you can hand out or leave at gigs

Even if you are just starting out and have only done a couple of gigs, an artist/band biog is still a good idea and can give you a head start, and hopefully a foot in some doors.

Imagine if you yourself were a promoter, agent or pub landlord and someone passes you a beer mat with ' any chance of a gig, ring Joe' written on it; chances are Joe will not get a reply.

Alternatively, a nice package arrives with a brief biog of the bands history including the band name and possibly a 'logo', description of

band line-up and who plays what, a recent photo/poster of the artist/band, a brief of recent history and gigs,
- a brief description of genre/style of music, if possible some newspaper cuttings including any critical appraise, details of any recordings, a tape of any recordings,
- current gigs 'coming up' list, where to see the band next, contact details, website etc.

Who is more likely to get the gig?

Obviously the band can use the biog for other reasons besides getting gigs.

It's got to be done, it's a marketing tool that can make a big difference to people's perspective.

Ok, getting the stuff together at first may cost a little money but once it's done it can be mass produced using copiers, etc, and again it's got to pay for itself in promotion alone. In any case it's no use writing a book about your band, all you need is the basic info.

Example
The L.A Biffs
(band logo)
Biog: July 2005
Line-up: Long Sumners—Lead vocals, Dick Shrimp—lead guitar vocals/harmonica, Ronny Nose—keyboards/b/vocals, Al Teeth—drums b/vocals

The L.A Biffs got together quite by chance after two ex monsters of rock—'The Sharpest Knife' & 'Killing for a Living'—decided to split. The new band has the best of both worlds with Long Sumners screaming lead-vocals paired with the multi—award winning guitar slayer Dick Shrimp.

The band is ready to knock the world off it's axis. Be afraid, be very afraid! The band take no prisoners and recently blew 'The Wild Mothmen' off stage whilst supporting them on their recent tour of St Helens, UK.

Critics have described the band as the "next best thing since Sliced Bread". 'Sliced Bread' themselves say "the band are—simply the best—and will be the next big thing, in fact they're that good we wouldn't have them as a support as they would blow us off stage". "Simply awesome"—Mean Machine magazine. "They kick arse"—Hit and Miss magazine. "Electric raw power"—Stringbreaker magazine.

The L.A Biffs have arrived, check us out before you can't afford the tickets or you simply can't get one. Hard, aggressive, total awe inspiring rock, not for the faint hearted (don't bring your nan).

The L.A Biffs are currently recording an album of original songs penned by master songsmith and drummer extraordinaire 'Al Teeth' and will be touring this summer and appearing on these dates below.

The Mayflower Club	16.7.05
Flannigans Muzzy Bikers Club	17.7.05
The Bin and Dunnit Club	18.7.05
Radio Baghilt live session	19.7.05
The Rag and Spanner	20.7.05
Little Dicks Club	21.7.05

For further details, contact…or visit our website www.theLAbiffsareloudenuf.com

That should do, not too much boring info, but enough to tempt someone who may be interested in either checking you out or possibly booking you or even signing you—whatever.

If the only review you have managed is something like "extraordinarily average"—'Which Fridge Freezer' magazine, or "Amazing teeth"—What Toothpaste magazine, you need to work harder to get some good reviews. It's amazing how useful a good review can be.

BAND PHOTOGRAPH

This bit is especially interesting to me. I have a section in the book with band's photo's in and it really was quite difficult getting decent photographs to use—some of them were great—but not only did I have problems with the quality but also the actual pose or image that the band or artist created. I couldn't actually use some of them. And yet a good photograph is really essential and can fulfil a variety of purposes, most notably the first impressions for anyone who sees it. I think it's important for artists/bands to scan the music press or their record collection and agree on something that might also suit them. It's a well known fact that a photographer will take dozens of shots just to get one good pic, so if you are doing it yourself you could be into the hundreds before you come up with something suitable that creates an image you like (it could also be your first attempt). It's not a bad idea, and quite legal, to recreate someone else's idea if it looks good—after all, they probably copied someone else anyway, there's only so many things you can do with a band photograph.

Full length band photos tend to have too many things that could spoil the shot, and can also look insignificant when reduced in size to use in a publication or a flyer. Top half shots always seem to look best and can capture faces and expressions.

But it's completely up to you as regards what you may decide suits your image. You should however consider the background. We have all used trees and bricks, so why not consider other background options.

BAND WEBSITE & THE INTERNET

It's a fact that two out of three homes now has a computer, so it goes without saying how important a band website could be to your band's development.

SO WHY SHOULD A BAND HAVE A WEBSITE?

To help promote your band and have your material listened to.

Think about it—the internet is hooked up to billions of people and music lovers throughout the world.

To give a direct form of promotion from a household PC that can include a sales forum for your CDs and merchandise, etc.

To collate a data-base of your fans.

To collect feedback from fans.

To be able to notify any fans of forthcoming gigs and events 24 hours a day.

It's also a great way to empower the band with all the bands affairs and become much more self reliant.

How does the band market the website?

OFF LINE MARKETING

Well apart from the obvious 'word of mouth', interviews on radio or even television if you can manage it. Gigs are also a great place to market the website on flyers, tickets and posters.

All promotional biogs and demo work should also promote your website.

Your bands business/contact cards.

ONLINE MARKETING

How do your fans get internet access?

Apart from the obvious home PCs, anyone can use local libraries. Students can use further education colleges, universities and most schools to go online.

THE VENUE

LOADING IN

One day soon you may have the good fortune to be chauffeured to the gig in a large black limo. On arrival you will receive a slow massage, a manicure and a facial rub. A large bowl of fresh fruit, a packet of your favourite biscuits and a pot of freshly ground coffee will be waiting in your dressing room. Meanwhile as you lay back and enjoy the coffee etc, several dozen road crew are setting up your hired equipment, tuning your guitars, testing your microphone, preparing the light show, liaising with the promoter and press and placing strategically placed ice cold drinks just where you can reach them during the gig.

But don't hold your breath! Unfortunately for the time being there's more chance the 'black limo' will be a old dented rusty 1988 Ford Transit with some old bus seats fitted, and the words 'clean me please' scrawled on the back door.

So until the good times come, you will probably be doing your own roadying and will need to consider the following.

If at all possible, sometime before the gig physically check out the venue as regards any problems loading your equipment.

A quick phone call to the venue and having a quick chat with the cleaner the day before is not recommended. However, if the venue is simply too far to visit beforehand, you may have to rely on phone calls—but get as much info as possible before setting off.

Are there any stairs? Stairs for example can be a nightmare when using heavy equipment (even a bag of *spuds soon becomes heavy when using stairs). If it's an outside metal staircase it can be extremely hazardous, particularly if it's raining. Also look for long corridors, small doorways, etc. Remember there is no excuse not to use wheels on heavy equipment.

*Spuds—otherwise known as potatoes used for making chips, roasties, mash etc.

Can your transport or van be parked near the stage area of the venue?

Have you arranged to meet someone with the keys to let you in?

Is there clear access to the stage itself?

Do you need extra cable extensions for power points?

Is there room for all your equipment on stage?

You could always ask the booking agent or promoter but unfortunately they don't always get it right, and besides that it's not really their problem. You will have to consider the gig arrival time with all of the above—stairs alone can triple loading time in and out.

Also, in some venues equipment has to be carried through the audience. This again can add on time and a lot of aggravation (people do not like being moved, particularly if they have been drinking). Also consider that at the end of the gig, the venue may not want you to move equipment until the night has completely ended. If you are in a nightclub for instance and the performance ends at 12.30am, you may not get out until at least 2.00am. That may not actually be the club's fault if their entertainments licence has residential noise restrictions. You also have to remember that in any gig situation, wherever it may be, there is always a certain time you have to be set up and sound checked by. It goes without saying that there is simply no excuse for not arriving at a gig early, even if you have checked the place out beforehand. It's so much easier if you have time to play with and no one in your way.

MUSIC GENRE OF VENUE

If possible, you should really check out the venue's recent music genre history. Don't make the mistake of turning up at a biker's club with an hour and a half of

Barry Manilow material—there's nothing worse than trying to hit a high 'C' with a microphone stand wrapped round your head.

This is actually a common mistake, though not so bad in original music venues where usually anything goes. But even some original music venues are genre specific regarding the kind of music they prefer. Don't make the mistake of arriving and being told to pack your gear up just after the sound check has given them a clue as to what kind of music you play.

There are dozens of types of music—never set out with the presumption that you are going to be able to play anywhere and everyone's going to love you (ever seen the 'Blues Brothers'? If not, check it out!)

BACK-LINE (ON STAGE AMPLIFICATION, ETC)

If you are doing a gig at a name venue, particularly with other bands on the same bill, you are going to need to know if any back-line and a PA is supplied.

If there are three or four bands on the same night, it's quite common for the venue to have some equipment that should, whenever possible, be used by all the bands, in order to save time setting up and sound checking. Particularly drum kits—if a sound engineer had to sound check four different drum kits in one night, he just might lose that last marble!

Bands are however expected to bring their own effects, symbols, pedals etc.

Musicians, including myself may I add, don't actually like using other unfamiliar equipment that we are not used to, but unfortunately sometimes it's inevitable, given a certain time scale for the change over of the bands. Again getting to the venue early is the key issue here. I ran a night at the Cavern club recently (3rd March 05) and the three bands appearing (The Mirrors, Ivan Campo and Polaris) thankfully all turned up early (as requested by myself—very professional, thank you lads!) so the fact that some of them used their own personal equipment (guitar amps) didn't actually pose that much of a problem. (They all used the Cavern's house drum kit.)

If they had turned up late they would have had to use the amps provided (which incidentally are superb amps, but as we said before—it's what you are used to.)

HEALTH AND SAFETY AT THE GIG

There are some important health and safety issues regarding most venues.

For example a few you may come across are **public liability insurance.** Do you have any? If not, I recommend you join the **Musicians Union** as soon as possible. **Portable Appliance Testing (PAT)** on your equipment—some venues stipulate (to cover themselves as well as your safety) that all equipment should be tested for any wiring faults by a qualified electrician. The electrician then puts a 'PAT' sticker on the equipment with a dated signature. Other things to consider apart from these points are obvious safety issues such as your PA stands or lighting stands causing a trip hazard or falling on somebody? It's easy to overlook these points in the heat of a gig but if your speaker or another piece of equipment falls on someone's head, it could be your head that rolls. Even worse, you could fatally injure somebody.

Other things to consider:

Check all mains plugs and extension cables for bad, loose, damaged wiring and any loose connections, etc. Remember even your guitar cable carries a potentially lethal current. You should always avoid touching one piece of equipment whilst touching another. I have had several light shocks and they are not pleasant.

I have also witnessed another musician on stage receiving a serious electric shock and ending up in hospital (it could have been worse). Myself and another musician ran to the stage, keeping clear of the person in trouble, and switched off the electric socket supply. The other band members did not even realise it was happening. The lad recovered and it turned out that he had wrongly wired a plug to his effects pedal.

Wherever possible use a circuit breaker or RCD (residual current device). The device cuts off any dangerous electric current. You can buy them for around £20-£40.

UK POWER SUPPLY

You may find that in some venues there may be only one plug available to power all your equipment, this will not happen in most good venues but lets look at the worst scenario). So how do you know if it's safe to do so?

You can draw up to 13 amps from a normal 240 volt UK power supply.

As a rough guide, a 1000 watt P.A rig draws just over 4 amps when it is working flat out. Using that formula you can use simple maths to work out roughly what you are going to need to supply your equipment. Wherever possible use different power points/sockets to power your equipment. Also wherever possible use a different source to power any lighting, not only do lights use up high wattage, they can also cause noise interference if using the same socket as normal amplification equipment.

STAGE HUM.

The dreaded stage hum can be a nuisance and is usually caused by a number of items that are using the same power supply or simply cables connected or crossed in some way. Cable screens—the braided metal protective layer of leads or cables—together with protective earth wires—form loops resulting in mains 'hum'. Never remove earth connections, instead try and rearrange the equipment so that wires do not cross or try using alternate power points for different equipment. If you are still having problems finding the piece of equipment or cable that is causing the 'hum' use a process of elimination by unplugging or switching off—in turn—each piece of equipment or cable till you find the source of the problem.

PERSONAL HEALTH AND SAFETY

Watch your back whilst lifting—always use your legs and knees!

If you can't play at low volumes use ear-plugs. There are special ear-plugs now that cut the volume without altering the overall tone too much.

Unfortunately, smoke causes a lot of problems but a fan can help.

THE PUNTERS HEALTH AND SAFETY

You have to make other people around you aware of any possible danger, use risk assessment—safety tape around any protruding gear is recommended—supervision, and common sense.

VENUE CONTRACT

All venues providing regular live music and use of musical equipment will have a basic **venue contract.** The contract is a stipulation from the venue's insurance company and has to meet certain criteria in order to be deemed viable.

It's also basically an information document explaining the way the venue operates.

Below is a dummy contract (based on a very well known venue) that will cover most items of a venue contract. NB. Well known Artists may have their own contracts drawn up but they would be based on similar criteria. Also note, there may be a 'rider' included, this may be in the form of free food or drink, free admission for an agreed number of guests etc, the 'rider' would usually be agreed in advance with the venue booker.

You won't be handed one of these at your local working mens club, although that may change in the near future.

The Tavern Club
Abbey Road Liverpool Merseyside
Tavern Contract

1. **The Blogheads love noise**… shall herein be known as **'The Artist'**

2. **The Tavern Club** shall be referred to as **'The Club'**

3. **The artist** is engaged to appear on stage on Saturday 15th April 2005 at approx ? TBC (time subject to number of flyers returned on night) Headline will be band with most returns. All musicians should stay in concert room until running order is confirmed by the sound engineer.

4. Unless otherwise arranged the **'sound check/arrival time' is 6.00pm**. If you are going to be late for either sound check or arrival time you **MUST CONTACT THE CLUB** and speak to the sound engineer, failure to do so may mean no sound check.

5. **BACK-LINE**—Artist MUST use the Club drum kit (unless otherwise arranged) Artist is expected to provide their own snare, cymbals (but not stands) and pedals.

The Artist may use their own guitar amps. Club amps for use by bands inc Fender Twin Reverb, 2 x Fender De Ville amps, 1 x Ashdown Bass guitar stack. (All free of charge. Great care must be taken with any equipment used)

Please inform engineer of channel requirements e.g. 3 x vocals, sampler etc unless you are a conventional 3/4 piece. (There is a lift available)

6. All equipment must be treated with respect and care. Any damage caused to any of the club's equipment by band members or their associates will be charged to the Artist concerned.

7. The Artist is expected to move their own equipment on and around the stage (this includes the Club amps when used by the Artist). Assistance is available.

8. When the Artist has finished their performance they must **immediately remove** their own equipment from the stage to allow any changeovers to be quicker (if using the clubs amps, check with the engineer to see if they need removing)

9. Dressing rooms are to be used by the Artists and management only.

10. All club personnel must be treated with respect at all times, we want everybody to enjoy the night.

11. Bands may cancel without penalty at least 21 days before the gig. Failure to comply for any reason, even medical, will result in the Artist not being booked again for a period of 26 weeks.

12. PAYMENT—the club will provide the Artist with 100 flyers or a sheet by email. You can reproduce as many as you require by photocopying and can mail a sheet to your fan-base The flyers returned will be counted at the door. If the Artist has over 15 returned the Artist will receive £2.50 for EVERY flyer over the 15 returned on the night.

Entry is £3.00 with flyer £4.00 without (flyers valid only till 10.00pm—if your fans arrive later than 10.00pm then the Artist may not be credited with their flyers—unless agreed otherwise by prior arrangement)

13. The Artist is responsible for their own electrical equipment which should be PAT (portable appliance tested) and also Artist should have Public Liability insurance.

Please return signed contract or send under the subject of Tavern Contract

Signed.................The Artist

Signed.................The Club

THE MUSICIANS UNION

'Everybody who plays a musical instrument knows that it can be a source of tremendous enjoyment. But if you have ambitions to make your living—or even part of it—from any kind of music, then it can become a serious business. You will need the help of the only organisation that cares about every kind of musician'.

The Musicians Union is the largest organisation for musicians in the UK.

Using any of the services the MU can provide will save you much more than the cost of the membership.

Legal service Advice is given on all matters relating to musical employment and limited advice on other legal matters is available to members through other schemes.

Rates The Union negotiates fees with broadcasting, TV, film and video companies and the recording industry—in fact, all the major employers of musicians in the country. They also negotiate or set rates for every type of live engagement.

Money MU officials recover thousands of pounds owed to musicians every year.

If they should fail, then back-up can be provided by their legal department.

Contract advice A free advisory service on all music contracts, including specialist vetting of complex recording, managing and publishing contracts, is available.

(NB. The last recording and publishing deal I signed cost over £1,400 in solicitor's fees alone—1992)

Careers advice Comprehensive advice on all aspects of your career including personal interviews.

Insurance Free cover for up to £500 worth of instrument/equipment can be arranged. A 'musician friendly' motor policy is also available (motor insurance for musicians can be notoriously expensive).

Public Liability Insurance Whilst performing—either solo or as a part of a group/band/orchestra—and/or whilst teaching in a public place or your home.

Limit of indemnity—£10 million (for any one loss or event).

Teacher service Lists of instrumental teachers are published in the MU Directory

Information The union produces a constantly expanding range of leaflets, covering topics such as contracts, copyright, managing, recording, etc., and maintains a comprehensive web site—**www.musiciansunion.org.uk** or email **info@musiciansunion.org.uk**

Directories A directory of MU members is produced annually and supplied free to members on request with an optional entry on the MU website.

Contract forms Free standard contract forms are supplied for every kind of live engagement.

Magazine The MUs award winning Musician magazine is sent free to members four times a year. You will also receive the MUs annual diary and 'The Key' which is full of useful information.

SUBSCRIPTION RATES 2005

Your Previous Yearly Earnings (before tax) From Music
Cheque/Credit Card/Direct Debit

A	Up to £15,000 (standard)	£116.00—£110.00
B	£15,000 and over (premium)	£227.00—£220.00
C	(concessionary) under 21—or student—full time education (proof required)	£50.00—£48.00

*Concessions are available to Under 21's—Full Time Students—New Deal Applicants Under 21's, earning in excess of £15,000 must pay at the premium rate

MUSICIANS' UNION NATIONAL OFFICE,
60-62 Clapham Road, London SW9 0JJ
TEL: (44) 0171 582 5566/FAX: (44) 0171 582 9805

MUSICIANS' UNION—NORTH/NORTH EAST,
327 Roundhay Park, Leeds LS8 4HT
TEL:(44) 0113 248 1292/FAX: (44) 0113 248 1292

MUSICIANS' UNION NORTHWEST,
40 Canal Street, Manchester M1 3WD
TEL: (44) 0161 236 1764/FAX: (44) 0161 236 0159

MUSICIANS' UNION SCOTLAND,
11 Sandyford Place, Glasgow G3 7NB
TEL: (44) 0141 248 3723/FAX: (44) 0141 204 3510

MUSICIANS' UNION SOUTH WEST,
131 St. Georges Road, Bristol BS1 5UW
TEL: (44) 0117 926 5438/FAX: (44) 0117 925 3729

chapter 10
choosing which route to take

COVERS V ORIGINAL

Basically, deciding whether to do covers, original or a mixture of the two depends on what your ambitions are and your skill level as a musician.

If, for example, you are aspiring to earn a weekly wage or at least some regular income from music then covering other people's songs may be your best option.

However, if earning a fast buck is not in your remit and you would rather try your luck at the big time, then maybe original material is the most suitable avenue to go down.

The latter of course depends on talent and whether you possess the creativity to produce original music to a standard which may result in a recording or publishing deal, and then sell the product in a variety of guises sufficiently in order to bring in money via various royalties.

It also depends on how you want to be perceived as a musician. Some musicians would not dream of covering other peoples songs, others do not have the slightest problem.

Lets consider all the options:

There are differing degrees to a covers/original band and you could put them into as many as five possible categories.

It has to be noted that this may seem a very clinical way to go about choosing a route to take, and that you may inevitably fall into one of the categories below naturally, via a series of trials, but what I have tried to do is create a simple guide tool that could be used. This may just save you several years of 'ifs and buts'.

It is all from my personal experience as a musician, my added experience of being a musical careers advisor and also studying hundreds of other musician's careers over the last thirty years.

A) An out and out covers band covering anything from the 'Birdie Song' to 'Agadoo', whilst wearing nice, well ironed, pink frilly shirts, white trousers and shoes to match, topped off with a Shadows dance routine, all immaculately rehearsed.

This type of band/artist has no scruples and will do anything to try to please the audience and although it may make money, you could say it borders on musical prostitution.

But after all it is an option that has been taken up by thousands and thousands of musicians throughout the world, going back years.

This concept even dates back to the ancient times when ancient Greeks had cabaret shows, wore bright clothes and probably even had their own Shadows-type dance routine.

You have to ask yourself the question of whether it is better than working in a factory from nine till five. Personally I would consider the factory option but some musicians actually prefer this choice and there is a lot of work out there on the cabaret scene; holiday complexes (UK and abroad), cruise ships and social clubs.

(Incidentally, some of the most famous faces in television entertainment have come via this route and have gone on to become major stars commanding millions of pounds a year; Sir Cliff Richard, Des O Connor, Jimmy Tarbuck, Shane Richie, Brian Connelly, Dave Allen and Bradley Walsh to name but a few who came good via their work in the Butlins and Pontins holiday camps so maybe it's not a bad stepping stone).

B) A top covers/tribute band who cover strong songs that both the audience and themselves enjoy.

This usually requires more talented musicians as the songs covered are usually of a higher calibre than the songs mentioned in the first option (a).

(That's not always the case though, as their are superb musicians in every genre of music entertainment).

There will always be work available for this grade of band/artist, if of course, they are dedicated and talented enough to put on a good show/performance. (Saying that, there will always be plenty of work for even the most mediocre tribute bands throughout the holiday hot spots of Spain and Greece).

This situation also requires less compromise as it is quite cool to do quality songs no matter who they are written by.

When we say a tribute band it can mean either a tribute to a certain period;
for example
a tribute to the 60s or 70s or the 80s, 90s by various artists,
or it can mean a tribute to a certain genre of music
for example
a tribute to Motown or Soul music by various artists,
or a complete **tribute to a particular band or artist,**
for example
a tribute to Queen
a tribute to Oasis
a tribute to The Steroephonics
a tribute to David Bowie

In actual fact over the last five to ten years these particular tribute bands, who concentrate all their efforts to cover a particular band or artist, have really come to the fore. The better known bands often sell out at large capacity venues where the original band may have once played.

To illustrate my point look no further than the Australian 'Pink Floyd', 'Rumours of Fleetwood Mac', 'Thenesis', 'The Bootleg Beatles', 'The Backbeat Beatles', 'Cavern' and numerous others.

In fact almost every successful band or singer you can think of has someone cloning them. Apparently there are around a million Elvis impersonators throughout the world and thousands of Beatles tribute bands.

All of these bands or acts are, at the end of the day, actually just covers artists. But some are taking it to such a high level that they can almost convince people that they are the real thing.

It may not always be visibly stunning, but certainly sound wise it can be—sometimes it's both. I know most of them take it so far as to use the identical instruments and amplification the original band will have used.

The other thing to consider is the fact that the bands who are copied are usually by now retired or sadly no longer with us.

So, all things considered, it is usually the only way a fan can capture the original band's excitement. There is also a lucrative market in private function/corporate work for good tribute bands who are not quite up to the larger venue gigs, or may be simply uninterested in taking it to that level.

The bands mentioned above can usually be on the road for months on end and obviously this does not appeal to a lot of musicians due to a number of factors including family ties, age and the fact that they may want to be winding down after years upon years of gigging.

Once a band has established themselves in the private function/corporate sector, the work can be well paid and lucrative.

Each gig is a marketing tool within itself, with the musicians getting offers of work from members of the audience, who may well be having their own function and would like them to perform at the occasion.

It is not unusual for a good band to be offered one or two gigs at the end of a successful gig and this creates a continuous succession of work.

Personally, I know bands who are booked up to twelve months in advance. Some even further ahead.

There is also good money to be earned via merchandising and selling live/studio recordings/CDs, as long as royalties are paid to the original writers/artists via the MCPS (Mechanical Copyright Protection Society). (See Royalties.)

C) Original & Covers:

This combination could be considered to be the best option and can give the band members the enjoyment, rewards and gratification of such a venture.

It can also benefit the band's members with regard to looking 'cool' with the original part of their set whilst also having the added bonus of earning some money from the covers circuit.

A band who also plays covers and has to learn parts, timings, phrasing, harmonies, lead solo's, licks and riffs of other people's songs should find it will dramatically improve their own musicianship.

This route was certainly my personal choice as a young up and coming musician. Having to learn the guitar parts of my favourite bands like The Eagles, The Beatles, Thin Lizzy, etc, certainly helped me improve as a guitarist, vocalist and general musician to say the least. I would sit there for hours with a vinyl record, lifting the needle every two seconds (there were no CDs in those days), learning every chord and lead guitar solo note by note 'parrot fashion' until I had perfected the part.

In my opinion, today's greatest musicians are those who have had to diversify at some time in their lives in order to put bread on the table.

Take note, the Beatles started off as a covers band and Sir Paul McCartney has admitted it was the best way to enter the industry and improve his playing and writing skills. He also added that these influences helped his creativity.

As a young musician, my greatest tip ever came from my mentor; the late, great Bobby Arnold. He said "If you want to work as a musician and be successful and earn some money, you have to learn as many styles of playing as possible and practise like hell ".

This musicianship then comes to the forefront when bands thrive writing their own original pieces based on the influences gained over the years of covering other artists work.

In fact, a local band (name withheld) have just been asked by their record company to learn a ten song covers set in order to prove their musicianship, stagecraft and basic gigging technique.

A covers band will earn more money than a band doing original music, unless of course the band are extremely successful.

I know of many bands who have had moderate success and yet will never earn the money that a covers/tribute band can earn.

Obviously the lifespan of the money earning capacities of both covers bands and original music bands are different in that a covers band can be more of a long term ride (depending on the original band's success and longevity).

A band doing covers can also afford to purchase superior equipment and therefore sound better when doing their original songs. Therefore, they should have a good chance of being asked back for a return gig at the venue.

Myself and most musicians I know, actually consider that doing a pub or club covers circuit acts as a band's apprenticeship. It certainly helped me to understand the industry from an early age, which was crucial as the music industry is an extremely complex business. And again, the fact that the band are out there doing the gigs gives massive exposure to the original side of your set, and also makes your songs sound tighter and more professional.

From experience, when you start playing your own songs in the mix of a mainly covers set, the audience actually starts to consider your songs as covers, due to them becoming familiar with the song.

I wrote the songs and played guitars/vocals in a band called ' Now Hear This'—a band who had great local success with a couple of singles released. Over a period of a couple of years, we managed to move an almost 100% covers set into a 95% original set by adding one or two good original songs every month or so.

The punters became familiar with the songs, learned the words and sang along as if they had known the songs for years. I can honestly say we were one of the very few bands who were actually being paid money to play an original set.

d) Original only:

Before we start this section, it's important to realise that the results are all taken from an average outcome. Obviously luck, 'being in the right place at the right time', and sheer hard work can and will alter outcomes for any artist/band taking this route.

After working with hundreds of promising musicians as a music careers advisor and teacher, I can say for a fact that 80%—90% of bands doing original music are paying to play. In other words they are certainly coming out with less money than they are putting in and that doesn't include beer money and fish and chips on the way home, let alone paying for expensive equipment, instruments, strings etc.

"You have to learn to survive, and as for equipment, it's a case of 'beg steal or borrow' but we have to keep going because, as musicians writing original songs we are cursed. The curse is we know we can make it, but we don't know when"

(Chas—The Bo Weevils)

If you are taking this route you have to be seriously good, simple as that. It's a fact that most songs written by young up and coming bands are usually, if we are to be perfectly honest, not really good enough. This is a harsh reality, but it is true. A band may be good enough to play the local circuit but their songs may not have enough quality, class or originality to become hits.

It seems that most bands/musicians are under the illusion that it's fantastic to write forty or fifty songs. Then it usually transpires that they have penned forty or fifty very average, and in some cases very poor, sometimes unfinished songs.

It would be far more beneficial to the band, the industry, and all concerned if that band worked on what they would consider to be, say, their best ten songs, and improve every single aspect of each of them, including the live performance of each song in question.

Therefore, they should hopefully end up with a good, strong, well rehearsed forty/fifty minutes set of songs which the music moguls may be interested in. Even then the ten songs in question could be further edited to a three or four song recorded demo used to approach A&R music industry personnel, DJs, radio programme producers or record/publishing companies.

The lesson that should be learnt by musicians who are serious about this business is that quality by far exceeds quantity. Some record companies have admitted that if a band were to be signed and they had a repertoire of say thirty songs but possibly only five or six possible hits, they would simply place two or three of the hits on to each subsequent album.

There would be no point in using all the best songs on one album. Two hits will sell an album, the album would then be balanced out with the bands weaker songs.

With regards to today's music scene; there are too many songwriters or bands who are delivering what you would call average songs. There are some great songs out there, but usually demo songs are not as good as the bands seem to think they are.

Again there are obviously exceptions to this and you can suddenly play something that instantaneously grabs your attention. But the problem is that this great demo or song usually ends up in the same chaotic system as all of the other inferior demos.

It is very important not to take offence regarding the above but instead to be more determined to get out and gig, rehearse and work hard to improve your material.

It is common for original bands to want to play 'name' venues and they simply are not bothered about making money. This school of thought is fine, you have to go for it and give it your best shot, after all you are only young once!

"If you fail, it's because you took a chance; if you succeed, it's because you grasped an opportunity."

The problem is that bands may survive like this for a few years as it is wonderful time of your life and should be good fun, giving you great memories you can look back on all your life and talk about with your grandchildren! Like 'The day you fell out the van on the way to a gig in Bolton' (done it).

But what happens when your equipment develops a fault or your guitar is stolen or members of the band are faced with personal or financial dilemmas (that probably relates to around 95% of musicians).

This is the time in a musicians life when they realise there has to be some sort of a reward for all the gigging, driving around in noisy cold rusty vans and getting home at all hours of the night, stinking of smoke and ale.

If that musician would have been in the last chapter (original covers) and had been doing some covers, he may have earned money over the years and may have had something to show for all the hard work and late nights, even if it was just a few pieces of good equipment.

He or she would certainly not be as disillusioned by the industry, and in fact may even be earning good money as a musician.

The dream of the original music band is usually securing a massive recording/publishing contract, therefore catapulting them to fame and riches.

The reality is that even if they were lucky to be offered a recording contract, it would not necessarily result in riches and fame.

Quite the opposite seems to be the case in that most bands who are signed usually end up either being dropped or brushed aside when another outfit comes along, or simply trying to succeed, but unfortunately failing in the market.

Ultimately the music industry is a money making business and it's a ruthless cut—throat business that can sometimes do more harm than good to a band.

I know bands who have been signed on major and minor record labels (and I include myself in this category), who have either been dropped or they have split up due to the problems caused by the intricacies and complications of record/publishing deals.

And with the exception of a few, even if they have had a single or album released, they have simply never made enough money to live on and have now inevitably moved into other ways of earning money.

Fortunate musicians who come from this section should manage to find work in the industry mainly due to past industry connections and obviously because of the vast knowledge they will have gained over the years, but others I know are actually working on building sites. A former musician friend of mine was so disillusioned by the industry after several years at the top, that he bought a sand blasting machine and now plies his trade in the very same area he used to sign autographs. It is strange to think he would ever turn his back on the music industry—but that shows how stressful the industry can be, even at the top.

Another important thing to consider on the original music route is the artists USP (unique selling point). This does not necessary have to be the band's image, (although that is very important)—it could be the band's sound. Maybe they use unusual instruments, maybe they have a singer with an unusual voice or a superb stage presence. It can be anything that makes them stand out from the hundreds of thousands of other bands.

Some current examples would have to include:

Travis—with their use of multi-layered capo fretted guitars which creates a 'mandolin-ish' type sound.

The Darkness—with their unashamed 'tongue in cheek' dig at the 1970s rock era.

Keane—have chosen to use a piano, high in the mix. The piano is the focal point for some of their best hits to date and they have capitalised on introducing a piano into their songs where many modern day artists and bands have shunned it.

Rebbeca—At the time of writing this book the band will be relatively unknown

(2005) but with superb songwriting skills incorporating all the great   classic rock artists of the past, I have to give them a special mention.

E) A band with two names:

There is of course another option available which can solve a multitude of issues and problems. Imagine your band could actually be two bands in one with two names; one name doing the club/pub covers circuit and another name doing the original music circuit.

This option covers all the previous options, in that all scenarios are catered for.

A band can do 'cool gigs' and still earn some money doing covers gigs. For example: On a Saturday night you are called 'The Beagles'—an Eagles tribute band. Wednesday night you may be called 'Bedlam', an original music rock outfit.

It is a simple way to keep all members of the band happy and also gives the opportunity to earn some money that can then be used to purchase better equipment. If you can afford better equipment you will sound better whatever music you are playing. There is no reason why more bands do not actually take this option. It is so simple and easy to set up; the hardest part may actually be choosing the two names.

Summary:

So there you have it. Remember, it's only my opinion and we all have different views, however it's important to remember that music is there to be enjoyed—I personally enjoy just playing music and writing, even if it's never heard by anyone at all—and it all depends on the reward you want from creating it. If you are happy to just keep plodding away with the dream of becoming a rich pop star and you can afford to do that, good on you. If however you are looking for some regular income you may have to consider your options. The majority of musicians I know, some of whom are remarkably talented, but for one reason or another have never had the breaks, have at some time in their musical career touched most of the categories above.

There is no shame in doing covers, ask Paul McCartney. But never stop writing and going for the big one because someday someone may be covering your songs.

> "The misconceptions surrounding the workings of the pop industry are many and varied; one misguided belief chief among them is that if you've strutted your stuff on "Top of the Pops" you must be rolling in it! Nothing could be further from the truth. I am living proof of that.

I am one of those unfortunate journeymen of pop, always on the periphery, never quite hitting the pay dirt.

The industry exists by allowing gullible kids to believe the myth. The dream machine that feeds on it's own legend.

Throughout my misguided quest for unlimited world wide fame and fortune, I have strutted my stuff with two bands on 'Top of the Pops'—

"Black Gorilla" *in 1977 and* **"Fun Boy Three"** *in 1982.*

There is NO Lear jet in my driveway!

During twenty-five years in the fairyland that is the pop world, I can point to over forty record releases. I have also worked/recorded for many major and independent record labels and signed megabucks recording/publishing deals associating with world-name pop icons and producers.

There is NO Lamborghini in my driveway.

–John Barrow....session Tenor sax and author of 'HOW NOT TO MAKE IT IN THE POP WORLD'— (THE DIARY OF AN ALMOST HAS BEEN)

available via www.trafford.com

So why do so many original music bands fail—or at least what are the most common reasons? It could be any of the following; the fantasy of being a star is far easier than working to be a star; unoriginal music is rife, laziness is rife; misunderstanding the reality of the music industry; misuse of any funding available as regards recording ventures and promotion; lack of commitment from fellow musicians in the group can hold everybody back; the belief that someone will come along and discover you; discouragement over the lack of support from the people you think you need; poor musicianship—although it has to be said that poor musicians have made it in the past—it's a lot easier if you master your trade as you may not have the connections or luck that the inferior musician/s had.

SENDING OUT DEMOS

If you are going to send out demos to record labels, managers, management companies, journalists, concert bookers, agents or whoever you may wish to send them to, there are some basic principles you can apply and should adhere to, which will save time and money that you spend doing it.

Some basic points and tips can make the whole 'sending demos' process seem easier and should therefore lessen the chances of rejection by a recording/publishing company, music industry personnel, radio station, producer, DJ, etc.

FIRSTLY, LABEL EVERYTHING.

You should put your name and contact details on every item you send, including the actual disc or tape itself. It's very easy in a busy paper-ridden office for items to become separated, and trying to match a blank disc with a mound of biogs is near impossible unless you have the time and money to do some DNA tests!

DO SOME HOMEWORK, AND FIND OUT SOME CONTACT NAMES

Instead of sending out your demos 'willy nilly' to all and sundry, spend some time finding specific people to target. Obviously it needs to be someone who may be able to help you (a band I met recently sent out so many demos, even the local pizza shop received one).

If possible, call them personally (you may have to spend hours getting through to the right department) and then ask if that department/person can help you.

If you do manage to speak with anyone at all, never ever under-estimate the power of politeness.

At worse, the least they may be able to do is give you some other contacts, or advice which may be able to help your cause.

If you are lucky you could just be talking to the actual person who can help you, and is actually interested in listening to your demo, and then, because of the personal contact (albeit by phone), that person will know the name of your band/act in advance of a demo landing on their desk.

It's important to remember that the music industry has a lot of staff constantly on the move from one company to another. They may have started in one company making the tea and coffee, then been promoted to head cleaner, then to A&R, and then either been sacked or took a better offer from another company.

Make sure after all this hard work that you actually spell the contact's name correctly.

BAND CO-WRITERS AGREEMENT REGARDING SONG-WRITING CREDITS/SPLITS

If your band have started to write songs but you are still playing charity gigs at places like 'The Gilthorp Dockers & ex Miners Welfare Club', it's hard to look ahead more than a few weeks as regards any possible future songwriting royalties. But what if one day you start playing Wembley Arena and have a number one hit or even a number one album? Consider the following and it just might save a lot of heartache and squabbles.

If you are a solo songwriter—happy days, you get the whole pie to yourself.

Bands/groups however can be much more complicated.

If a book was written filled with all the legal wrangles of musicians in bands arguing over who wrote what bit of what song, and when, it would be thick enough to stand on to change the guttering on a high rise block of apartments. Why then, for the sake of a few minutes, don't musicians in bands have some sort of simple written agreement in place in order to show who actually did what as regards the actual songwriting. It's very easy to say 'we can sort it out when we get the deal' but the problem is by then, lots of things could have happened. Members may have left, members may have joined, and that's apart from the most crucial point being remembering who actually wrote what bit of the the song in the first place. Imagine you (the band) have written a superb catchy melodic song that's about to take the UK and US charts by storm. Inevitably there will be monies earned via royalties on that song's journey (and beyond)…Those royalties and future royalties have to be accredited and shared percentage—wise between the songwriters.

It would be very sensible and really useful if, after a song has been written and put together, the collaborators talk openly about it and agree on a fair split.

It's not unlike prenuptial agreements in marriage, in that splits and agreements as to 'who gets what' are agreed and noted on documentation before they can ever become a problem.

When I say fair split, it's important to remember that although there may be some members who have not actually written any of the actual parts of the song, they may be an integral part of the band's make-up and may have contributed with the arrangement and/or added some *'enhancements'.

* (Enhancements could include a particular riff, bass-line or even a beat that strongly contributes to the overall feel/melody and construction of the finished song. In particular a riff that is an integral part of a song and improves the song's overall sound can constitute a slice of the music/melody royalties.)

To what extent that riff or enhancement has made a difference to the song is for the band to decide; it could be as little as a 1%-5% or higher if it's really improved the song. (Some examples are given later on.)

You simply do not need a formal contract at this stage and to stop any bickering, a simple informal written agreement will suffice. At least then there will be some evidence of who wrote what and when (it should be dated, and preferably signed by all members). The Musicians Union can provide band songwriting agreement sheets or 'co-writers forms'. If in future you want to take it a step further and a major deal is pending, you can then employ a specialist music lawyer to take up the agreements and make them all legal. (The agreement should state that each member has taken legal advice and this should be put in writing, otherwise an unscrupulous member may claim they didn't understand what they were actually agreeing to sign at the time.)

SO HOW DO YOU GO ABOUT SPLITTING THE SONG ROYALTIES UP?

Basically it's completely negotiable, it's as simple as that. Gone are the days of 50%: lyrics, 50%: music (although obviously you can use that if you deem it to be the fairest split).

There is also a "thirds" split being Lyric/obvious overlying melody/music.

Some bands may have one writer who takes all (although this can cause a number of problems, for obvious reasons).

Other bands—like Blur, for example—may have a totally equal split which is obviously going to be the easiest way of whacking out any royalties and will keep the majority happy (and keep the lawyers at bay).

It all depends on the main songwriter's thoughts on whether they think their hard work and ability to write songs should be shared equally with other members who may have been lazy, uninterested or may have only just joined the band. As I have already covered in the book, writing good songs is not easy, and if someone spends countless hours locked away working on turning a few melodic ideas into great songs then they should, in my view, take a bigger piece of the pie.

A good idea that can keep everyone happy is a song arrangement/enhancement percentage put aside before the main songwriters take their share.

If the main songwriter really does everything as regards writing the song—which is quite common—then he/she could still have the above percentage put aside for the band, but could have it written into the legal agreement that it is a purely financial split and that all rights to the song remain solely with the main writer. In other words, although the writer/s are agreeing to share some of the royalties, they are not letting go of the song rights. Therefore the songwriter will not be restricted in his use of the song in the future (for example, if the band splits and he/she signs a publishing deal in the future, there will be no ties).

Let's do some examples of possible percentage splits using this system.

Two members Both write equally—easy peasy—50/50% split.

Five piece band All members met as friends, been together three years. All muck in and rehearse and arrange original songs together, gig together, share ideas etc. Two main songwriters, but all help towards arranging the songs. A starting point formula could be, per song—

5 x 20% equal split (but is that is fair on the actual songwriters?)
or
Arrangement percentage split of 50% equally shared by five members = 10% each
Song music and lyric 50% shared by two writers = 25%
Songwriters = 35% each x 2 = 70% band members 10% each x 3 = 30%

Four piece band One main writer, band been together six months, not much effort to help songwriter.

A starting point formula could be, per song
Songwriter = 100% (that may cause band to split!)
or
20% arrangement percentage split equally, shared by four members = 5% each—Songwriter 80% plus his 5% arrangement = 85%

These are just a couple of the thousands of possible formulas. You could also just do it by name, per song—

Fred 45%—Joe 15%—Ian 15%—John 15%—Billy 10%

Another way is to simply have a starting split for all members of around 5/10% with the remainder going to the main songwriter/s.

Don't forget, it's **completely and utterly negotiable**, but remember that a little bit of pie will keep everyone happy and can be seen as a reward to all the band's members for actually rehearsing and arranging the songs. By all means, it should be kept as friendly and amicable as possible, after all the songs may never be signed anyway, but better to be prepared. I have seen the results of writers in bands taking the whole pie (with cream) and becoming rich and yet other members who were there from the very beginning coming out the deal with nothing at all—not even a crumb to show for their input.

Agreements made in advance under friendly circumstances will be much more civilised than agreements made after acrimonious bad tempered splits.

If you manage to come up amicable splits, it would be a good idea to put the names of the writers on any CDs/recordings with the main writer's name first and so on. It would then become another form of registration of writers involved.

PROTECTING THE COPYRIGHT OF THE SONGS

FIRSTLY—WHAT IS COPYRIGHT?

Copyright is a 'property' right. This means that the owner of the right, who can be the writer, author or for any person whom the author has assigned it, has the exclusive right to authorise or prevent others from using a 'musical work' in various ways. These 'restricted acts' are
- making a copy of the work, in any material form
- publishing the work
- performing the work in public
- broadcasting the work
- making any adaptation of the work

A 'musical work' consists entirely of music, and the words of a song are 'literary work'. They are protected in the same way.

There is no copyright in ideas until they take some material form usually a manuscript or tape—in other words under UK law—copyright does not exist until a musical or literary work is recorded in writing or otherwise as above.

Copyright in musical works lasts for seventy years (UK) after the end of the year in which the author dies. At the end of this period the musical work then becomes public property.

NB: There is no copyright in the title of a song, you can use a title of another song—think 'The Power of Love', the same title for three different songs, all hits by three very different artists in the 80s.

If you really can't get to sleep at night for worrying that another band/musician or thief may steal and rip off your favourite, personally penned original song, then you can use the most basic 'form of registration' system, regarding date of the origin of the works.

In other words, although the copyright is there as soon as an original lyric or piece of music is written down or taped, you may need some form of proof of the date of the works.

Then, in the extremely small chance of someone copying/plagiarising your works, at least you will have some proof of the date of origin to prove you 'gave birth to' and have a dated authorship of the works. It's also important to protect against unauthorised usage.

The simplest and cheapest method to prove ownership of a song is too simply place a simple cassette/mini disc/CD recording of the song, plus a lyric sheet, into a sealed envelope and post it to yourself by registered post leaving it sealed and unopened and keeping it safe alongside the registered post document.

It is a common misunderstanding amongst musicians that copyright

is in some way 'created' by sending a tape of your music to yourself via the above method. This does not create a copyright, it is simply a very cheap method of proving the date upon which you created the original works (sometimes known as the poor man's copyright—it may not actually stand up in a court of law, but it's infinitely better than doing nothing at all). It's actually very rare that a song is copied to the point that it would reach court proceedings, but it's a sensible step to take—who knows what can happen if the songs in question ever become hits.

You could also deposit a copy of any works with a solicitor or bank manager and obtain a dated receipt; beware though, as charges would certainly be made for this service.

Consider this:

You write a song, but you never perform the song live or have it aired via any media what-so-ever. You place the song in a self addressed envelope, send it to yourself as described above and keep the only copy in a sealed envelope. Two years later you hear a song very similar, has your song been copied? It's quite impossible if your song as never been in the public domain, how can someone copy something they have never heard. The point I am making is, sometimes—every now and then—a song will sound like another song simply by chance. Remember I mentioned in the practise section earlier in the book that almost all Rock & Roll or Blues songs use the 1st, 4th and 5th modes of any given key therefore all of them sounding very similar as regards the back drop to a song. Most Country and Western songs also use a similar pattern. The other very common songwriting formula is the 1st—6th—4th—5th of any given key (mentioned earlier in practise), so don't spend too much time worrying about other people copying your songs, for all you know you may (without realising) be 'copying' someone else's song. There's always the chance you may also—without knowing—be heavily influenced by a song you may have heard just once, you may have heard it whilst driving along, listening subconsciously to the radio years before.

'Stories about accusations of music plagiarism appear fairly regularly in *Variety* and other more mainstream publications. Few of these disputes go to trial, and fewer still generate published judicial opinions. Since the 1850s federal courts have published fewer than 100 opinions dealing with this issue, and the frequency with which these cases arise is not likely to increase'. (Columbia Law School—Music Plagiarism Project)

Superb website **www.ccnmtl.columbia.edu** for comprehensive full listing of all the big plagiarism court cases (includes samples of the songs/music involved).

FAMOUS CASES OF PLAGIARISM

NB: There are other decisive factors besides the obvious one of a melody being copied (see first case below Isley v Bolton)

Isley Brothers (Love Is a Wonderful Thing) 1964 v Michael Bolton (Love Is a Wonderful Thing) 1991

In 1994, a jury found that Michael Bolton's 1991 pop hit, "Love Is a Wonderful Thing," infringed on the copyright of a 1964 Isley Brothers' song of the same name. The district court denied Bolton's motion for a new trial and affirmed the jury's award of $5.4 million.

Bolton, his co-author, Andrew Goldmark, and their record companies ('Sony Music') appeal, arguing that the district court erred in finding that: (1) sufficient evidence supported the jury's finding that the appellants had access to the Isley Brothers' song; (2) sufficient evidence supported the jury's finding that the songs were substantially similar; (3) subject matter jurisdiction existed based on the Isley Brothers registering a complete copy of the song; (4) sufficient evidence supported the jury's attribution of profits to the infringing elements of the song; (5) Sony Music could not deduct its tax liability; and (6) the appellants' motion for a new trial based on newly discovered evidence was unwarranted.

Ronald Mack (He's So Fine) 1963 v George Harrison (My Sweet Lord) 1970

This case found the late George Harrison liable for copyright infringement—given Harrison's popularity as one of the Beatles, it is probably the most commonly known music plagiarism dispute. The court's tone is almost apologetic in determining that Harrison's use of the melodic kernels of plaintiff's universally popular number, in the same order and repetitive sequence and set to 'identical harmonies', compelled it to conclude that Harrison unconsciously misappropriated the musical essence of 'He's So Fine'. The court made much of the fact that both songs have a distinctive 'grace note' in the same melodic motive. Harrison's use of this idiosyncratic musical device, along the lines of the court's reasoning, implicated him—it was akin to copying a mistake.

An important point in both cases above is the ability of each of the above defendants to have access to the songs—as regards having heard the songs before—in order to be able to copy them. In both cases the songs were in the public domain and had received considerable airplay, and therefore would have been highly likely to have been heard by the defendants. In fact in the second example the song 'He's so fine' sang by the 'Chiffons' was actually number twelve in the charts in June 1963 the exact time the Beatles were enjoying a number one hit, it had also reached number one in the American charts for five weeks prior to it's UK chart entry.

BAND PARTNERSHIP AGREEMENT

If it looks like your band are going to be around for a while, earning money, sharing costs for equipment etc, another thing to consider is some sort of partnership agreement. Basically this will outline the fact that you are all entering a business venture together and that all members should be aware of the business side of things and that there are no misunderstandings which could cause problems in the future. The agreement should cover earnings from live performance, exploitation of any recordings, ownership of any recordings, ownership of any artwork, band name and logo and equipment. In fact it's very useful to agree upon what will happen if a band member/s leave the band; who will then be entitled to carry on using the name? As we pointed out earlier in co-writers agreements, these things are better sorted whilst everybody is singing from the same hymn sheet! Depending on whether you will need a lawyer or not is down to you, but it is recommended if you are starting to run the band as a business. A simple partnership agreement should suffice and although we don't like paying for the lawyers next pin-stripe suit, it's something that has to be considered.

ARTISTS TO KEEP AN EYE ON

I have chosen a few bands/artists to 'keep an eye on' (In no specific order).

Over the next few years I shall update their progress and see how they get on in the industry. The very best of luck to them all.

'NEW YORK HERE WE COME' HOPEFULLY NEXT YEAR WE CAN AFFORD A PINT EACH!

Band name—The Mags—from Runcorn, Cheshire UK **Line-up** Mike Kennedy—Lead vocals, Wilko—Lead guitar/b/vocals, Greig Wilding-bass guitar, Mark Bleasdale—drums. **How did you meet up?** Friends from school—met Wilko in a pub! **Rehearsal schedule—**We are off to New York in two weeks to record an album (honest!) so we are actually rehearsing four days a week at the moment and writing new stuff. We pay £10 when we can afford it to rent a barn in Helsby, the people who own it have been great and I think they know we're a bit skint. Hopefully we can pay them back one day for their kindness—thanks to Andy and Angela, it's only a matter of time. **Equipment** We own our own stuff, just had to sell my Fender bass though. **Original—Covers?—**Original 100%. We did rehearse some covers but when we realised we needed 2 x 45 mins, it just got in the way of writing the original stuff. **Influences?—**The Beatles—The Kinks—T Rex—Led Zep. **Gigs?** Yes, around Liverpool. A good friend (Bill Heckle) owns 'The Cavern' club too which is handy. Big, big thanks to Bill for all his help, great guy, also pay him back one day. He even sent the open top 'Cavern City Tour Bus' to pick up our fans for a gig. **Band songwriting co-writers agreement?** Yes, basic one, but it'll do for now. **Any management?** No but looking, some people have shown interest. **Recordings?** Yes plenty, but over in New York next week to record an album with Will Schillinger and Danny 'Kooch' Kortchmar. **Any**

interest? Yes loads, plus Fierce Panda sniffing, though we need to follow that up and re-stoke the fire. Also have producers (Will Schilling & Danny Kortchmar) investing in recording an album in New York—Manhatten. **Any radio play?** Yes, plenty of local stuff in Merseyside etc, big thanks to Billy Butler. **Member of MCPS/PRS?** No, not yet. **Musicians union?** Yes.
Wesite photo biog? Yes—www.themags.info—watch this space!
Band name—**Reece** from Liverpool, Merseyside—**Line-up** David Wilcox—Lead vocals, Stevie B—Lead guitar and b/vocals, John Conner—bass guitar and b/vocals, Toby Smith—drums and percussion, Paul Garrett—Rhythm guitar and b/vocals. **How did you meet up?** Been friends for years, a lot of the lads went to music college together or have played in bands together before. **Rehearsal schedule**—We rehearse at crash studios twice a week, it costs roughly £40 a session with a PA provided. We also have a lock—up there so we don't have to carry our gear there every time, which makes great sense. **Equipment** We've all recently purchased new guitars etc, usually use venue's backlines when possible though **Original—Covers?**—Were all original. At the moment about 1 hour and 30 min set. **Influences?**—Each member has there own influence ranging from Guns and Roses, Bon Jovi and Train to Stevie Wonder and Prince. **Gigs?**—As many as we can. We have played all around the country and have recently toured out in Mozambique although we prefer to play the Cavern in Liverpool—it feels like home to us—a great stage, great sound, top staff

and management. All in all, a great venue. **Band songwriting co-writers agreement?** ?

Any management? Yes, with lots more interested, so our manager had best keep up the good work or else!!!! Ha ha we love ya really Dave. **Recordings?** Only a few demos at the moment, but hopefully that's all we need. Getting great interest at the moment, been offered a deal very recently off the strength of the demos.

Any interest? Quite a bit, we're not chasing though, we are firm believers in

the motto 'if they want you, they'll come and get you'. It seems that they want

us at the moment thank God!! **Any radio play?** Yeah, we're listed at Radio Merseyside. Billy Butler is a big help to all the local bands and has been a great supporter of Reece since we began. City FM have played us in the past thanks to Joe Ferguson but unfortunately he's left now and no other DJ there has his courage. We're played constantly on Radio Mozambique and BBC world service.

Member of MCPS/PRS? Just Paul, our songwriter is a member at the moment as he works with many other artists and companies including writing for Disney. The rest of us will join when necessary. **Musicians union?** Not yet **Website/photo/biog?** Yes www.reeceonline.net

Rebbeca: L-R Colin White—Drums/Percussion, Tom Keys—Vocal/Guitar, Paul Tong—Guitar/bv, Neil Harris—Keyboards/Bass

'Halfway In Love'—debut single release 16th May 2005—Fat Northerner Records

This song blew me away when I heard it on local radio. Bought it on release. Superb stuff—imagination and talent at it's best, off of the beaten track, brave and bold, love the stuff (me).

"Standing clear of the stereotypical Merseyside sound, Liverpool born four-piece, Rebbeca, have developed a fresh outlook on guitar music, gaining them comparisons to legendary ground breaking bands and illustrating their collective ability to envelop the unusual with the commercial." www.rebbeca.in

Name—Katie Skilling **Line-up** Solo, sometimes have another acoustic guitarist **How did you meet up?** A friend

Rehearsal schedule—Try to write or play everyday **Own equipment**—yes, all own equip **Original—Covers?** All original written by myself and some co-written

Influences?—Bjork, Alanis Morriset, Hanson, Gwen Steffani, The Beatles, The Eagles, The Doobie Bros. **Gigs?** My manager gets the gigs and I also get my own gigs

Band songwriting co-writers agreement? Not yet no, but in process **Any management?** Yes I have a manager, **Recordings?** Yes, demo CD and fully produced demo CD thanks to Stephen Lironi **Any industry interest?** Yes

Any radio play? Live sessions and interviews, BBC radio Leicester, **Member of MCPS/PRS?** Not yet **Musicians union?** Not yet **Wesite photo biog?** yes www.katieskilling.tk

Photo by Dan Chaloner (after a few attempts!!) **Name of band? Rambo and Leroy**—From Macclesfield Cheshire UK—**Line—up** Jake Evans—guitar vocals, Matt Evans—drums vocals, Ash Earlem—Bass guitar vocals. We tend to swap instruments in the studio. **How did you meet up?** Two brothers and a friend of a friend **How long been together ?** Two years but serious stuff one year **Rehearsal schedule** Two x Two hours a week **Own equipment/transport** Yes, but have to hire a van **Original/covers?** All original **Band agreement re songwriting?** No not yet **Influences** "Hendrix, The Who, Rolling Stones, Stone Roses, The Doves" **How you got first gigs and where?** Liverpool Institute for Performing Arts (LIPA) sorted it, in the Magnet bar. **How often gigging?** Whenever we can **Manager?** No but looking. We know a few people in the industry, we are getting on with writing and recording for now **Any interest so far?** Yes, some lads at the Cavern Club, Liverpool are looking to start a label and they want to do something with us **Any radio play?** Yes—GMR (Greater Manchester Radio) **Any recordings?** Yes we have our own studio plus some in local studios. **Band biog/website?** Yes it's www.ramboandleroy.com

176   THE ART OF GIGGING

Band name—Tiny Tin Lady from St Helens Merseyside, **line—up L/R** Helen Holmes—Danni Gibbons—Beth Gibbons, played acoustic stage at this years 2005 Glastonbury

Manager? Yes **Band biog, photo's, website?** Yes www.tinytinlady.com

Band name? Ivan Campo—From Preston Lancashire UK—**Line-up** Will Rogers, Adam Shaw, John O'hare, Paul Dilworth, Ben Atha **How**

did you all meet up ? Fate. **Did anybody audition?** No we were all friends.

How long been together? Current line up, one year. **Rehearsal schedule** About six hours whenever we can get together and chill. **Own equipment/Transport?** We have all of our own equipment, we have access to a van. **Original/Covers %** No covers **If original 100% ever going to consider doing covers?** It would have to be the right one. **Band agreement- regarding songwriting?** We register what we write. We all write, sometimes separately, sometimes together.

Influences? At the moment, I'm into Beck and Erik Sate, Adam's into Mark Bolan. Nick Harper deserves a mention and of course the Beatles.

How you got first gigs and where? We just went and gave cd's to venues.

How often gigging? Once, sometimes twice a week. **Manager?** Yes

Any interest so far ? Yes **Any radio play?** No, not yet **Member of MCPS/PRS?** Yes **Any members work besides music career?** We have to earn a living, not easy to do just through music **Recordings? How and where? Producer or self done?** We have done all of our previous recordings at home. **Band biog, photo Website ?** Yes Yes, Yes www.ivancampo.net

Band name—The Bo Weevils—from Liverpool, Merseyside UK

Line-up Chas—guitar vocals, Ste—guitar vocals, Andy—bass vocals, Ian—guitar piano, Gav—drums/vocals **How did you meet up?** We are all friends really, oh—and two cousins, and we all live near each other. **How long have you been together**? As this line up, one year. **Rehearsal schedule**—We think it's really important and we actually pay £100 every week plus we had to pay £400 in advance just to get the room. Although we have access to the room 24/7, we actually rehearse twice a week for four hours. We have band meetings on a separate day to discuss things and plan rehearsals. **Do you own your own equipment/transport?** Some of it, we scrounge, scrimp and beg, borrow and steal from friends and vice—versa, we help them if we can, we also borrow a van for any gigs. **Original/covers?** Original 100%, we're not interested in doing covers—only a record deal. Our other guitarist Chas says "as true musicians we will never stop trying…in some ways we are cursed even if we never make money off it—we will never stop trying ha…ha. Are we cursed..ha..ha ! **Influences?** Anything good really, but we are open minded.

Gigs and how you got them? Play a lot around the Liverpool scene and got them ourselves by approaching other bands, asking for support slots and also from promoters and venue bookers. **Band agreement regarding song writing?** No, not yet but thanks to you we may look at an 'arrangement' percentage of 25% split equally before main royalties are taken out. In other words each member will take 5% x 5 = 25% the other 75% going to the main song writers, in that scenario we all get a piece of the pie. **Have you got a Manager?** No but we are looking for one, getting a lot of help from local bands done good, The Coral, Zutons, John Power and some mates at LIPA (Liverpool Institute for Performing Arts) Keith Mullin and Peter Hooton and you, thanks. **Recordings ?** Yes got a new CD recorded, again by beg steal or borrow, various funding, scams, scrounging, back—handers, whatever it takes. At one point we even considered breaking into a studio just to record a new song. **Any radio play?** Yes a bit from local station KCR. **Member of PRS/MCPS?** No, not yet but considering it. **Musicians union?** No, but we are joining asap. theboweevils@hotmail.co.uk—web—www.theboweevils.com

Band name—The Second Floor—**Line—up**—Nolan Watkinson—lead guitars, vocals/Jonathon Crosby-bass guitar/Mark Cody—Drums vocals/Matt Hirst—keys **How did you all meet up ?** Friends at college **How long been together?** 3 years as this line-up **Rehearsal schedule** 3/4 nights a week but varies **Own equipment/Transport?** Yes **Original/Covers %** Original 100% **Band agreement- regarding songwriting?** No not yet **Influences?** Velvet Underground—The Who—Bob Dylan—Joy division

How you got first gigs and where? Manchester mainly but started local pubs inNewton **How often gigging?** monthly **Manager?** No **Any interest so far ?** Yes Island, London records **Any radio play?** Yes GMR radio **Member of MCPS/PRS?** No not yet but sorting it **Any members work besides music career?** Yes some of us half band **Recordings? How and where? Producer or self done?** Yes self produced **Band biog, photo Website ?** Yes www.thesecondfloor.co.uk

Band name—Paul McDowell & the Peppermint Pigs—Merseyside—**Line-up** Paul McDowell—vocals, guitar, Alistair Ligertwood—cello, bass, Joe Roberts—drums **How did you meet up?** Paul and Al went to the same school, but in totally different years and classes. **Rehearsal schedule** As much as possible, usually a few times a week—we're constantly gigging around Liverpool, so need to practice all the time. **Originals—Covers?** Originals. All songs and lyrics are written by Paul McDowell. **Influences?** From Nick Drake to Incubus to the Pixies to Nirvana to Bonobo to the Doors…and so on… **Gigs?** Yeah we've gigged loads in Liverpool, and Paul McDowell has been over to Germany to do some solo gigs in Oberhausen, Bochum and Cologne, Germany. **Band songwriting co-writers agreement?** At the moment, we have not agreed on the details, but are in the process of thinking about these issues and will be signing an interband agreement in the near future.

Any management? No official management yet, but Paul has taken control of the band's management—DIY style **Recordings?** Yes—we sell CDs at gigs and via our website. **Any interest?** Not saying **Any radio play?** Yes loads on local stations in Liverpool and on various internet stations and websites. Paul presents a radioshow playing the best unsigned music from Liverpool, the UK and Germany. The show's called The Unsigned Show on www.radioliverpool.co.uk **Member of MCPS/PRS?** Yes and yes **Musicians union?** Yes **Website photo biog?** Yes, www.paulmcdowell.co.uk

LOCAL RADIO AIR-PLAY

Let's presume you are now at the stage where you are recording some of your original songs in some form (usually CD), and you are seeking some air-play.

Most musicians and songwriters are under the illusion that in order to have a song played on a radio station, they have to have a 'record deal'.

This certainly is not the case and the fact is that radio play in any form could actually be a good route to securing a recording or publishing deal.

Most local radio stations have some sort of show or slot for local bands/acts/artists to showcase their original songs, and even if they don't it's not impossible to gain some air-play if you go about it the right way.

It's important not to be fussy as regards the radio station; any air play whatsoever has got to be good publicity—even a hospital radio is better than nothing, after all who knows who could be lying around!

First let's look at the importance of some local radio air play for your songs.

Publicity alone is obviously an important factor and the fact that your songs and band name are being aired to thousands of people is a fantastic marketing tool which can create awareness of your name.

One single local radio air play slot could actually create as much awareness of your band/act/songs as one thousand gigs.

The majority of people who become fans of any particular band are usually people who have heard the artist/band's song on a radio.

(The last three albums I have purchased, I have done so because I have heard that band's songs or music on the radio, most recently being 'Rebbeca' (halfway in love).

It can also create as much publicity for a future gig as a thousand flyers could, with people having a good idea of what your bands all about and then hopefully making an effort to catch your act live. It's important therefore to always give a 'forthcoming gigs' date sheet to any DJ, along with the recording.

Personally, radio air-play was the best thing that happened to my band 'Now Hear This'. In the late eighties, we were doing the odd gig here and there, bits of charity work, working men's clubs and some real sticky carpet dives, etc.

After recording a few songs; 'Dream about the girl', 'I don't know' and 'September' and gaining considerable air-play, we suddenly became the band to book and to see. The diary became completely full and we became a household name (albeit locally/north west coast). This created packed crowds at our gigs, therefore giving the band even more publicity.

Bigger/major national radio stations then took to playing the songs and the whole thing just spiralled from there. The next thing we new we were in Hamburg, Germany recording an album (not released, but that's another book!)

That's enough about me for now but it's a good example of the importance of air play as a marketing tool.

If you can raise the attendance of your gigs, your band/act should soon get a good name around town and then you should be able to look at the possibility of raising your fee and becoming more fussy with regard to possible venues.

It's a wonderful feeling to be able to move away from the sad sticky carpet gigs you have had to endure so far—don't get me wrong, they were the gigs that you needed to learn your trade—but it's always good to move on.

Also, once your band has a good name it becomes easier to gain attention from managers, bookers, promoters and even record companies.

Another added bonus from being in a 'name band' is that the name stays on the local 'network' scene forever. People will always refer to you as member of that band/act. You would not believe the amount of musicians I know who have gone from one great band to another, simply because they had been in a well known band before.

There is also the added bonus of royalties (see MCPS/PRS).

HOW DO YOU APPROACH THE RADIO STATION?

A radio station producer, along with the presenter, usually chooses the songs and programmes that make up the radio station's play-list/agenda.

Every radio station has a producer. To find out his or her name you can simply ring the station direct or look in local press for details.

It's then simply a case of asking the producer if he or she could possibly set aside a few minutes for you to meet and possibly listen to your material. Whoever you manage to speak to, always remember to be persistent but very polite.

It's important to remember some DJs and radio stations are pestered by unprofessional kinds and this can cause problems. However, If you are lucky and go about it the right way you could then arrange to meet personally, but sometimes it's better to have a representative or obviously a manager (if you have one) to meet them.

It's is vitally important to have a professional package and also the best possible recording of your material.

If it's at all possible, it's always a good idea to have a radio edit of your best songs. Some stations, like Radio 1 for instance, in the 80s and 90s played (with the odd exception) approximately just on three minutes of a record no matter how long the song actually lasted.

To start you should approach some local stations and if that goes well and you gain some air-play you can then consider trying some national radio stations. (It's not easy but if your material is very good, you are half way there.)

You may be surprised how different your recording will sound on the air-waves. It may be a pleasant surprise or it could turn out that you may be booking some more studio time.

"It was something like 2 months later when we had our first Peel Session. As soon as it was broadcast our lives changed overnight. The record companies were on the phone immediately. We eventually signed our own Sylvan Records to the Arista record company. We recorded 'First Picture Of You' with Nigel Gray."

Peter Coyle (The Lotus Eaters) www.petercoyle.com

What a great song, I remember lying in the garden when it was first played and it was just a perfect Summer song. In case you are wondering Peter now lives in France and is still writing.

SELLING YOUR CD/RECORDING VIA LOCAL AND NATIONAL RETAILERS

If you are lucky enough to receive some air play—albeit locally—you should consider approaching local record shops with the view to having your CD available via their outlet. Smaller independent record shops will certainly do it for a small cost but you should also approach bigger, high street outfits like Virgin and HMV. A percentage will have to be negotiated as regards how much the shop will deduct before your cut is taken. You will need to meet the manager who may use his or her discretion as to whether to even bother stocking the CD/recording. For example, they wouldn't be too interested in a recording that had no air play what-so-ever, so again, air play is the priority. The product label (see MCPS) and package or cover should also look as professional as possible to help your cause. The bigger shops can provide bar codes for till sales but they will insist that your product should have a unique catalogue number for identity purposes (if you are not doing it via the MCPS—who will provide one). Anything will do as a catalogue number as long as it is unique, if your name is Richy Van Flute for example, you could use the initials plus some numbers =

RVF 001 or even Richrecords 001, whatever, it's up to you. In effect you are actually creating a name for your own mini—label. (Make sure the name hasn't been used)

Obviously if the radio play becomes more national and the song starts making waves—which can happen—you may have to consider a distribution deal to make the product more available to the punters living where the radio stations are giving the song/s the air play. Unless of course you are snapped up by a record label who may just take over the whole thing!

chapter 11
your image

Sometimes your image can come naturally simply due to the personalities in your band, but sometimes it needs work. One thing is for sure, you need one.

Again the direction you are aiming at would obviously be a good start. You wouldn't for example wear a pin stripe suit if you were playing in punk rock band would you? Wrong, why not? Wouldn't that be a great image? Imagine it, at first the audience would look at you a bit strange, but after a while they'll probably warm to it and think it's cool. That is then your image; 'bankers playing punk'.

Pretty soon (if your band is good) you'll find fans turning up with pink hair and pin stripe suits.

I would like to think I was exaggerating there, but at the end of the day an image is an image, and is there to make you look slightly out of the ordinary, and hopefully give your act or band more of an identity.

Go off the beaten track, it's usually who dares wins in the image stakes.

Particularly in the entertainments industry, and if some people don't quite get it, that's not a problem—at least they will be talking about you and therefore giving you the publicity and identity your image was there to create in the first place.

The image of a band can be carried over individually or the band as a whole. Sometimes one person (usually the front person) can give the full band an image. Your image can, and should, compliment your music and style.

All you need is a decent chest wig, Kevin Keegan haircut and some bryl cream, a long black leather coat, black tights, some sweat, a nice shaped guitar, oh and some socks 'strategically placed'! and hey presto, you have an image. (Me! in 1985, A.O.M gig, Firestation, Bootle, Liverpool) Aah…those were the days!

You can not underestimate your visual style/image in that it becomes a part of every pop acts identity, and therefore something your fans will associate you with.

Even something as simple as a tee shirt, trainers and jeans can create a simple style/image (think Mark Knoffler, Status Quo) although more flamboyant images tend to be remembered more. (I still have people say to me after all these years 'were you that dip-stick in the black leather with no top on?', so the image worked!)

If you look back at most bands or artists over the decades you will always associate someone with their image (think David Bowie, Elton John, Queen and more recently bands like Franz Ferdinand, McFly etc).

THE FRONT PERSON

It's no exaggeration to say that a band can only be as good as the main person, usually (but not always) being the vocalist, the front person.

A good front person can and often does, carry an act/band to the extent that even if the rest of the outfit was weak he or she could still command an audience and sell the show.

There will always be bands/acts that have so much talent and charisma collectively as a 'group' that there is no actual 'front person', but it's quite rare.

A great front person can actually convince the audience into believing that they (the front person) is actually much more talented than they actually are, by simply taking stage and performing. To take that a step further, if we look at some of the great frontpersons of the past, you would have to say with all due respect that some of them may not the best singers in the world—but who would 95% of the Rolling Stones fans be staring at if they attended a 'Stones' gig at the Wembley arena.

It goes without saying that if a great front person also has a great voice, then the sky's the limit. Amongst the greatest ever frontperson's you would have to include the late great Freddy Mercury of Queen, who not only had fantastic stage charisma but also had superb instrumental skills topped off with a wonderful vocal range.

If we look back at the biggest bands ever they have always had a great frontman/woman.

The common theme being that if there is a good front person fronting the band it's usually contagious, in that it seems to bring the best out of the other members. It certainly breeds confidence and gives other members more reason to go that extra yard themselves.

The only problem here is the fact that you can't really teach someone how to become a front-person; it's usually a natural talent, a charisma that person has when they perform in front of an audience.

Sometimes they can be quite introvert off stage, but once on stage they become someone different—it's almost like they were born to entertain.

Some people naturally command an audience and become a 'star' even if, as we mentioned before, they may not actually have that much talent as regards instruments/vocals.

SO HOW DO YOU FIND THIS PERSON?

Unless you already know somebody who fits the bill, you are going to have to do some serious advertising, networking, scouring through the classified's and some serious auditioning to try to find this person, after all they are a very rare breed. There are plenty of singers around but that extra ingredient is extremely hard to find.

If you are able to find a good front person, hold on tight because other bands will try to attract them.

It would obviously help if your band were good as regards musicianship and even better if the band already has a good name on the local music gigging scene.

A good frontman/woman wants to join a good band which they can then enhance with their own input and talent. They will also perform better and with more confidence if they know there is a good 'team' behind them.

You may have to consider looking further afield than your local pub to find this person, and you should consider advertising in national publications alongside local papers. Who knows? The very person you are looking for could be working in your local plumbers merchants or could well be someone in your neighbourhood.

If you simply can't find the right person, which is not uncommon, you may have to try developing someone who may, in time, just fit the bill.

There must be many 'stars' out there, fronting bands and doing a superb job, who may well have started off 'not too good', but developed their frontmanship skills over the years.

When auditioning possible frontpersons for your band you have to consider every aspect of their performance and try not to be too strong on vocals alone. Looks, style, charisma, banter and general personality have to be considered. Great vocals alone may not be enough—as we mentioned, before I think we all know more melodic singers than Mick Jagger, but he's just got that touch of magic when performing on stage.

The frontman/vocalist to die for, Philip Franz Jones (pictured with myself) at the Royal Court Theatre, Liverpool, 1985. (Afraid of Mice 2)

Phil is really the dream frontman; he even had me watching him and I was in his band! Guitar, flute, sax, amongst other instruments and a magical voice that could grace any stage in the world. And the most important thing for a frontman—the ability to completely command an audience. Add to that the ability to create and write wonderful songs and you have the perfect package. There has to be something special in order to command a full house at the Liverpool Empire. Phil had record deals with CBS and Charisma amongst others.

CHOOSING A NAME

Every band, act, performing artist obviously has to have a name in order to be identified.

Again, the name you choose depends on the type of act/band you are in and whether or not you need your 'name' to say something about you.

A covers band for example need not be too concerned about the name of their act, as long as it's a name that's easily recognised and remembered.

Regarding covers bands, the genre of music can also be attributed to a name to give the public an idea of the type of music the band actually perform. In other words, 'Country Devils' for example would not lend itself to a punk outfit, nor would 'The Dead Leather Bikers' relate to a barber shop quartet.

This can also cross over to the 'original' circuit as regards the 'name' making a strong statement even before a chord has been struck.

How many times do you see a band advertised in a newspaper or on a flyer or poster and think to yourself ' they sound good', when you haven't even heard them? It can therefore be the first important decision you will make within your band/act.

It has to be recognised that if it works like that for the general public, it may well work like that within the industry, maybe even more so.

A good name/title is important for any product be it washing powder, a book or of course the name of a band.

It can (and often does) therefore take several name changes before a band actually settles on one they think is strong enough and portrays a good image of the band. A good name may help a bad band (at least until they get found out); a bad name however could hold up a good band.

If you think of any famous band, chances are they may have gone through one or two names before settling with the one you now know them as.

A few good examples would have to be...

The Black Jacks—The Quarry men—Johnny and the Moondogs—The Beatals—The Silver Beats—The Silver Beetles—**The Beatles**

Sigma 6—The Abdabs—The Screaming Abdabs—The Meggadeaths—

The T Set—and finally taking their names from two American pop musicians Pink Anderson and Floyd Council we have **'Pink Floyd'.**

Two examples of two of the worlds biggest 'names' who obviously went through the very process we have just covered.

It's very important (though not quite as important for the covers circuit) that after all the hard work of finding a name you are happy with, you then stake a claim to the name by registering it through 'band name' registering organisations. Note the plural; you really need to register the name with as many different systems as possible. It's quite pointless registering the name with one company who may give you a name clearance, but that clearance will only be cleared and searched through their own particular database. Another database may not clear the name and so on.

It's also important to register as soon as possible. Don't do hundreds of gigs or wait until your first single is released; you don't want to be going through the slog of getting everything sorted and then end up with a law suit from another band who happen to have the same name under copyright.

* You could even turn up at a gig and a band has the same name. Imagine it !

> **Tonight for one night only**
> **Dirk Thrust Promotions**
> **Presents**
> **Battle of the bands**
> 8.30 from London -The Biffs
> 9.30 from Scotland -The Biffs
> 10.30 local band -The StrollingTones
> 11.30 special guests -The Biffs

Apart from doing the obvious and simply visiting music shops and record shops to see if the name has been used, you can use the net to do a search. You can contact all of the Band name registries, and then (presuming you have the 'all clear') you can pay a small fee to register the chosen name.

Also, remember which member of the band actually thought up the name in the first place. If that member ever leaves the band he or she may just stake a claim to the name and take it with them.

This has been the cause of many massive legal disputes over the years with bands splitting up and various ex-members of the band all using the same, original, band name. Particularly in live situations or tours where ex-members with very small connections to the original band market themselves as the original outfit. Sometimes the only original thing on stage is the snare drum.

NAME REGISTERING SITES

- www.bandname.com
- www.bandreg.com

Other sites to search for used names (music retailers);

- www.cdnow.com
- www.amazon.com
- www.towerrecords.com

You could also type in your proposed name in the common search engines and just see what comes up.

If you finally get that unique name you love because it's 'catchy', easy to remember and encapsulates what the band stands for, you should start to market it straight away.

You can trademark a band logo, so you need to consider a unique design or even a special design of your actual name. Logo's can be incredibly useful as a marketing tool, if you consider that 'Nike' rarely uses it's actual name but uses it's logo to great effect (I am sure you know the logo).

Trademark. A word, phrase, symbol or design (or a combination thereof) that identifies the source of particular goods or services. This would apply to your band name as it appears on your CD, flyers, website and other merchandise and to any logo your band uses.

A trademark can be applied for if you establish your band as a business. Again this isn't too difficult but does cost you around £200 from the UK patents office.

Check USA trademark information at the US Patent and Trademark Office—www.uspto.gov

Don't be put off by a few legal hoops, it will all be worth the effort if your band has even moderate success. Note that an original work of art for your band logo requires both a 'copyright' and a 'trademark'.

It has to be pointed out that you could go through the whole process above but still come up against problems. For example, say a band in America with the same name as you has a massive hit album and releases three videos, etc. You may feel a little silly ringing up their manager and explaining that you own the name and you have been playing a residency on The Dulthorp Anglers Social Club for the last five years using the name. Chances are the other band will have rights to the name, even if they have only been using it for two years simply because they have taken the name past the finishing post first.

SELF MANAGEMENT/MANAGERS

Sometime in your band's future, it's going to be essential to have some form of management, whether that be a band member's parent, relative, friend, or if you are lucky to have sufficient commercial potential, even professional management.

Until that time arises it's important that the band has some form of self management system in place in order to progress and move to that point.

By self management, what we mean is a band agenda—some form of discipline within the band's structure and members in order to move forward and make the band progress.

Too many musicians join a band, rehearse in a garage for years on end, never actually do a gig, fall out, split up and do the same thing over and over again with different musicians in different garages.

That situation could be brought on by the simple fact that the band never really had an agenda, or even an identity, because no members of the outfit were willing to take some responsibility.

So let's look at how you can actually start to manage your own band affairs till someone takes over.

First it's important to decide whether it's going to be done by a single member, two members or a shared venture.

If you decide, as a band, that one member will do it alone it's then important that the person delegated has full control of all affairs.

Will the band be happy with one person running the show and making all the decisions?

It may be a lot simpler to give each member a different role within the band. For example, one member could be in charge of transport, one member in charge of bookings, one member in charge of the equipment and income (if any) and even a member in charge of the marketing and band publicity, etc. These are, after all, some of the areas and affairs a manager would look after.

Regular meetings can then be arranged to keep updated on any progress made and targets should be set, and adhered to.

As mentioned before, a big problem for up and coming bands is not setting specific dates to aim for.

For example, if you were to book your first gig on a specific date, that date then becomes a target the band can aim for and then you simply have to be ready on time. So all of a sudden the sloppy rehearsals and band members treating the band with a 'take it or leave it' attitude will have to be addressed and sorted out. Musicians can fall into a lazy rut all too often. I know, and have met, a lot of young musicians who are quite happy to be able to say they are in a band and seem quite contented to do some jam sessions and garage practise. If that's you and you're happy staying at that level then you shouldn't have bought the book.

If it's not you, then consider my advice.

The other big headache of many bands is collating enough equipment to get out and actually gig, so again it's another important issue and one you should sit down and discuss in detail. Many members seem to be able to scratch together their own guitar, amp, drums, etc. but there's one big thing missing and this could well be your most important piece of kit.

It's called your PA system (see Public address equipment PA). There is a part of the book dedicated to PAs but let's look at how you can afford one.

As you start to do gigs you will probably be borrowing a 'PA' to sing through from other kind hearted musician friends you may have. Any money earned from these gigs, however small the amount, should be saved and put towards purchasing your own equipment. It's not really a good idea to borrow money from finance companies at this stage of your career for various reasons, the most important being that you have to pay it back (usually with extortionate interest added).

Bands and musicians by nature can be very fickle and rifts amongst members are very common in the early stages of a band's life, causing splits and therefore causing financial cash flow problems to the surviving members who could be left to foot the bill. Even a promise of regular gigs cannot really justify going into major debt, for the simple reason that it's going to be difficult doing the gigs if the vocalist and drummer decide they have had enough and move on to another outfit.

All these points can be added to your band's agenda and discussed at your meetings arranged by whoever you have chosen to look after band finances.

WHEN DO YOU NEED A MANAGER?

That question may well answer itself when all the above becomes too much for you to handle and you suddenly realise that you don't have the knowledge, self discipline and experience to do the job effectively, or at least to take the band any further.

It's a fact that many bands and artists can be, and have been, successful in releasing their own records, negotiating distribution and arranging tours themselves without ever actually having a manager. Some bands have even had major success and still continue to manage themselves, but if you think it's time to bring someone in because you simply do not have the time, skill and tenacity to do it yourselves, then it may be time to look for someone to become your manager.

THE ROLE OF A MANAGER

A manager will normally look after the business side of an artist's career from bookings right through to negotiating royalty settlements with record and publishing companies. The manager's role will obviously depend on what stage the artist or band may be at regarding their career. In the early days of a band or artist's career, a manager would be looking at arranging gigs and negotiating fees, sorting publicity, transport and all the 'coal face' practical issues a band may come across.

THE MANAGERS FEE

All the above can add up to long unsociable hours and very hard work and for that work a manager would be expecting a commission of around 20% of their artist's gross earnings. This 20% figure would be negotiable with 15% to 25% (there are exceptions) being the usual guide markers. It should be stipulated from the start and written into any contract what earnings are actually 'commissionable income'.

In other words you should try your best to put in any contract that 'live performance' commission is paid after expenses (net income) and not before expenses (gross income). This again is completely negotiable and situations can differ from artist to artist. If, for example it's a band starting off and perhaps the 'manager' has invested his or her money into the equation for equipment, recording costs etc, then maybe it's only fair that he or she would expect to be repaid via the gross earnings—at least till any monies invested have been repaid. If however there has been no monetary investment then it's down to negotiation—but the terms 'net' and 'gross' (as regards earnings deduction) are completely different and will make a big difference to artist's and managers earnings.

EXAMPLE (A) NET EARNINGS

(commission calculated on earnings after costs have been deducted)

Fee—live performance	£ 1000.00
Booking agent commission at 15%	£ 150.00
PA hire, equipment hire, lights	£ 240.00
Van hire	£ 80.00
Fuel, Meals, miscellaneous	£ 60.00
Total costs (net of VAT)	£ 530.00
Fee:	£ 1000.00
Less costs:	£ 530.00
Balance:	£ 470.00
Management Commission at 20%	£ 94.00
Band Income:	£ 376.00
Earnings per band member (x 5)	**£ 75.20 each**

EXAMPLE (B) GROSS EARNINGS

(Commission calculated before costs have been deducted)

Fee—live performance	£ 1000.00
Management Commission at 20%	£ 200.00
Balance:	£ 800.00
less costs: (as above)	£ 530.00
Balance:	£270.00
Earnings per band member (x 5)	**£ 54.00 each**

As you can see by these examples there is a big difference in the managers fee.

Also consider that a booking agent—or talent agent—plays the largest role in securing live engagements for an artist or band and that their fee is usually fixed at a non negotiable 15%. The manager may co-ordinate the activities of the booking agent but the manager usually functions in the wider role of helping the musician with career development and obviously management. In the early days however a manager may also arrange any live engagement bookings (gigs).

CHOOSING A MANAGER

Careful consideration should be used when looking for possible managers and the cost of employing them. Will the person you choose have the potential to take your career further and actually improve your prospects and/or income within the music industry?

Can the person achieve things that you alone could not?

All possibilities have to be considered before any contracts are signed. Unfortunately if you do sign a manager early in your career and you have chosen the wrong person, it could hold you back and cost you valuable time.

Good management can be a sound investment; inadequate management can cause many problems for an artist or band. Again it can depend on what stage you are at and, of course, your potential as an artist or band.

Let's face facts, if you as an artist or band are not quite as talented as you think you may be, then you may not attract a good manager. If you have the potential to be the next 'Beatles', then obviously you can be more fussy as to who you choose to become your manager.

In the early days, it may transpire that you need someone to help you with the entry level stuff, like sorting gigs, moving equipment, representation, etc.

It's not uncommon for a friend or a relative to step in as a make-shift manager. If that friend or relative (usually a band member's father) is genuinely interested in you and can assist in any practical issues then it's got to be better than having no one at all. It often works out that this person can go on from being a make-shift manager to full blown management of the artist/s. Many managers of very successful bands and artists started via this route. Another good thing a friend or relative can do is to become the band's anchor man and dissolve any band disputes before they become a threat to the band's very existence. (Every band has members who fall out with each other from time to time and it's easy for bands to split up. However if there is someone to act as a go—between, the band are more likely to stick together).

You could consider a trial period to see how things work under your new manager, but remember any big improvements may take time.

A six month trial period would be useful for both parties and you can keep tabs on exactly how your 'trial' manager has improved your situation, also giving any prospective manager time to see if you are willing to put the work in. Bands usually pull their socks up when they have someone to impress.

If things go well and you are both satisfied with each other's efforts and you decide you would like to make the situation contractual, a three year contact is becoming the norm. Again, this period is negotiable and there should be 'escape' clauses for both artist and manager.

Bench marks and time limits should be written into a contract with specific targets for both parties; if the bench marks are not adhered to it gives power for the artist or manager to terminate the contract. For example you could have a one year term with an option to further the contract if certain criteria are met.

THE MANAGER'S RESPONSIBILITIES

There are no hard and fast rules but to put it basically there should be an understanding and written agreement that the manager should use his/her best endeavours to move the band or artists forward within the industry and enhance their career prospects.

A manager should also ensure all monies earned are payable to you (after commission) and properly accounted for.

THE ARTIST'S RESPONSIBILITIES

As it's a two-way agreement, the manager will want assurance that the band or artist will also endeavour to fulfil certain obligations towards them.

Some contractual requirements may be;

That there would be no impediments to you entering into a management agreement (for example, no other similar contracts are ongoing with another party).

The management deal is exclusive for the 'Term' of the contract.

That all referrals for gigs or live engagements should be via the manager and that you will not negotiate any contracts on your behalf.

MANAGEMENT COMMISSION AFTER THE CONTRACT HAS EXPIRED

This can be a very messy time in any artists/managers career and it may well depend on what stage you have reached at the time. It won't be too difficult if you haven't secured a recording deal or something major, as the relationship and any commission should just cease (unless there is money owed—or there is a clause in the contract). However if the manager has secured and negotiated deals he or she may refuse to forgo claims to commission on such income even after the management term has expired. You may have to negotiate (if it's not already written into the contract) a reduced rate as a compromise (better then to have these things written into any contract from the outset—that way all parties know where they stand). One thing is for sure, you may struggle to afford to pay any new management fees together with your old manager's fees. If of course your old management had nothing to do with any success you may have—after any agreement has expired—then it should be a much cleaner break.

It's important to remember that many managers are extremely hard working and have genuine interest in their bands/artist's. They may work countless hours trying to secure a deal or a tour, etc, usually against the odds. It's a fact that for every tale of an unscrupulous manager or management, there will probably be another one of a good sincere manager working his socks off for years earning next to nothing, only to see the band split due to 'musical differences'. Good management will more than pay for itself and as we mentioned before under agents fees, 80% of something is much better than 100% of nothing.

TOUR MANAGER

If things start going well and a tour is imminent you or your manager may wish to employ a 'tour manager' who's sole responsibility would be to do just what it says on the tin! The tour manager would be responsible for the complete organisation of a tour which would include the overall budget, transport, hotels, visas and *carnets, insurance, health & safety, punctuality and behaviour and making sure the musicians get out of bed and do their bit (which isn't easy). The tour manager has to be highly organised and able to make tough 'on the spot' decisions.

*Carnets = carnets are a kind of passport for musical equipment. They are required by the Customs and Excise department whenever you take any equipment out of the country to stop the illegal import and export of goods. The carnet will consist of a complete listing of every single item of equipment and the list will be checked).

The MMF (Music Managers Forum) represents the interests of Managers or would-be Managers in the music industry and provides comprehensive training. **www.ukmmf.net**

chapter 12
studio & home recording

Somewhere along the line you are going to record your band, whether that be via a simple four track home studio, a professional recording studio or even a live recording.

Strangely enough, even though you may have been together for years gigging and rehearsing, it could be the first time you may have heard a true reflection of your band.

STUDIO RECORDING

If you are considering booking a recording studio for the first time, it could be the single most important thing your band may have done so far. The excitement and in some cases trepidation of making your first studio recording will be something new to you and will be yet another learning curve for you as a musician.

Gigging songs and recording them are two completely different things.

You are about to commit your material to tape and it's so much more difficult to get it right than you can imagine.

Live performances can usually disguise many small errors like flat or sharp notes, timing and simple errors that are just not heard by the human ear under the cover of the actual performance.

When recording, every single note of each members performance will have to be scrutinised and listened to over and over again. It's imperative that it's done right or you'll be listening to any minute mistakes on the recording for years to come, knowing they could have been sorted at the time of recording.

We have all recorded things and heard very slight errors and thought at the time they would just have to do or thought 'maybe no one will notice' and then later on thought 'why the hell didn't we just re-do the part?'. Don't opt for the easy 'that will have to do'. Studio recording can sometimes be very stressful for a musician and therefore problems can arise; a simple riff a bass player has played for months can become quite a difficult piece once the player is under stress.

It's imperative therefore that every part of each song is rehearsed to the death prior to the actual recording by each band member, so as not to use too much time re-recording specific parts.

Vocalists, no matter how well they may think they know the lyrics, should always have a clear, large print of the lyrics including all breaks and choruses, etc. Vocals can usually be one of the most time consuming parts, and re-recording can mean starting the song at different segments (drop ins) so it's important to have a lyric sheet to know where about in the song you may be at any one time. Even though the singer may have been performing the song for years, it's amazing how difficult lyrics can be when starting from a different section of the song.

It goes without saying that the song's structure and format should also be agreed on before any valuable studio time takes place. If, for example, you wish to change a song format by adding another verse or guitar solo, that should be decided before you even book your studio session.

Put simply, the more you rehearse the actual song before recording starts the less time it will take to record it on the day.

Also, there is the equipment involved—make sure you have access to spares like strings, drum skins, amps, etc.

Do you have a spare backup disc if using sequenced material?

See if you can scrounge a bit of extra time by turning up early and having all of the equipment ready for the start of your session—it amazes me how many bands actually turn up late, never mind on time, therefore eating into their very valuable recording time.

Setting microphones at recording sessions can take up to an hour alone and unfortunately this valuable time is wasted (though it should be pointed out that microphone usage is an extremely important process in recording).

When you book a recording studio, you book an engineer and when you can afford to, you will also have to consider a producer.

For your first recordings and if you are on a very tight budget (which is usually the case) your engineer will become the person responsible for any basic ideas as regards the recording of the instruments and vocals; a bit of delay here, a bit of reverb there, some crisps and chocolate here and there, maybe some chorus on the rhythm guitar etc. He is not, however, a music producer as such and will not be responsible for the arrangement of the song or take control of the song's structure, instrument brakes, overall sound, and ultimately the final mix down.

Therefore, if you can't afford a producer, it's not a bad idea to take someone along who has experience of recording studios and preferably some production knowledge or your recording may end up sounding dull and unexciting. Some engineers try harder than others and it's a fact that many have gone on to be top record producers, but the fact is that an engineer is just there to record your songs, not to produce them.

When you can afford it and you really want to make a big difference to your recorded material, it is important to get a producer involved.

Most producers are usually very experienced sound technicians and more often than not musicians themselves. They may well have spent more time in a recording studio environment than a rat spends in a sewer.

That's how they have come to learn their trade, through years of recording their own and other people's songs, experimenting with sounds, effects, arrangements, song structure, different instruments, amplification, vocal harmonies, mix—downs, etc. Also working with every possible genre of music—again very important when you consider the different sounds needed by all these artists.

Though top end of the industry producers can, and usually do, choose the bands or artists they wish to work with, there are usually some good local producers who may not have quite hit the big time yet, who may just be within your price range. Even if it does break the bank a little, a producer may just give your material the edge it lacks.

Obviously it all depends on whether you are looking for a finished article or just demo quality. If it is demo quality you are looking at, the shortest time to book a studio should usually be two or three days, to record three or four songs. Never underestimate just how long it takes to put down all your parts and of course the final mix down alone can take a day.

Remember, if time is getting tight, it's so much better to have two or three great recordings than four or five average recordings. Rushing that last song could well be to the detriment of the other songs, it's a very common occurrence, although it's equally important to remember that a great song should shine through even on a relatively poor recording. Again, it depends on what the demo or recording is going to be used for and what you can reasonably afford.

THE MASTER MIX

If you have spent three, four or even more days in a studio eating nothing but crisps, Mars Bars and Pot Noodles and listened to a constant noise, you may be getting to the stage where your brain and hearing are totally muddled. You may even have come to temporarily dislike the songs after hearing them constantly over and over again. Therefore, it's a good idea to have a separate day to do the master mix. Even better if you can skip a day or two and come back to it, though obviously this will have to be prearranged with the studio. Take a rough mix of the recording with you and have a listen on different audio systems to get some ideas for the final mix. Once you have done your master mix and you are happy with the end result the you can then commit the mix onto a master copy, which would be a digital format such as DAT (Digital Audio Tape) or MiniDisc.

MULTI-TRACK RECORDING AT HOME BY NICK MURPHEY

A BRIEF HISTORY OF MULTI TRACK RECORDING (JUST IN CASE YOU WANTED TO KNOW)

Multi-track recording is the ability to record separate parts of a musical composition onto separate areas of a recording medium so that they can be mixed and treated to create the desired result. It also allows for one person to reproduce the sound of a number of musicians playing together, limited only by the number of tracks available and the talent of the individual!

TEAC were a company famous for their studio multi-track studio tape machines. In 1982 they released a product that would revolutionise the music industry—The 144 PortaStudio. This was a cassette based four-track recorder and four channel mixing desk all in one unit. Songwriters, solo artists and bands could record themselves with the same basic studio format that the Beatles recorded Sgt Peppers on, in their bedroom, garage or garden shed!

Over the next 15 years, the cassette based multi-track units became more advanced, even managing eight-track recording. But although they were great for demo's to send to record companies, or to your local pub to try to get a gig, these cassette based, analogue machines were of limited quality when it came to 'pro' recording. This didn't stop a lot of people from getting very creative with this equipment and producing some exceptional music, without the expense of using a commercial studio and constantly clock watching as the drummer replaced his third snare drum skin whilst paying £80 an hour!

But as with everything that has a plug on the end, the digital revolution began to take over. Compact Discs, (CD's) were taking over from vinyl records and cassettes as the playback medium of choice, although you couldn't record to them. Multi-track stayed with tape, but TEAC, Akai, Fostex and others developed new cassette tape formats that recorded digitally. But they were expensive and still of a limited capacity.

In the background, while the small time musician wondered how best they could realise their ideas without remortgaging the semi, a computer company called Atari introduced a machine that would lead ultimately to how most contemporary music is recorded, and to a large degree composed, today.

The Arari 520, 1040 and ST were among the early home computers that became affordable to the average musician. What made them attractive to musicians was that they had MIDI built in. MIDI, Musical Instrument Digital Interface, is just a standard that allows all kinds of musical electronic equipment made by different manufacturers to communicate.

At first, just a few keyboards were fitted with MIDI. This meant that if you had one of these and an Atari computer, you could record the notes played on the keyboard into the PC using a recording program called a sequencer. The sequence of notes played could then be played back into the keyboard and it would generate the sounds. This meant that you could record a piece of music slowly, then speed it up to play it back, or fix any 'wrong' notes afterwards, or even play the part back using different sounds. No audio was being recorded, just the data from the keys being pressed. A German company called Steinberg had been working on simple sequencer programs for early home computers, but the MIDI equipped Atari was perfect for their first serious multi-track MIDI sequencer, the Pro-24. Now practically all electronic musical hardware has MIDI as standard.

We musicians are never satisfied. We wanted to be able to record real audio as well as MIDI. Vocals, guitars, brass and woodwind etc. Real sounds of real instruments, not just synthesised simulations. As the PC developed and prices fell, the technology allowed affordable multi-track audio recording at better than CD quality. Steinberg developed Cubase, a MIDI and audio multi-track recording studio in software that could also produce it's own audio effects, automatic mixing, and even it's own instruments that could be played and recorded, all within the PC. Other software developers have produced similar musical environments, giving the modern musician an amazing choice.

Today we have PC's, Apple Macs and laptops that can run music recording software that rival commercial studios of just a few years ago. And for those of us who don't know a mouse from a floppy disk, there are many units available that take on the old stand alone Portastudio format but using digital technology for outstanding results, recording to Mini Disc, hard drives or chip memory. The only limit to how many tracks you can record now is down to the power of the computer processor and the memory capacity. The general term now used for any of the above is a DAW, Digital Audio Workstation.

SO HOW DO YOU DO IT?

Many good books are available covering the depths of modern home recording. This is an overview of what you need to get started and what to be wary of when parting with your hard earned cash.

There are many arguments over whether to use a PC or a Mac, not just in the world of music. It's really down to personal choice. Both have good and bad points.

The Mac is well built, reliable product made by Apple. The current models are very powerful and are used by many professional people in all areas of media production.

The PC was originally made by IBM, but the format means that any company can make separate parts of varying quality and price that can all be put together by a computer retailer or even an individual. This means a powerful PC can be built more cheaply than a Mac, but there are some issues over reliability.

The Mac runs on an Apple operating system, currently called OSX. The PC runs predominantly on Microsoft Windows, currently XP, but other operating systems can be used. The operating system basically tells the machine that it is a computer, how to present it's information on a screen for us to read, and how it should store and process the things that we input to it.

One big advantage of a PC for musicians is that there is a lot more music based software available than for the Mac, and the upgrade possibilities are far greater. But at the pro end of the market, some of the top studio software will only run on a Mac! Why isn't anything simple?

So these are my opinions based on my experience of working with a PC in the real world.

Here is a list of what you will need to be able to record and manipulate sound in a desktop PC, and what each thing does. It isn't essential that you know what these numbers mean, but as a guide these are the numbers quoted when buying a PC.

THE PC

A Pentium 4 processor with a speed of 2.5 GHz or more. This is a fast processor that handles audio in a way that suits multi-track recording.

512 Mb of RAM or more. The RAM, Random Access Memory, is where what you are working on at any given time is stored.

80 Gb hard drive or more. This is the storage memory where all your recordings, software and any other data is stored.

A CD drive that can read and write CD's. This lets you load software and to 'burn' your finished masterpieces onto CD to impress your friends or nan.

A sound card. Most PC's bought in the high street will have either 'on board' sound or a basic sound card. These are fine for normal PC use and even playing back CD's but for recording, a decent sound card or stand-alone unit is a must. Prices are falling, and a pro quality sound card starts at around £60. The important things here are the bit rate, 24 bit, and the sampling frequency, 96 KHz, minimum. So you will see 24/96 or 24/192 on the box and it should be OK. The card should use the ASIO (Audio Stream In/Out) standard. This ensures low latency. Latency is how long it takes for the sound to be heard after you have pressed the key or spoken down the microphone. There will always be a slight delay but you cannot notice it below about 20ms (milliseconds-thousandths of a second).

The sound card will also have MIDI **(Musical Instrument Digital Interface)**, which is very useful. More on that later.

A monitor screen. Go for at least a 17-inch monitor. You will be looking at a lot of stuff on screen at once, and the less cramped it all appears, the better. LCD or TFT screens are becoming more affordable, take up less space and are much kinder to the eyes after a long session than traditional CRT monitors.

A printer. This can be useful for CD artwork, set lists, publicity, etc. They can be quite inexpensive, but beware the cost of ink!

Other than the sound card, all of the above can be found at your local computer fair at surprisingly reasonable prices. Choose an established fair, and look for the stalls where the queues are biggest. Take a friend who is PC literate and explain what you're looking for, and get some kind of warranty when you make your purchase. Alternatively, go to your local high street computer store, but be prepared to pay more.

ADDITIONAL EQUIPMENT

An amplifier and speakers, and headphones. Purists would have you spend a fortune on audio monitoring, but really a decent hi-fi amplifier and some decent speakers will be fine. **An alternative is powered monitors**, speakers with a built in amplifier. Your ears will tell you what sounds good. Take a favourite CD to the shop and listen to a few combinations. Good, comfortable headphones are useful, particularly for late night inspiration! But remember, listening at high levels for too long will damage your hearing for good. Headphones are also needed if multiple tracks are being recorded with a microphone. You need to hear the previous tracks that you are playing or singing with but they can't come from the speakers or the microphone will pick them up.

A microphone (mic). If you are going to record real acoustic instruments or voice you will need a mic. The standard PC type will not be up to the job, but good mics are available at a reasonable cost. For example, a Shure SM-58 is a world famous professional vocal/instrument mic and costs around £69 on the internet. This can also be used as a gigging mic. It is a dynamic mic, which means it can handle high sound levels from drums or rock vocals, but the high frequencies are not as crisp and defined as with other types of mic.

Capacitor or condenser mics tend to be more expensive but produce a more detailed sound, particularly with softer vocals and acoustic guitars for example. They are less robust than dynamic mics, and are often seen held within a cradle of elastic bands on a mic stand, called a shock mount, to suppress vibrations being picked up through the stand. Unlike dynamic mics, condenser mics need a small amount of power to function. This comes from either an internal battery or from 'phantom power' from a mixing desk. Recently the price of some condenser mics has dropped and a company called Rode produce the NT range starting at around £120.

SOFTWARE.

This is where the fun starts! The PC is a box full of processors and memory. The software tells it what to be. In a musical context, this means it can be a digital multi-track audio recorder, multi-effects box, sampler, synthesiser, CD burner, all at the same time, and can also produce art work for CD covers, t-shirts, publicity. Also, connection to the internet means you can keep in touch with fellow musicians and if distance is a problem, collaborate on a project by sending files to each other.

PRODUCTION MUSIC LIBRARIES

As a musician we all have to consider adapting our skills in every which way possible to boost income and earn a living.

Gigging, whether that be original, covers or a mixture of the two, instrumental teaching, or seeking a recording or publishing deal are all the obvious routes within the industry. But there are less obvious routes, one of them being being music production for the media.

Television, for example, at any one time communicates to billions of people in the world and the television networks need music to create up to hundreds of thousands of programmes. That's staggering amount of music which needs to be written and produced and someone has to do it, that's where another possible income could be made.

Some figures collated by Screen Digest World Media claim that, at any one time there are over 16,000 channels on air with over two billion people watching a TV at any given time. (There are currently over 2,000 channels in the states alone.) So it doesn't take much working out to realise that there is some money to be made writing the kind of music that TV producers may want to use.

To break the types of music down doesn't take too much difficulty either if we consider the networks and programmes involved.

We have food networks, gardening networks, travel networks, health & beauty, movie networks, horror channels, comedy, country living, parliament, property networks, quiz shows, documentaries, etc, etc and one of the most lucrative of all being the good old advertising networks.

All that music has to come from somewhere and most of it comes from everyday musicians who create and produce music for what's commonly know as production music libraries.

The networks rely on musicians creating and producing samples of music and scores that can be stored in a music library, waiting for the right moment when a certain piece of music can be used in whatever circumstance the particular piece may suit.

Production music libraries buy most of their music from musicians who may work from simple home studios or professionally fitted studios.

You do not have to have a full out and out recording studio, a simple 8 track studio (preferably digital) with midi capability is sufficient. Digital recording is industry standard and should always give a clearer recording of the piece of music.

It's important to remember that music recorded for production music libraries should be of 'Master Quality' or as near as possible. The companies that will be buying or licensing your music do not want the hassle of re-recording compositions; they want the completely finished 'Master Quality' article. The mix of the composition should be recorded to industry standard, being DAT (Digital Audio Tape) or at least mastered on to a CD. Put simply, It has to be complete, finished and ready for the job.

Most music libraries have categorised CD volumes of every kind of music you could possibly think of, anything from Didgareedoo sounds to full blown orchestras. The most common categories that may be requested by the end user are typically Dramatic, Horror, Romantic, Country, Rock, Blues, Bluegrass, Classical, Military, period, 60s, 70s, Rap, World, etc. You name it, they will have it on disc.

Even the most unusual music you can think of may be needed sometime. If you dropped a snare drum down a few steps and recorded the sound, chances are there will be someone, somewhere who may just need that particular sample. PC game music is also increasing in demand with literally thousands of new games coming on the market every year.

It's important to remember that samples of music compositions can be requested in any recorded length of time from two seconds to up to as much as three hours. Usually music libraries will request specific pieces in all the aforementioned lengths; they can then use the samples to suit any situation.

If you consider that some lengths are used for t.v commercials, some for radio jingles, corporate work, film scores, etc, you can see why it's obvious that different lengths of the samples or full blown compositions are needed.

Therefore you should have your tracks with definitive endings and easily editable sections. Various lengths of the same composition is always a good idea.

It's also important to know that if a piece of music is requested for say a sixty second slot, then it should not be a second longer.

That's the basic format that you should try to adhere to and the rest is up to you. First you are going to have to find the companies who are willing to take up your music. You can find music production libraries on the internet and if you get the chance to send some samples or even meet up with the main players, be polite but persistent. You could also start up your own music production library if you have the marketing power to actually get it off the ground.

It's extremely hard to make a complete living via this route, as it is in any route within the industry. Look at it as another string to your bow as a musician and you never know, with persistence and a bit of luck, it could pay a few bills and get your name on some TV or movie credits.

chapter 13
music & the industry

On average from the moment we are conceived we spend anything from 4 to 20 hours per week listening to recorded music. Some people spend nearly every minute of there life listening to some form of music.

THE RECORDING INDUSTRY

The UK recording industry alone is worth billions of pounds. We spend around £3 billion pounds in total on music. That's a staggering amount of money but that's how important music is to us.

Considering we are only a small island, UK artists have around a 15% share of the world market. And the UK exports twice the amount it imports. Therefore it really is a truly massive industry.

WHO BUYS THE MUSIC

United States = $12 Billion
Japan = $6 Billion
Germany = $2.5-3 Billion
UK = $2.5-3 Billion

RECORD LABELS

There are literally thousands of record labels throughout the UK, however there are now only four Major International companies, at present being **Sony/BMG, Warner, EMI, and Vivendi Universal**. Each of these companies have a range of smaller labels, and they can also license from independent labels. There were five majors until Sony and BMG recently merged.

Each major has a number of subsidiaries (sometimes known as imprints);

EMI—Blue Note, Capitol, Chrysalis, Heavenly, Hut, Mute, Parlaphone, Positiva, Food, Source, Virgin, Innocent. (**UK market share 2004 = 18.5%**)

Sony/BMG—Arista, RCA, Columbia, Epic, S, Creation, Sony S2, Camden, Jive, J,
(**UK market share 2004 = 23%**)

Vivendi Universal—Go Discs, Interscope, Def Jam, Island, Interscope, MCA, Mercury, Motown, Polydor, Verve, Decca, Phonogram, Fontana, A&M, Talkin' Loud
(**UK market share 2004 = 25%**)

Warner Music—Atlantic, Warner Bros, Asylum, Elektra, Infectious, Rhino, East West, Maverick, Mushroom, Reprise, Sire. (**UK market share 2004 = 13%**)

INDEPENDENT LABELS

There are hundreds if not thousands of smaller independent record labels in the UK, ranging from small one-man-band bedroom operations to multi-million pound businesses. Some examples of successful indies would include Ninja tune, XL and Beggars Group. The indies are represented by a trade organisation called AIM (Association of Independent Music).

If you are writing songs and seeking a deal, the A&R department is the one you'll be looking out for.

THE A&R DEPARTMENT

You've heard the term mentioned, but what what does A&R actually stand for?

ARTIST & REPERTOIRE.

The term was coined a long time ago to describe the function of people at record labels who are basically in charge of searching and weeding out and then developing new talent that may be 'of use' to the label. I emphasise the words 'of use', as basically the record company uses bands and artists to make them money.

Development typically includes finding the right material for the artist to perform, if they don't write their own songs, (even if they do, they may prefer them to do a cover to start of their career), hooking them up with the right producer, engineer, studio, etc., deciding which of their songs are the most viable, and then basically going through the whole process of making a record.

Meanwhile, it's not unusual for the A&R person to be responsible for getting the other departments such as retail sales, radio promotion and pluggers on board to help get the recording in the spotlight. If all departments work well together, there's more chance of developing a hit from the end product.

Today, A&R people are much more fussy with regard to the finished article. Whereas years ago they would be prepared to develop an artist or band, nowadays they are looking for artists who have developed themselves and may just need some 'fine-tuning'.

HOW DO YOU GET YOUR MUSIC HEARD BY A&R PERSONNEL?

A&R departments are constantly bombarded with material and receive hundreds of demo's a week, so don't be too surprised if yours ends up as a door wedge, propping up a table or even a coffee coaster. Contacting them via an unexpected phone call is also not recommended, as they are simply too busy to be handling random queries. If you think you have the right material, the best way is to make them to come and see you. If you are causing havoc on your local music scene and having to hire crowd control barriers for your gigs, then it's quite possible word-of-mouth may just cause the record companies A&R personnel to attend your next gig (if there's room for one more person !). Relentless gigging, self promotion, marketing and selling your CDs added to the building of a solid fan base will always attract A&R people. If they know you are capable of causing excitement and commotion in a small scale environment without any backing—they can visualise what could happen with the full backing and 'might' of what is the record company 'machine'.

WHAT IF YOU, AS AN ARTIST/BAND, ARE NOT ACTUALLY GIGGING?

If the only way you can get A&R to listen to your material is via a recording and not a live show, then consider that A&R personnel are extremely busy people, and generally may only listen to the material that comes to them from a trusted source such as a high-level manager, a publisher or a music attorney (there are exceptions but they are rare).

RECORDING CONTRACTS—THE BASICS.

All recording contracts will set out an exclusive agreement between you (the recording artist) and the record company. This agreement will allow the record company to exploit the rights in the recording of your performances. It also means you cannot record for anyone else other than the record company during the 'term' of your contract—unless special permission to appear and perform on another artists recording has been sought and agreed.

Whilst small back street 'Independent' labels may just knock out a two page contract, major players like Sony, EMI, BMG etc, usually produce contracts that may have up to 40 to 50 pages of terms and conditions, clauses etc. In many contracts the **'financial terms'** alone, can run into 15 pages.

Reading these contracts yourself and trying to understand the wording and phrasing may be just a little out of your league—a Latin version of War and Peace comes to mind.

But strangely enough all such contracts should have a basic lay out—it's just the finer points, wording and phrasing that can hide the devil within.

Better then to always seek legal advice from a lawyer with experience of music business—related contracts. A slight change of wording here and there can dramatically change the financial impact of a contract.

The basic principles of a recording contract usually contain the following

The Advance—an up front payment—this advance will differ obviously depending on the deal itself and will also depend on the size of the record company involved. Some minor independent labels for example cannot afford advances, whereas major record labels tend to have large amounts of money to invest in their artists.

Remember the advance that is paid to you or invested in the artist or band is set against record royalties earned whilst under the contract, in other words you will not receive any money till any advance has been recouped. This is commonly known as the ' recoupable advance'. This advance should only be set against any record royalties—there should be no liability to repay the advance if you do not generate enough money to do that from actual record royalties.

Cross—collateralisation—is a phrase used for moneys recouped from further albums if the money is not fully recouped from the first album or single. It's a very important term used in many contracts and again leans to the side of the record company and enables them to recoup money from future releases if any loss was made on a previous release.

You should be aware that if you are signed to a Recording Agreement and a Publishing Agreement with the same company they may try and cross—collateralise publishing income against any recording income. **Do not agree to this.**

The Duration or Term—how long the contract lasts. The term of the contract will depend on options included within the contract and will nearly always be in favour of the record company. In other words—contrary to popular belief—a five album deal does not mean you will be guaranteed to release five albums, it merely means that the record company have the option of keeping you tied to a five album deal if it all goes well. If it doesn't, and the first album is a flop, there will be clauses in the contract that will enable the company to drop you. Also look out for the **'minimum commitment'** clause that sets out how many albums or singles you will be expected to deliver to the company usually by certain dates, set in the contract.

A record contract should have included—to the artists benefit—an obligation to release any recordings by a specified time period. If this obligation is not met, the rights to the recordings should be given back to the artist. This is commonly known as **'reversion of rights'**.

EMPLOYMENT WITHIN THE MUSIC INDUSTRY (UK)

Just how many musicians are employed in some capacity in the UK is almost impossible to answer. As I mentioned earlier in the book literally millions of people learn to play an instrument at some stage of their life, they may even go on to perform in some capacity, but the majority give up for one reason or another. Many people also pick up an instrument later on in life and may end up doing some paid gigs or they may do it as a hobby, so it's very difficult to collate accurate figures… but a recent government report together with some research of my own resulted in these figures.

There are around 3/4 of a million musicians actively involved as amateurs or in the voluntary sector (unpaid).

Around 48/50,000 people are musicians and composers, although only around 33,000 are full time.

Those 48/50,000 musicians and composers' jobs are roughly in the following categories:

Live performance: (Covers, Cabaret, Function, Rock/Pop etc) 31,000
Recording 4,200—Orchestras (full time) 3,500—Musicals 2,100
Opera 3,500—Freelance classical musicians 2,000—Military 1,200
Composers not included elsewhere 3,000

Other music related jobs include around 160,000 individuals who are actively involved in the creation and distribution of music in the UK of which 115,000 are full time.

The recording industry employs around 11,000
- 6,400 in record companies,
- 3,000 in manufacturing
- 1,600 in studios or as producers
- Music publishing employs around 2,000
- Music and education employs around 15,000
- Retail and distribution employs around 19,000
- Music venues, concerts, festivals   11,000
- Musical instrument (production, retail) 9,200

The remainder are employed in other music related occupations such as administration, music press, merchandising, management, promotion, agents etc.

It's important to remember why only a small proportion of people manage to make a full time living out of music. If you have managed to read this book, you may have realised that being involved in the music industry—in any form—may not result in a lucrative income and it's certainly not a simple profession. Many musicians have other non music related jobs simply to afford to be a musician in the first place, or at least they may have two or more music related jobs which together may just add up to a decent income. For example a guitarist may be a gigging musician of a weekend, a guitar teacher one or two evenings per week and may also do guitar 'set—ups' or repairs.

ROYALTY COLLECTION AGENCIES

Basically if you have recorded your own material or you are considering recording or remixing other people's music, the following societies will need to be informed.

You really could do with learning about these societies anyway as you may use them sometime in your career. They are now affiliated as the MCPS/PRS alliance.

THE PERFORMING RIGHTS SOCIETY (PRS) THE MECHANICAL COPYRIGHT PROTECTION SOCIETY(MCPS)

The Performing Rights Society (PRS) was established in 1914 and is a non profit making membership organisation for composers, songwriters, authors and publishers of all musical genres and styles including pop, jazz, classical, music for films, adverts and TV.

The essential roll of the PRS is to collect and distribute music royalties on behalf of it's members.

The composer or creator of a piece of work can expect to receive between £5-£20 per 3 minute broadcast on local radio, £30—£50 on network/national radio (radio 1/2 etc), and £150—£300 for television satellite broadcasts.

PRS is commonly known as a 'collection society' because it's primary role is to collect royalties from music users in the UK who, daily, publicly perform or broadcast in any shape or form.

PRS has agreements with other collection societies outside of the UK and, in fact, throughout the world.

WHO CAN BECOME A MEMBER OF PRS?

- Music composers and songwriters.
- Authors, writers of lyrics or poems that have been set to music.
- Arrangers of non-copyright music.
- Music publishers.
- Successors (beneficiaries of deceased members).

WHY BECOME A PRS MEMBER?

Basically to receive royalties for public performance and broadcast of your music, a new item has been added to the society (2004/5) as regards royalty payment schemes for small venue Gigs and Clubs.

PRS SMALL GIGS AND CLUBS SCHEME

Members who perform at small gigs and clubs can now send PRS details of the music they perform and receive a royalty payment under a new scheme being launched on 1 January 2004.

WHO IS THE SCHEME FOR?

All performers who regularly play in smaller UK venues such as pubs, bars, community centres and hotels. Touring performers, resident performers and DJs will be able to submit event and set list information direct to PRS.

DOES IT COVER ALL EVENTS?

No. The scheme does not cover:
- a) concerts that are licensed under the concert tariff arrangements; mainly concerts with bigger box offices.
- b) gigs and club events that are picked up by the PRS Music Survey. If one of their researchers visits the event, it will receive a payment automatically and this event will be excluded from the scheme.

HOW DOES IT WORK?

You can take part in the scheme if you perform a core set at ten or more gigs in any twelve month period. The scheme is email based and applicants must register via email by sending your full name, address and contact details to:

gigsclubsscheme@mcps-prs-alliance.co.uk

Upon registration the participant is requested to return the set list and event information on a template supplied by PRS, back to the same email address.

This scheme removes all paperwork from the distribution cycle and any information must be supplied electronically.

IS IT THAT EASY?

Yes…but, you must have a minimum of ten relevant UK performances, you must email the information and the performances can't have been picked up under the concert tariff arrangements or picked up under the PRS Music Survey, and at least some of the works must have been written by PRS members.

What kind of royalty can I expect? Each event will generate a net royalty of around £4.50 net. Therefore, the minimum of 10 performances necessary to qualify

for the scheme would generate a net royalty (after PRS administration reduction) of around £45, to be divided amongst the composers, songwriters and publishers of the works performed. Obviously if you do 20 gigs it would be 20 x £4.50 and so on.

PRS are organising a series of marketing strategies including road shows to advise qualifying members of the benefits of the scheme (starting late 2005).

WHAT ARE THE CRITERIA TO JOIN THE PRS

Composers, songwriters, lyricists and arrangers must have a work/composition that has been broadcast, performed live or played in public.

WHAT PROOF IS NEEDED?

Composers, songwriters, lyricists and arrangers will be required to provide a letter from either a broadcaster, promoter, concert agent or venue owner confirming the broadcast or performance has taken place. (Check with PRS direct to obtain latest information regarding becoming a member, as new criteria has been added due to the introduction of the small venue scheme.)

Publishers must have contracts covering at least fifteen works (songs).

(Your music does not have to have been published or recorded for you to become a PRS writer—member.)

THE MEMBERSHIP FEE

The joining fee is currently 'for Composers, songwriters, lyricists and arrangers' a one-off fee of £100 (inc. VAT). (Correct at May 2005.)
   Music publishers are required to pay a one off fee of £400 (inc.VAT). (Publishers must have contracts covering at least fifteen works.)
   There is no annual membership fee.

HOW TO BECOME A PRS MEMBER

For information on how to actually become a member, or obtaining a membership application form, contact:
   website: **www.prs.co.uk/new members** or **www.mcps-prs-alliance.co.uk**
   email: **admissions@mcps-prs-alliance.co.uk**
   call: O2O 7306 4805
   write to: Writer/publisher Admissions
   MCPS-PRS Alliance
   39/33 Berners Street
   London W1T 3AB
   Members will automatically receive more information about the role of the PRS, but general questions and information and latest news regarding PRS and it's membership, etc. can be found on the PRS website: **www.prs.co.uk/members**
   On application for membership, you will also be given advice on whether you will actually benefit from joining at this time.
   If you (or other performers) play your original music at live venues on a regular basis or you gain radio air play for your songs, or even have club DJs playing your music (on a regular basis) it should be worth you joining but consider that according to figures collected by PRS for 2004—only 5% of their writer members receive a substantial income (i.e. more than £10,000 per annum) for the public performance of their works.

WHO NEEDS THE PRS LICENCE?

A PRS licence is required by anyone using or intending to perform music in public, by whatever means (live, DJ, jukebox, TV, radio, satellite, cable, etc.), also in venues as diverse as concert halls to discos and all manner of places such as shopping centres, doctors waiting rooms, etc.
   Every UK-based radio station and television broadcaster, cable operator and website owner using music also requires a PRS licence.

DO SONGWRITERS NEED A LICENCE?

Songwriters, publishers, musicians and performers do not normally need to hold a PRS licence, unless they are also the music user; normally the promoter of the performance or proprietor/owner of the venue where it takes place. This could be a club manager, owner of a shop, pub landlord or a managing director of a radio station.

Obtaining a PRS licence gives blanket coverage so that the licence holder does not have to seek individual clearance for every single piece of music used. Millions of works then become available without the likelihood of being sued for infringement.

You can also find out about the **MCPS-PRS** alliance.

The MCPS (Mechanical Copyright Protection Society) is another collection society affiliated to the PRS.

Acting on behalf of it's composer and publisher members, the MCPS negotiates agreements with those who wish to record music, ensuring the copyright owners are rewarded for the use of their music. It collects and then distributes the 'mechanical' royalties which are generated from the recording of music onto many different formats, including CDs, cassettes, audio visual and broadcast material (including online).

Every time copies are made of your work, a 'mechanical' royalty is payable. In other words, every time a record company makes another CD, cassette, recording in any format of your material, a royalty is payable. That rule also covers any person/company at all who makes copies of other peoples works. For example, if I decided to release a cover of another artist's work, I would have to pay the MCPS a royalty for every copy I made—that's regardless of how many may be sold. If I press 1,000 CDs, I would be expected to pay 1,000 x the royalty (there are some exceptions regarding a percentage for promotional usage; more info supplied by MCPS AP2 Licence Agreement).

Record companies have to supply details of all the different recording formats, CDs etc, that they manufacture every month, and then pay the 'mechanical' royalty.

WHO ELSE PAYS THE ROYALTIES TO MCPS?

Every time a musical work is copied, or a copy of a work is issued to the public

a mechanical royalty is generated. This includes not only the recording of a song for sale on a record, tape, CD or any other sound carrier, but also where music is copied into TV and radio programmes, feature films, TV and radio commercials, videos, the internet, retail multimedia, premium products (e.g. a free CD with a packet of cereal or newspaper) and mobile phone ring-tones.

MCPS levies a variety of commission fees, depending on the source of the royalties and the administration necessary to process the royalties.

MEMBERS

MCPS currently has just on 13,134 members and 4,921 publisher members (figures correct at 12th January 2005). The 2004 distribution to MCPS members was £219 million (unaudited figure).

ANTI—PIRACY UNIT

MCPS also operates an Anti-Piracy Unit that works alongside UK enforcement agencies to investigate infringements of MCPS members' copyrights.

The Alliance Against Counterfeiting and Piracy, of which MCPS is a member, has estimated that around £11 billion is lost to copyright and trademark thieves annually, and that the cost to the UK government in lost taxes was around £1.9 billion in 2003.

OTHER USEFUL CONTACTS

- **PPL** Phonographic Performance Ltd, 1 Upper James Street, London, W1R 3HG
  tel: 020 7534 1000 Collecting Society. Licensing broadcasts and public performances of sound recordings in the UK on behalf of record companies and performers.
- **PAMRA** Performing Arts Media Rights Association, 3rd Floor, 161 Borough High Street, London, SE1 1HR
  tel: 020 7378 9720/020 7378 6777
- **AURA** Association of United Recording Artists, 134 Lots Road, London, SW10 0RJ
  tel: 020 7352 4564
- **MU** Musicians Union, 60-62 Clapham Road, London, SW9 0JJ
  tel: 020 7582 5566 Representing and advising its members in contracts and good practice. Publishes practical information sheets.
  The MU also has regional offices.
- **AIM** Association of Independent Music, Lamb House, Church Street, London, W4 2PD
  tel: 020 8994 5599 British independent music companies' trade association

- **BPI** British Phonographic Industry, 25 Saville Row, London, W1X 1AA
  tel: 020 7851 4000 British record companies' trade association
- **ANA** The Article Number Association (UK) Ltd, 11 Kingsway, London, WC2B 6AR
  tel: 020 7836 3398 Administers the allocation of barcodes including the barcodes required by retailers on records for sale.

MUSIC INDUSTRY WEBSITES

Here are a few of the thousands of websites dedicated or related to the music industry. Please take care, some of the sites are subscription based (you pay)

- **Guide to Survival & Success in the Music Business**
  web: www.musicindie.org
  t: 020 8994 5599
  e: info@musicindie.com
- **Music Business Resources**
  A great website clear and simple to use, providing advice to those who wish to launch a career in music
  web: www.musicbusiness.free-online.co.uk
- **AIM (The Association of Independent Music)** British Association of Independent record companies and distributors.
  w: www.musicindie.org
  www.bemuso.com—superb music business resource
- **OneMusic**
  An initiative of BBC Radio1, providing a free comprehensive range of advice for musicians.
  w: www.bbc.co.uk/radio1/onemusic
  e: onemusic@bbc.co.uk
- **Networking opportunities**
  w: www.songlink.com
  Vocalists, Superb comprehensive website covering anything to do with vocals and singing, busking etc.
  w: www.vocalist.org.uk
- **www.thefreedictionary.com**
  just type the name in rather like a search engine and very useful.
- **Music Biz**
  w: www.theessentialguide.co.uk
- **Getsigned.com**
  A huge music career information website from the US, with loads

of tips and advice on signing, performing, promotion, artist management, publishing, etc, by a variety of industry experts. You can ask questions online, join for email updates, etc.
w: www.getsigned.com
e: media@getsigned.com

- **Fourfront Media & Music**
Comprehensive US information portal on how to promote, sell, publicise, and market your music.
w: www.knab.com

- **The British Academy of Composers and Songwriters.**
w: www.britishacademy.com

- **CMU/The Update**
A 'creative network' aimed at music industry and music media people—especially those interested in the student and youth sectors.
Membership is free for anyone working in music at any level—check the website for details.
w: www.cmumusicnetwork.co.uk
t: 0870 744 2643
e: cmu@unlimitedmedia.co.uk

- **Music Business Journal**
A collaborative online resource about the entertainment and music industry owned and operated by Ligo Publishing Limited. It features extensive interviews with industry experts and a collection of articles and fact sheets that provide a real insight into the business of music.
w: www.musicjournal.org
e: info@musicjournal.org

- **Jazz Services**
The national service organisation for jazz in the UK. Contains free fact sheets on subjects such as manufacturing CDs, marketing your gigs, plus lots of jazz info and news, including gig listings
w: www.jazzservices.org.uk

- **TheSiteWizard.com**
A comprehensive guide to creating and developing your website, from hosting and designing through to promoting and generating revenue and with jargon free tutorials and articles.
w: www.thesitewizard.com

- **Hitquarters.com**
Huge US-based resource website featuring 1000's of international music industry links, with an emphasis on A&R contacts.
w: www.hitquarters.com

- **Editors Media Directories**
  A collection of guides listing all UK national and regional media (TV, radio, magazines and newspapers) with their full contacts details and other useful information. Available in hard copy only.
  t: 01494 797 230
  e: editors@mediainfo.co.uk
- **PA Listings**
  Free service supplying entertainment listings to the national newspapers and their supplements. A minimum of 2-week deadline applies for all listings.
  t: 020 7963 7707
  e: paul.stump@listings.press.net
- **The Knowledge**
  A resource website for the UK TV, film and video industry with the contact details of all traditional and digital TV channels and other related organisations in the UK and abroad.
  w: www.theknowledgeonline.com
- **Music Industry News Network**. Up to date news and what's going on.
  w: wwwmi2n.com
- **Student Radio Association**
  The SRA is an advisory body for UK student radios.
  w: www.studentradio.org.uk
  t: 07005 35 1 999
  e: exec@studentradio.org.uk
- **Soundgenerator.com**
  'The essential resource for music' is the culmination of three years research and development. Soundgenerator.com is fast becoming the UK's largest independent music site providing an array of music industry information including news, reviews, features, charts, message boards, education and industry directory for music fans and music industry professionals alike.
  w: www.soundgenerator.com
- **Showcase International Music Book**
  Music industry directory. Full online version accessible free of charge.
  w: www.showcase-music.com
  t: 020 8977 7711
  e: info@showcase-music.com
- **Musicians-web.co.uk**
  A network of web resources from around the UK to help you find

music contacts in and around your area, including, teachers, venues, performing opportunities, etc.
w: www.musicians-web.co.uk

- **Realukmusic.co.uk**
A music industry directory searchable by either genre or region.
w: www.realukmusic.co.uk

- **Music Business**
The UK's leading monthly trade magazine for musical instrument retailers, distributors, manufacturers and recording studios.
w: www.musicbusiness.co.uk
e: music@dgoldstein.enterprise-plc.com

- **Music Industries Association**
MIA is the trade association representing the interests of all UK businesses selling musical instruments and associated products and services. An extensive list of suppliers and retailers can also be found on the website.
w: www.mia.org.uk
t: 01372 750 600
e: office@mia.org.uk

- **TAXI**
A US, subscription-based, independent A&R Company which helps unsigned bands, artists and songwriters get their music directly to top A&R people at Major Record Labels, Music Publishers, and Music Supervisors working on Film & TV projects.
TAXI is the only legitimate company of its kind in the world, and they work with over 600 major companies including: Arista, Atlantic, Capitol, Columbia, Disney, Dreamworks SKG, EMI, Epic, Interscope, Jive, Maverick,
MCA, RCA, Universal, Virgin, Warner Brothers, and many more.
w: www.taxi.com

- **Hitquarters.com**
Huge US-based resource website featuring 1000's of international music industry links, with an emphasis on A&R
w: www.hitquarters.com

- **1212.com**
Free online searchable database of music production/promotion services, labels, and artists in over 50 countries.
w: www.1212.com

WEBZINES (ONLINE-MAGAZINES)

- **Metallville.** Artist interviews. CD and show reviews, and general info re heavy metal scene in the UK
  w: www.metallville.com
- **Bigmouth. UK.** Music info with tour dates, music events, and artist information.
  w: www.bigmouth.co.uk
- **Fly Magazine.** Jazz, hip hop, R&B, dance and indie music from around the world.
  w: www.fly.co.uk

in my liverpool home

Some boring bits about me (just in case you wanted to know!).

Most people talk about the 60s when they talk about the history of music in Liverpool and I have to agree that it was the greatest era. Although I was riding around on a small bike with scuffed knees whilst the Beatles and all the Merseybeat stuff was going on, I couldn't miss the excitement of the music—even listening to it on the radio and everyone generally walking around singing or whistling a Beatles song.

I was brought up in the heart of Liverpool just next to where the Royal Liverpool Hospital is now. Jubilee Drive then Chapel Place (which is now factory units which personally I think is very sad). The Beatles soon took over my life and they were the reason I first started playing—I think that's the same story for hundreds of thousands of musicians.

My 'live music' era was Liverpool mid/late 70s and my first taste of music venues came in the form of The Sportsman, The Star and Garter, The Moonstone, Oscar's, Rudy's, The Mayflower and The Cumberland.

Some of the bands knocking about were simply wonderful—Thunderboots (featuring Mark Parry), Colonel Bagshot, The Bingo Brothers, 29th and Dearborn, Export, Next, Rocking Horse (I used to think Stan Metcalf and Art Caravan were Gods, in fact they were!) and it was around that same era that I started the Liverpool gigging scene myself. I had moved to Kirkby at the age of seven and by the age of 13/14 joined my first band. We called the band 'Gambler' (it sounded like a good name at the time!) and we hit the road (literally—I fell out the back door on the way to our first gig and scuffed my arse, leg and elbow—there were no back doors on the van). Besides that, looking back now, we were remarkably professional for such a young band.

Every Sunday without fail we would practise in a 'scouts hut' at the back end of Kirkby Industrial Estate. Even through the coldest days of winter we would be there—coats on, two pairs of socks, a flask of soup, finger-less gloves, etc. I remember it was so cold one day we couldn't actually play our instruments so we practised harmonies huddled around a small heater.

However we plodded on for around eighteen months and rehearsed a two hour set that consisted of The Beatles, The Eagles, Thin Lizzy, some of our own and other songs of the era. We were also determined to learn the songs as perfectly as possible, learning every note 'Parrot fashion' from vinyl records. The Thin Lizzy twin lead guitar breaks were always extremely difficult to master, but we would always get it down to the last note in the end. We would then meet on the Sunday and rehearse the songs with the full band. The band then consisted of myself—guitar vocals, Kevin Kelly—guitar vocals, Arnie Stevens—bass vocals and Nick Bellis—drums vocals. We knocked up a quick image by dressing up as gangsters (don't laugh—it worked) and went on the road (starting with the local pub scene. We actually had a residency on 'The Eagle and Child' in Huyton—a notoriously rough legend of a pub—but a great place to practise our trade. I think we were paid expenses, plus lemonade and a pie each if we were lucky).

That was around 1976 (I was 16 at the time) and we were soon supporting and playing with the Liverpool bands we'd idolised. I think we surprised a lot of older musicians because of the sheer hard work we had put in to make the songs tight. We were always one of the best equipped bands in Liverpool as we all had a day job (I was an apprentice floor-layer/roofer) and every penny went into musical gear. We had bought a full range, three way H+H PA system (from Frank Hessey's) that at the time blew everything else away. We got a few funny looks when we took to the stage with gangster suits and hats—but the smirks stopped when we began playing. When we weren't gigging we would jump the bus to town and check out the other bands—studying their every move, note and word and getting any tips as to how we could improve our playing and sound. We then added around four or five original songs into the set influenced by the music we had been covering and it worked a treat, with the songs going down as well as the covers. We recorded the songs onto a tape album in 1977 and I still have a copy. Two of the songs still stand up now so we must have been good! Before long we were supporting some great bands—in particular 'The Steve Gibbons Band' (March 78) and 'Sweet Sensation' who sang 'Sad Sweet Dreamer' (June 79).

Kevin sadly left the band in 1980 and I moved to West Derby, Liverpool. I plodded on as the sole guitarist until we all finally decided that we needed to move on. I then joined up with The Bobby Arnold Scratch Band or 'Leo' as guitar/keyboards in 1982 and spent a few more years learning from the maestro guitar playing of the late Bobby Arnold. I had known Bobby since childhood as he worked with my father in the roofing game since they were both apprentices. I also worked with Bobby nearly every day so we became great friends and I couldn't have had a greater mentor. At the time, I had also hooked up with a friend (Dave Reilly) who had recently split with his then band 'China Crisis' (who were also friends of mine at the time, and still are—we work together). We got a little band together but it never actually got to the stage of gigging. (Years later we worked together in my band 'Now Hear This').

In 1983/4 I joined up with Philip Franz Jones, the singer and writer in a band called 'Afraid of Mice', as a guitarist/keyboards player. What a band, what a time, what great songs! But somebody must have double greased the top rung of the ladder, or maybe it was just never meant to happen. Just after recording a video produced by UK TVs Channel 4, the band unfortunately split in 1988 and I remember feeling physically sick. I was immensely sad and disheartened, not just for myself but for Phil who had put his heart and soul into his music and had gained major record deals with CBS and Charisma, sold out on both the Liverpool Empire and the Royal Court Theatre and yet still had to return to the sticky carpet dives in the back streets of Liverpool. I remember talking to an old AOM fan recently (Andy Hardwick) and he came up with the notion as to why Phil may have just missed out on the riches and fame of stardom--"he didn't kiss arse". When I put this to Phil he answered, "maybe he's right, and if I had the chance again I would probably do things differently. I was always a bit 'I am the star so what I say goes'—you just can't do that with the major companies, you have to be prepared to bend a little, I realise that now".

After I got over the disappointment, around a year later I started up a band with the other musicians and called the band 'Now Hear This'. Again, I ask myself what happened, what have you got to do? This (without sounding too self indulgent) was another great band playing original, catchy, commercial songs. We did however manage to gain considerable air play over a two year period with the release of 'Dream About The Girl', 'I Don't Know' and later 'The Closer I Get To Heaven'.

What happened next taught me a big lesson in my life as a musician/songwriter. As I mentioned earlier, the singles we had released had been receiving good air play, although mainly local radio—the odd national radio play too. I had also sent the singles to several record companies (two of whom had been in touch prior and requested some material) and suddenly, in the post, I had three very promising replies and a couple of promising phone calls. Fm-Revolver records (Rob James ?) Warner Chapel, BMG and Columbia also asked for more material as soon as possible. Before I had the chance to send any more songs or meet these people came a phone call from London from a man called Mr Dennis Sinnott. Mr. Sinnott explained that the record label he ran called 'Christel Music' was under license from EMI and basically told me to get down to London as soon as possible to sign publishing with Christel/Orange Publishing and to contact the rest of the band with regards to recording an album. After meeting Dennis in London and realising he had a very, very impressive background (he worked for the EMI group for most of his life and in addition to head administrator to the world's largest publishing group, he was also instrumental in negotiating deals for many super groups and solo writer/performers, including Queen, Sir Elton John, Sir Paul McCartney, the Rolling Stones, Pink Floyd, Deep Purple, Wishbone Ash, Jeff Beck, Mud, Medicine Head, Be-Bop Deluxe, the Hollies, Bob Dylan and scores of other hugely successful acts. Plus the added bonus that he was a good friend of John Miles of whom I was a big fan at the time. John was also signed to Orange publishing).

He was also a very nice chap, so I/we decided to go with the flow.

It all looked like the perfect deal and unfortunately I didn't even contact the other companies that had shown interest (mistake?—how will I ever know?). Dennis went on to explain that as soon as we had recorded the songs in Germany, EMI would possibly take over and the songs would be released with all the backing and might of a major record company. A music lawyer amended the contract several times (it was an inch thick) and we signed. It sounded to good to be true and the next thing we knew we were on our way to Hamburg.

Just one small matter delayed things by six months. The band was attacked at a gig by a gang of thugs (due to our scouse accent—yes, unfortunately these things do happen), two of them were jailed. I spent a month in hospital and had a few back—discs removed. When I managed to get up and moving again, which took around five or six months, we headed off to Hamburg to a superb studio with a top producer and an album full of songs to record. However, the tangled affairs of the recording contract, publishing contract, the delays (caused by my injuries) in recording, etc, came to a head and for reasons I may never know, the recordings were never released and are in fact probably still stored somewhere in Hamburg, Germany (this is not an unusual scenario, lots of recordings are never released). Recording costs are only a part of the investment by record companies.

As I had also signed a publishing deal, I had in effect signed away all rights to my songs for the foreseeable future, therefore I had burned bridges to the other companies who had shown more than a little interest. Don't get me wrong, I had a fantastic time recording in Germany and the experience is something I will never forget, but did I/we jump in too fast? Looking back and with hindsight it's obviously a yes, but who knows whether the other deals would have turned out any better—maybe I should have waited and studied all the offers before signing anything—but you live and learn.

So what do I do now?

I am the Regional Manager for the NW coast's government initiative MIC (Music Industry Consultancy) service. I work for a company called Access to Music and in conjunction with the Liverpool Institute for Performing Arts (LIPA) provide a teaching and mentoring service for up and coming musicians of any genre. Although mainly aimed at the 18-24 age group, we work with musicians of any age. Apart from instrumental tuition, advice and mentoring we also run nights at various venues in particular Liverpool's famous Cavern Club in order to give young musicians and bands the opportunity to play on a recognised venue (equipment supplied) to give them valuable experience of life as a gigging musician.

Excerpts from this book can be found in all 8 of the Music Open Learning Provision (MOLP) work—books supplied by various colleges throughout the UK including LIPA via the governments New Deal for Musicians programme.

I am happy, I have a lovely family, a wonderful job—working with the next generation of musicians—and great friends.

What more could a man want.

Good luck.

ISBN 1-41207402-9